KNIGHTS OF THE ROAD

The Autobiography of
Gypsy Dave Mills

KNIGHTS OF THE ROAD
The Autobiography of Gypsy Dave Mills

WISDOM TWINS BOOKS
wisdomtwinsbooks.weebly.com

This edition released in 2013

Photos © Dave Mills
Text Copyright © Dave Mills 2013
Cover design by Chris Wade, 2013
Editing by Dave Mills, Davy McGowan and Chris Wade

This book is dedicated to my late son, Matthew Sighdawn Mills and my daughter Michaela.

I would also like to thank Davy McGowan for all his help in editing a large part of the book

CHAPTER ONE
<u>LIVING AT HOME</u>

I was born in Dulwich, Peckham Rye, London SE15 - the year 1946, the month July, the day the ninth. My given name was David John Mills.

My mother was a country lass, my father a London boy. He was in uniform when they met. She was 18 and was sitting on the steps of a Cinema during the blackout, having taken her dog for a long walk. He tripped over the dog's lead and fell - first for the dog, then for the beautiful young girl serendipity had placed in his path. Unbeknown to her she had tripped up the man who was to become my father. It was wartime and, apart from the sheer hell that was war, a much more innocent time. Time wore a different clock face then. Within one month they were married - within two months her husband was sent off to Scotland for extra training; here she joined him for a week - it was the nearest thing to a honeymoon they ever had. It was there my sister Sandra was conceived - at the same time as the British Army conceived the idea of sending the new groom abroad. My father was a very lucky man in Love and War - he survived them both. I was conceived during a two week leave of absence from Austria, where my father was billeted with a local farmer, our forces being there to track down any German SS officers who had fled over the border when peace was declared. Mercifully for my mother my father was demobbed on his return to

England nine months later, just in time to be at her bedside for the great arrival - namely me.

I spent the first eight years of my life in Scylla Road, London SE15. The family house was as thin as skin, flat roofed prefab built at the end of the Second World War as temporary housing. The next seven years I spent in Welwyn Garden City. This delightfully named place was in Hertfordshire, eight miles from St. Albans where my mother's family, the Hawkes, had roots stretching back generations. Thus it was that the love of green and tree filled places found a special corner in my heart - though I could still be thrilled by the sights and sounds of a great metropolis of mankind's making.

A scholar of any account I was not, although it would seem that I had a natural intelligence that in this day and age would be called 'Streetwise'. In my day it was known as 'Common Sense'. This rather uncommon sense soon led me to want to stand on my own two feet. At fourteen and a half years of age I decided I was old enough to face the world and its myriad untold foibles. My best friend, Robert Thorby was having trouble with his parents, so the two of us talked over his problems and the answer was simple - he had to leave home. With the optimism of youth I decided to leave too and we headed for the open road and stuck our thumbs out on the A1 hoping to head for London.

Three cars passed before a Bentley, complete with chauffeur, stopped to pick us up. A nice old man, grand of manner and sitting in style on the leather interior seat, leaned forward and showed us wide-eyed boys the magic of his mini bar as he poured himself a drink. It was all very civilized and far removed from anything we were used to - but looking back now, strangely prophetic of where life would take me in the then not too distant future.

In due course we arrived at Robert's grandmother's house in the expectation of some money and sympathy. She lived in the East End of London, not a place renowned for its sympathy or generosity in 1960, but she did what she could - giving Robert and I some good advice and a little money. But what to do next? My suggestion was to look for beatniks.

A few months earlier, whilst playing truant from school, a friend Cuddles and I had discovered a beatnik's café. I was overwhelmed to see the beautiful beatnik chick who was the waitress. Her jeans were covered in paint in the most outrageous of ways, each colour artistically highlighting the split in the cloth at her crotch. Wow! It was love at first sight! At that precise moment in time I knew I wanted to be a beatnik, and if possible an artist.

The million dollar question for Robert and I was where to find these beatniks. I thought we should look in all the nearby cafes - but we had no luck with that idea, beatniks were few and far between in those days. Robert kept asking me what a beatnik looked like.

"Don't worry," I told him, "you'll know one when you see one."

However by nightfall we had not found a soul who looked remotely like a beatnik.

We came to a large park surrounded by a fringe of deciduous trees. Brightly coloured deckchairs sat with spread-eagled legs on the neatly cut lawns and orange lights shone street by street behind the pines, making a hazy backdrop that seemed to hurry dusk onward in its glow. It was fast becoming too dark to search further.

This was to be our first night sleeping rough. Robert suggested we might sleep in the trees. We dragged a couple of deck chairs into the cover of the branches and hoped we would sleep fairly well ensconced in the trees' leafy protection but, as Fate would have it, the powers that be chose that very night to clear the park of all tramps, reprobates or riff-raff who were loitering within its vicinity. The police scooped Robert and I up in their metaphorical net along with all the others.

It was something these inebriate tramps were used to, and they took it good naturedly, but we two youngsters were really pissed off. The police thought we were older than we were but, having decided there was something suspicious about us sleeping rough, they arrested us and took us to the local Police Station where we were questioned so persistently we realized there was no way they would let us go until we told them the truth. Our names and addresses duly taken, our parents were informed. First thing in the morning they were there to pick us up. A few days later back at school we were punished. Robert, being several months older than me, was held to be responsible and was expelled. I got a mild reprimand on my report and was made to depart my school a full term before I was due to. Thus it was that I started work before my fifteenth birthday.

I was a trainee electrician working for the *Fine Fare* supermarket chain and it was there I learned to drive an array of forklift trucks - to this day I'm an expert at judging distances in tight corners thanks to those experiences. My weekly wage, after deductions, was the princely sum of £3/4d. £2/10s of this went to my mum for food and lodging, leaving me 10/4d per week to live on. I felt like a King - after all a pint of ale was only 1/7d. Best of all I was standing on my own two legs and able to make and have my own opinions - opinions that included an interest in the CND movement, bohemian lifestyles, art, music and a lively interest in sex as experienced by the Swedes in their form of Free Love.

Weekends were spent talking about 'Ban The Bomb' marches that were being planned in Aldermaston where the Americans had an Air Force Base - and a store of atomic bombs. We few Welwyn Garden City CND members tried to make a show of strength, but to little avail so I joined the bigger St. Albans membership. I met some interesting young people there, most of them from St. Albans Art College. We used to meet up in a pub called *The Cock* in the middle of St. Albans. At last I was mixing with a more beatnik and arty crowd.

The alternative cultural straitjackets for the young at that time was to be either a Mod, a Rocker or just to fit in with the rest of the masses and be termed 'normal'

- 'normal' was not my forte. I tried to be a Rocker, encouraged by my sister Sandra who needed me as her dancing partner. The Rockers held dances called 'hops' in local church halls and social clubs - sometimes they could be violent. Motorbike chains and small hatchets became the testosterone battler's favourite weapons. I parted company with this crowd after my first serious fight - the cause was over nothing as usual, but I remember I did not like the way my fist felt when it buried itself in the poor guys stomach.

Through the CND and other sources I began reading about non-violent protesters, like the great Indian thinker Gandhi. He believed non-violence was the best way to effect change. I believed change was the only way - it sure as hell was in the air. I decided to give non-violence a try. I turned the other cheek by not fighting my friend's brother who was several years my senior. I let the bloke hit me time and again, telling him as he did so that I would not fight him back as I believed in non-violence. He had no idea what I was talking about - and for sure *he* didn't believe in non-violence - so he continued punching me until a lucky blow knocked me out. He probably thought I was a soft touch. I learned a few things by allowing myself to be beaten up:-
1. It takes longer than you think for black eyes to go down
2. A solid punch to the body doesn't hurt very much
3. Let some other idiot turn the other cheek if he so wished
4. I would be getting my punches in first if anyone was foolish enough to pick a fight with me from then on.

Soon after this incident I started going to local Jazz Clubs. The best one was in a pub called *The Cherry Tree* in Welwyn Garden City. Here I met for the second time a bloke named Donovan.

We had first met in an alcoholic haze - well, strictly speaking the haze was mine, not his. A friend of mine - also called Dave - was in the Army. Somehow he had managed to procure a load of miniature bottles of whisky - I suppose each bottle would have been a treble measure in a bar. Needless to say I was not used to drinking whisky at the tender age of 15¾. We became very drunk and as we both soon wanted a piss we found ourselves in the local public toilets. As I stood there, trying to keep it together and take a leak, I heard a voice talking to me and on looking up I saw a young man I had never seen in my life before.

"Who the fuck are you clocking mate?" I said in a threatening manner. "Do I know you or what?"

"It's OK Gyp," I heard Dave say. "It's Donovan - he's alright man - straight as a fucking die - can't go wrong with him mate - cool as a sodding cucumber."

"Well bloody lucky for him then ain't it? Or I'd have tied his cock around his blooming neck," I laughed, loudly and drunkenly.

Chance meetings can sometimes bring the strangest of results. In this casual way I had just met the guy who would be the best friend a bloke ever had; in whose company I would travel the world in First Class seats on the most luxurious aircraft; be a guest in the best suites in the most exclusive hotels; be ferried about by Rolls Royce's and hire mansions in the hills above Los Angeles from where we travelled to gigs in style by Lear jet.

 In our third encounter in a pub a few weeks later we knew nothing of this rosy future, but Donovan and I got on like a house on fire nonetheless. We talked our mouths dry about one thing or another for hours and the upshot of the evening was - we decided to go on the road together.

   For me it was my second leaving and I was determined to make a proper go of it this time. The Open Road called to me with more power and seduction than I thought it possible to feel. Not yet 16, and about to break the law again by leaving home before that sacred date, I gambled on my folks not calling the police - after all, I had been working for nearly a year - I knew a few things, didn't I? Didn't I? Well - like most youths - I thought I did.

CHAPTER TWO
<u>HITCHING AWAY</u>

Don and I decided that if we were getting the hell out then there was no time like the present. We planned to leave the very next morning.

During our conversation in the pub we'd had an audience - a nice fellow called Lockey and an old friend of Donovan's named Danny. These two were also keen to leave home, so with great enthusiasm we four plotted our escape. We would go to Cornwall. The route was duly worked out and we agreed to meet up at *The Cock* the following morning at 6 a.m.

At home that evening I tried to tell my parents I was leaving. They told me I was far too young and had no money - that was true - I had three pennies to my name. Nevertheless I left my folks house at 4.30 to get to St. Albans at the appointed time. I had a change of clothes, three pairs of underpants and six pairs of socks - this being all I could get out of the airing cupboard in my parent's room without waking them.

At a roundabout in Hatfield, four miles from our rendezvous, I met Donovan and a very pretty young girl named Pauline who had promised me her sleeping bag, then Dono and I rambled off like proverbial heroes, with kisses and hugs from the sweet Pauline, to meet up with Lockey and Danny at *The Cock* pub stables door. Fate was holding us squarely in its manipulative hands.

The plan was to double up - Danny and Dono, Lockey and me - we would see how that worked out for lifts. If we had to split up then our great idea was to meet up in Torquay. We would make our individual ways to the Clock Tower there on the hour, every hour and presumably this would get us all back together again. It worked well. We arrived at the Clock Tower within an hour of each other, still in the pairs we set out in and not too bad wear and tear wise. But it was later than we had anticipated. Obviously we would have to find somewhere to sleep - but where?

We were feeling a little crestfallen when out of the glare of the setting sun his long hair ablaze with sunlight a Beatnik walked the shining road towards us.

"Hey man," said Lockey, "know anywhere where we can kip down for the night?"

"Sure do," said our own Knight of the Road. "Just keep walking up that road ahead of you - turn first left, second on the right. You'll come to a fancy street man, but don't worry about that - half way up it on the left there's a derelict house - you'll get in around the back – there's a broken sash window on the downstairs level - the glass has been cleared out, so it's easy to get in - no cuts man. Smells a bit - but it's OK for one night - I wouldn't stay any longer though - they say it's haunted - that's why they can't sell it."

We looked questioningly at each other. "Shit," said Danny " 'aunted!"

We walked together in the direction we'd been given and arrived at the house as dusk fell. Climbing through the broken window we all four stood looking at the smashed furniture, the peeling wallpaper and the crushed glass on the living room floor. There was a musty smell, reminiscent of wet newspapers, rats' droppings and human turds.

"Fuck this!" said Lockey forcefully. "I ain't sleeping ere! I'm going down the local pub, pull myself a chick and sleep wiv 'er. Don't give a flying fuck what she looks like either."

"You can't do that Lockey - we came together, let's stick together," I said.

"But this is disgusting Gyp! Looks like shit on wheels," intoned Danny in abject horror.

"What the hell do you want man - a five star hotel? We're on the fucking road for Christ's sake!" I laughed

We peered into another room to see if that was any better. For sure it *wasn't* any better - if anything it looked even more tattered and spooky, though it was a little less smelly.

"It feels bloody haunted to me," came Danny's soft voice.

"OK - I know it's a bit weird - but let's look upstairs - it's not so dark up there and maybe it'll feel less depressing," said Donovan nervously. We four brave lads crept up the stairs as though our very lives depended on it, with Lockey and I out in front as we were the biggest.

On the landing things looked bleaker. There was a taste in the air of dead things; decaying animals; rotting hair; twisted bones; sticky sinews. We were getting carried away by a horror story of our own making as we climbed higher and higher until we found ourselves in the attic, thick with dust and grey matter reminiscent of brain tissue. Suddenly Danny farted with the pent up excitement of it all - and we cracked up with laughter. As our guffaws subsided, we heard it - a shuffling sound in the darkest, furthest corner of the dilapidated room, followed by a deep moan that could only have come from the lattice lips of the damned. An obscure figure arose before us, arms akimbo, dirt and dust falling from its body like thick viscous liquid. We four intrepid travelers stood stock still for two or three heartbeats....then as one we stormed the stairs.

Lockey, with his longer legs and quicker reactions, was first down followed in a flash by the rest of us.

"What the fuck was that?" he asked, his eyes alive with adrenalin.

Then, as if by premonition, I had the answer.

"Just some old bum sleeping off his alcoholic binge," I replied. "Harmless really."

"Yer - you think so Gypsy? Well let me tell yer - yer won't catch me going up them stairs again tonight," Lockey brayed.

"Let's just kip in the kitchen for tonight and leave it at that shall we," sighed Donovan.

"Yep, you're right Dono. We need to be up early tomorrow - we still have a way to go," I said tiredly.

With that we unrolled our sleeping bags, I with the delightful vision of the young lady who had loaned me hers dancing before me.

"You're right man," said Lockey yawning, "but if that old bugger comes down the stairs tonight we better stick together and clobber the stinking bastard."

With that gentle thought blowing through our minds we settled down for the night. Our first day on the road had turned into a wee adventure - a taste of many an adventure to come.

The morning found us refreshed and in good heart. Packing our few valuables into doss-bags we hoisted them onto our young hopeful shoulders. The plan was the same - this time we were to meet up in Brixham harbour by the Clock Tower as near to noon as possible. At the Tower we would change partners and continue to St. Ives.

Hitchhiking was fairly easy in those days. It was the main means of transport used by our Forces during the 2nd World War if they had any sort of home leave and often the first thing we were asked when entering a car was what service we were from - usually in a voice that held amazement at how low that service must have fallen to include lads of our decrepitude.

The hitching didn't go so well that day and each of us, in our separate ways, got stuck on the road due to lots of short hauls, detours and long waits between lifts. We were learning that a hundred mile journey could take 48 hours.

We arrived in dribs and drabs in Brixham - hopelessly out on our noon expectations. Knowing there was no way we could make it to St. Ives that day, we pooled our resources to make a meal of a large loaf and two tins of fish in tomato sauce. Donovan had left home with a fiver in sixpences; I had 3d. Lockey and Danny both had a few quid. Basically we had nothing at all - nothing but a huge great faith in life, confidence in abundance and a deep, deep feeling of comradeship.

"We ain't getting to Ives today," Lockey said, his face grim with frustration.

"You're right there," said Danny. "Let's make the most of what's left of the day by having a holiday - after all, we are by the sea."

With that we walked at a leisurely pace down the road that led to the coast. We felt so alive - so fulfilled - so unbelievably free.

The day was reaching its climax with a perfect sunset when Lockey and I spotted a pillbox that appeared to be fused into the rock surrounding it. Pillboxes were machine gun posts left over from the War that dotted the coastlines of Britain in the early 1960's. Lockey and I went to explore this modern day concrete sandcastle.

"Just sittin' there doing nothing', ain't it Gyp? Why don't we kip here for the night? Be as snug as a bug in a rug."

"Looks OK," I said, "bit dodgy getting in though." I jumped down from the rocks above the pillbox onto its roof. "Be shit if we have to climb in through the gun slit," I called out. "There must be a door down there somewhere - want to have a look for it Dono? Let's try breaking in - better that, than wriggle our way through this bloody porthole."

Donovan's eyes followed the 20 metres drop to where the ragged rocks below were being pounded by the evening tide. He took the long way down, step by step. Sure enough, there was a door - but it had a huge, rusty padlock on it.

"You'll have to get in through the gun slit Gypsy - there's no other way," Dono called up to me.

"Then we need a rope mate - that's the only way we're getting in and staying alive," I shouted down again.

With these words floating down in the evening breeze, Donovan walked off to the thin ribbon of sand nestled between the ragged concrete jetty and the grey-green sea.

"A rope," I heard him mumble to himself as he set out on his mission, "where am I going to find a bloody rope for fucksake!" Then, a few minutes later, to his utter amazement, he found a length of bright orange lobster pot rope wedged between two rocks. What incredible luck! Grinning from ear to ear, his legs wet up to the knees, Dono pulled for all he was worth until he freed the cord from the green covered rocks. Triumphantly he brought it up the cliff and threw it over to me.

I soon had it tied to some rusty iron reinforcing which was jutting out from the top of the building. Draping the cord over the side I tested its strength. *'It'll do',*

I thought as I looked over the drop. Twenty metres down the sandy coloured rocks glistened as we assembled to go one by one over the edge.

"Bloody nicaroonies - that's a long way to fucking fall!" laughed Danny. "Sure as eggs is eggs we're going to die if we fall down there. Better say yer prayers now you three - you won't get another chance unless you're quick on the way down."

"What about you? Don't you need to pray? Think yer got a first class ticket to Paradise tucked inside yer underpants do yer?" Lockey said laughing.

We cracked up with laughter as hand over hand, my legs dangling into space, I let myself down the rope until finally I felt the tip of the ledge of the gun slit. I threw my body outwards and then, like a pendulum, swung into the dark interior, perching like a parrot on the edge. Striking a match I saw there was a level floor of concrete.

"It looks cool enough," I called up to them as I jumped onto the hard floor. "Doesn't stink anyway - it's good and dry and should do us a treat for one night."

Slowly the lads followed my example and made their way into the pillbox. *'Fantastic,'* I thought, *'a clean space smelling of old ozone and the incense of sun-warmed seagull feathers. Couldn't be better.'*

We opened our sleeping bags out on the floor and lit a piece of candle, as it was quite murky inside. Danny rummaged in the bottom of his bag and triumphantly brought forth two tins of baked beans.

"There you are," he beamed, "that should do us for a treat."

"Fan - fucking - tastic," Lockey intoned, "but I'm damned if I'm going to eat them cold - let's start a fire and cook 'em."

That means someone is going to have to go down for some wood," Danny said, not liking the idea at all.

"I'll go," Dono said cheerfully. He had remembered seeing broken twigs and old wood piled up on the cliff sides a little way above the pillbox and two minutes later he was passing a goodly load from the roof of the building down to my outstretched hands.

Danny was in charge of the cooking and the fire and he began heating the tins by placing them directly in the flames - we had no pots or pans.

"Have you pierced the tins Danny?" Donovan asked after they'd been in the fire a little while

"What would I want to do that for?" said Danny in all innocence.

"Shit Danny! You wanker!" Dono shouted. "Take them out now! Knock them out of the fire for fucksake!"

"Knock what out of the fire?" answered Danny completely oblivious to what all the fuss was about.

"The bloody beans you idiot!" Lockey shouted as he skittered across the floor away from the flames. "The bloody tins will explode like bombs - they'll rip us apart in a small place like this!"

"Bombs for fucksake," Danny cried as he knocked the swollen tins away from the fire. "Never 'eard of Baked Bean Bombs before - know they make you fart - but that's too much that is." he chuckled.

We laughed our heads off at Danny's comments and once the beans had cooled off a bit we ate their contents in complete contentment.

'This is great,' I thought, as I looked around our cosy encampment. Dono put some more wood on the fire as the high pitched screams of sullen seagulls, scampering for a place to rest on the nearby cliff face, entered our shelter. The dancing flames made shadows of consorting fawns on the backdrop of the crumbling plaster of the wall. What more could we want? We had a safe, warm, dry place to kip and beans in the belly as a bonus. Each in their turn blew out the candles placed at their sides. The warmth made us drowsy. Our retreat became as dark as space as the flames of the fire slowly extinguished. We slept.

I awoke on the wings of fear - what was that bloody noise? It was Lockey, coughing fit to die - soon I heard Dono coughing too. I felt a cutting stab in my lungs like spitted with a blunt knife.

"My eyes are stinging like fuck!" Lockey spluttered between coughs.

"Shit man - what's going on here? I can't see a thing - I'm blind as a bloody bat!" Danny called out in panic.

The reason was obvious - no chimney. No chimney for God's sake - nothing to let the hot smoke out except the gun slit we had crawled in by. We had to get out. The fire and hot smoke had replaced the oxygen in the enclosed space and we couldn't breathe.

Like fiends from Hades we rose from our sleeping bags - which caught at our ankles, intent on keeping us trapped in the quagmire of smoke. This was no joke - we were close to being suffocated. Knocking into each other with our eyes streaming and coughing fit to wake the dead we stumbled around the pillbox.

"Put your arms out at waist height and slide around the walls till we find the gun slit," called Danny

"Here - over here - I've found it!" Donovan called out.

We veered to his voice like iron filings to a magnet and dragged the clear air into our lungs like nectar. What idiots we must have looked, with our young stained faces peering at each other through the foggy smokescreen of our own stupidity. Lockey took a deep breath, re-entered the smoke and put the remains of the smouldering fire out by pissing on it. That was a beautiful sound that hiss. More smoke wafted by - scented this time courtesy of Lockey's waters. I searched from face to face and knew what we all knew.

"Thank God we weren't deeply asleep," Donovan intoned gravely.

"If we had been," I said stony faced, "we would be dead meat right now."

Lighting the candles - and wiser now than we had been on lighting them earlier that evening - we laughed at our dirty faces, got into our sleeping bags and called it a night.

We woke to a magnificent day, with the scent of ozone wafting its way through the gun slit opening. Rolling up our few belongings, we carefully climbed out of the pill box. Once on the roof of it Dono untied the rope and hid it under an overhanging rock. The rope was our secret - something to share with other Knights of the Road. It was a passport for a night's doss in the gypsy hotels of the road.

We wandered down to the sea and cleaned our faces and hands as best we could. The scent of wood smoke had permeated our clothes, but we hoped the sea breezes would take care of that sooner or later. Ready for the journey again we four climbed up the incline of rocks and onto the open road where Dono and I paired up and walked off. Within ten minutes Danny and Lockey passed us - thumbs up - in a small car. 'Never mind,' I thought, 'there's plenty of time before nightfall - we'll make it to St. Ives today.'

CHAPTER THREE
ST.IVES

St. Ives was love at first sight. Not quite sixteen, two adventures behind us, Donovan and I mooched along through the quaint town so full of romance and history. The air itself smelled different. The aroma was of cleanliness and tidiness. St. Ives smelled of ice-cream, saffron cakes, coffee, tea, beer, pub lunches and ozone by the bucket load.

Seagulls sat like sentinels on the rough stone wall that bordered the sea front and once in a while screeched out their apology for a song, just to make sure they and the world were not dreaming this dream alone. How could we, so young and so free, not help but take this day to our hearts?

Thrills of freedom ran up and down our bodies; our minds expanded into a space that was timeless, endless and limitless; this was the Open Road - and we were proudly on it. We were young, full of delight, and out for the learning experience that adventure would bring us. There is a wise old saying that states *'Youth is wasted on the young'*. Usually true - but Donovan and I didn't waste our youth - we lived it to the full, exulting in each God given minute.

We were drawn inexorably to the beach where we met a very pretty young lady who stated boldly that she liked to meet all the beatniks that came to St. Ives. She was the youngest daughters of one of the most famous of the potters of St. Ives - and this was her town. The more I talked to her the more attractive I found her, then I asked her age.

"Fourteen," she said proudly. "I know I look older than my age," she added with a cheeky look that was directed at Donovan.

"Well my little love, older or not I won't have you put my mate here in prison for any hanky-panky you might have in mind - so you keep those wonderful green eyes of yours to yourself," I joked.

She laughed good naturedly as she walked us to a place known locally as The Island where she showed us the best kip in town - the beach huts that sat squarely on the seafront sand.

"Don't spend any more than two nights here, otherwise the locals become suspicious," she told us seriously. "Tomorrow I'll show you an even better place, but that's some way out of town. Now I have to go home or my parents will be worried about me. See you both later," she concluded, dashing off with the energy of a young antelope.

"Well that's a bit of luck, she's a find and no mistake," said Dono with a leer on his face a mile wide. "How do you think she knows all she knows Gypsy?"

"Don't let's look a gift horse in the mouth," I said. "And you watch out - she's jail bait, she told you so herself."

Inside one of the beach huts we scooped out a shallow hole to deposit our sleeping bags in.

"I hope none of the kids piss on our things while they're changing in here," Dono said seriously.

"Why? Is that what you used to do you old bugger?" I laughed out loud.

"Come on Gyp," said Dono, smiling to himself, "let's go and tell the others about our find - I'll treat you to a Cornish pasty if you're hungry."

"Hungry? Are you joking? I could eat three horses - saddles and all! It must be the sea air getting to me," I laughed.

"Sea air my bollocks - it's the thought of all those sweet young chicks getting to you Gypsy. Did you notice how full the seafront was of them as we walked by?"

"Notice? I would have to be blind as a bat and slow as a possum to have missed 'em - Fantastic, eh? Art School lassies most of 'em - intelligent I would bet yer. I like 'em bright," I said with a twinkle in my eye.

"Well you should do well me old mate. You're definitely the thinking girl's crumpet if ever I saw one," said Dono.

We met the other lads soon after our meal and told them of our good fortune.

"Great stuff you two!" Lockey said, a smile on his face a mile wide. "Just look at all those birds - the place is overrun with 'em. I'll buy us a pint apiece to celebrate our first night in Ives." As good as his word he took us to a pub on the seafront where we soon made ourselves at home.

Lockey was a very handsome fellow; he could charm the pants off most girls, so it wasn't long before he was chatting up a raven haired beauty. Donovan, Danny and I soon got talking to some girls from Bristol - sure enough they were

Art School lassies as I had predicted. After hearing of our adventures they dipped into their pockets to buy us a round.

Later that evening Lockey waved to us happily with a big wink in our direction as he departed the bar. He had scored well and was off to spend the night in the rented room of his new girlfriend. 'Well, you lucky bastard, maybe ours is still to come,' we thought.

But not that first night. Our Bristol girls decided it was too complicated, as the three we liked all shared the same large room, so Danny, Dono and I wound our half-drunken way back to the beach huts enjoying as we did so the clear star filled night and the euphoric feelings a few hot kisses, and even hotter promises, will put in a young man's mind.

"What a gas Gyp," said Dono as we climbed into our sleeping bags.

"You can bet it's gonna be a gas alright," I replied sleepily.

St. Ives was an experience never to be forgotten - It held so many 'firsts' for me. It was where I first fell deeply in love; first felt the knowledge of brotherhood; first realized that you aren't going to die before you're supposed to; first understood the true meaning of 'freedom of spirit'; first knew for sure that each man is his own island; first welcomed the fact that God was in no man's church, but lived in the very core of our own being; first got drunk on something other than alcohol; first became aware that colleges didn't hold a monopoly on intelligence; first understood that sex is a responsibility as well as a fantastic pleasure; first realized that governments don't really govern, they only make a show of it.

These are the 'firsts' of youth - and youth is the only time to put these feelings into any sort of perspective. They are thoughts that sit in the very essence of ourselves - our minds need time to understand the power these thoughts evoke in the heart. There in St. Ives both Donovan and I gave ourselves time to understand these revelations, thus to a greater extent we knew who we were - a useful knowledge - for the man we become in youth is the man we are going to be for the rest of our lives, however hard we might try to hide it. These understandings are the building blocks of our character.

In Cornwall we found understanding in the simplicity of our lives. In the stream of innocent pleasures we were washed clean by the clear waters of 'not needing'. By not pursuing the puerile we placed ourselves on the path of wisdom, a wisdom usually associated with that of eastern philosophy, but the fact is that Truth isn't only to be found on the banks of the Ganges - Truth by its very nature is universal, found often in the cracks and crannies of that journey to the mountain of our higher self, where if we are at all aware, we touch the never ending vastness we call God; we become as one with the universe - one small electric thread in the picture of Life's Great Tapestry of Illusion.

In the years that were to come Donovan and I never forgot that fertile ground that was our discovery of the open road.

A little more daring than most - or a little madder - we threw ourselves into living. We lived in beach huts, pillboxes, tents, the occasional paid room, a hut on Crab Rock and out on the open sands of a moon and star encrusted beach. Also for a time in a cramped dwelling made of branches and plastic bags that a friend and I had made in the woods of the grounds of a swanky hotel. I never had money in my pocket; never knew where my next meal would come from or how I would get it; things turned up or they didn't. We needed very little and, like the birds that wake up singing, we cocked our heads in the hope of finding that proverbial daily worm. Most days we found it within reach.

Full of warmth and good cheer in St. Ives and heated by feelings evoked by the brotherhood of man I decided it was time to look into the sisterhood as well and search for the special one. *'Seek and ye shall find'* as the saying goes - and I found her. But the difficulty lies in knowing whether what you seek is fantasy or reality.

Ann was fantasy, though at the time she felt as real as London Bridge.

She was a beautiful, blonde waif of a girl; a blue-eyed, elfin faced lass with a devil-may-care attitude to life in general and an air of Northern honesty - and all this was tucked up neatly in a shapely little body that was under no pretensions of being anything other than what it was. Ann was a good soul and I wanted to eat her all up - little blue and white striped t-shirt and all. Being about 20 she was older than me by several years but as she looked three years younger and I looked five years older than my 16 years things worked out well for us looks wise.

Having just found my path to freedom I was concerned about not committing myself to a girl too quickly. Mostly I met Ann in the daytime - it was easier that way. She had a Grandmother and an Uncle living in St. Ives. The uncle wanted to put her under his wing and chaperone her - nice really, albeit old fashioned - but it got on Ann's nerves. She was used to looking after herself and doing as she pleased in Manchester. As the new generation we had a responsibility to once again go forth and multiply - spread that seed man. Around our camp fires lit on deserted beaches, we would discuss these thoughts with great gusto, while grilling a mackerel or two. The amazing flying sky was everywhere, burned through with shining holes in the firmament poked by God's sticky fingers.

It was easy for the Government and the Churches to say, 'What is the Youth of today coming to' - well I will tell you what they were coming to - A great respect for peace; a love of Mankind for Mankind's sake; a disgust of war; a silly idea of honest government for the people by the people - and of course a little more freedom to choose our own pleasures without Big Brother breathing paranoia down our necks.

It wasn't till Ann's brother turned up one morning that I realized she had gone. He informed me that my old mate Donovan had taken Ann away and seemed very concerned for her well being. He asked for my help in finding her but I told him that if she'd left with Dono she'd be fine.

"He knows the ropes, there's no need to worry' I said. 'Annie just needed to get away from it all."

"I'm sure you're right Gypsy - it's just that they have no money and that spells trouble to me."

"You need less than you think mate," I told him in all honesty.

"I heard Donovan lost his job - something to do with a near fatal accident in a boat that involved my sister. You can see why I worry Gypsy. Please help me find her. Have you any idea where they might have gone?"

"Not a bloody inkling - but listen man, what do you intend doing if you find them? For all I know you might call the cops and blame Dono for the whole shooting match. No way man - if you want my help then I'm coming with you."

"Great Gypsy!" Ann's brother replied. "That's exactly what I wanted."

"There's no guarantee we're going to find 'em you know. I ain't seen Dono or Annie in quite a while," I said.

"Is that so? I was told you were seeing quite a lot of Ann," her brother volunteered.

"Was yer now?" I answered suspiciously. "Well, there was a time when I saw quite a bit of her but nothing too serious came of it. Right, if we're going there's no time like the present."

He grinned at me and went to fetch the car. He was a cool cat this one - told me his name was Peter. We got along well and he chatted about Ann - seemed to really love his sister. Nice, I thought - I had a sister myself. We were on the only road out of Ives when he asked me my plan.

"Only thing I can think of is that they may be on their way to St. Albans. If so Don will want to spend the night in a derelict house we know of in Torquay. He'd think that a safe place to kip down - not sure if Ann will think much of it though," I laughed.

"OK Gypsy - you're the boss. You know what's what - all this is new to me. Never knew you lot existed before today - it's quite exciting really," Peter volunteered.

"I suppose it is," I said, though I was becoming a little blasé of the lifestyle.

The journey to Torquay was uneventful and when we arrived at the derelict we found it boarded up good and tight. I knew that Dono and Ann had not stayed there.

"Sorry mate, the whole trip's been a waste of time."

"Yes, well that's not your fault Gypsy, it always was a long shot."

"Like I told you - if she's with Donovan then she's cool as a cucumber. You'll hear from her when she's good and ready. Just keep yourself together till then mate."

Such was my advice to Peter - but a funny thing happened to me as we sat in the long silences of the return journey. It dawned on me just how much I would miss my little Annie. The last time I had seen her she was a bit pissed off with me to say the least - and I couldn't blame her.

It was in the little wooden hut on Crab Rock. I was using one of the beds in there in a most delightful manner with a lovely young lady named Veronica, when out of the blue the door burst open and there stood Natalie.

"She coming!" she blurted out. "She coming Gypsy! Ann's on her way here now man - be here within minutes she will."

I noticed the startled yet inquisitive look in Veronica's dark Kohl enhanced eyes but I knew I had no time to explain.

Natalie and I had been talking in the pub the previous night and I, in my cups, had been waxing lyrical about my love for Ann. Needless to say the romantic Natalie had been amazed to see me enter the hut with another girly on my arm the very next afternoon. 'So much for deep loving feelings,' she must have thought, when to her horror she saw in the distance the wee figure of Ann approaching. When it became obvious she was heading for the hut Natalie panicked and rushed ahead to warn me.

I jumped out of Veronica and into my trousers, determined to meet Ann on the other side of the door leaving Veronica and Natalie inside.

"Hi Annie love, what are you doing here?" I asked as calmly as I could.

"Looking for you," Annie beamed up at me. "You sound a bit breathless Gyp - what you been up to?"

There was a pregnant silence - and in that pause there came a feminine voice, loud and strident.

"He's been fucking the arse off me and Natalie!"

I turned in distress to see Veronica, a demonic grin on her pretty face, stride briskly out of the little hut.

"That's not true," said Natalie, "he was only fucking Veronica."

"And I suppose he was only licking your sweet pussy and not fucking it," came the very pissed off voice of Ann. I had to laugh at Annie's tone of voice and hilarious comment, the wicked look on Veronica's face and the even more guilty look in Natalie's eyes. The three girls gave me long looks. Each expression said something different - but the meaning was the same.

"Fuck off Gypsy, fuck off!

Oh well - you can't win them all.

Sitting in Peter's car thinking over this interlude I began to realize how unfair I had been. Annie was fantastic - really someone special - I saw now that she was deeper in my heart than I was prepared to admit to. As we journeyed back to St. Ives my feeling of loss became almost unbearable, Bloody hell - what was happening to me? If this was love I didn't like it. The ice cold thought was getting through to me that I had just lost my best mate and the girl I loved.

Dono had helped her leave. It was not unusual for us young Knights of the Road to be asked by teenage girls to hitch hike with them back to their homes.

We boys knew it could be dangerous for these pubescent young ladies to travel alone. We also scored rather well when we arrived at their parents' house as they, being grateful, gave us a shilling or two for the return route.

'That's what Don has done - taken Ann back to Manchester,' I thought to myself. It was possible - might just be probable. I told my thoughts to Peter.

"Could be you're right Gypsy, but somehow I doubt it," Peter mumbled quietly to himself. "We'll soon be in St. Ives, maybe they'll have heard something while we've been gone."

But there was no news when we got back in town. Peter offered me his hand, thanked me for my help and gave me three quid   "That's a little something to keep you alive for the next few days Gypsy. You're a good guy you know - the world would miss you if you weren't in it , so take care of yourself man."

He was a good bloke our Peter - albeit a great liar. I gave him a hug and rambled off to the pub. I owed a few drinks and a meal or two to those who had given me recently. Peter's three pounds would release me from their kind debt. I saw Natalie in the pub so I sat down and joined her. At the end of the night we wandered off into the sunset together, three sheets to the wind, and made our way to the hut I'd help build in the grounds of a first class hotel. By the time we woke up and made our way to town next morning the news was everywhere. Dono and Ann had returned.

Strictly speaking only Ann had returned, the police having taken Dono to the border with Devon telling him to stay out of Cornwall for good. 'Great,' I thought, 'Don's sure to return by evening then I can ask him what the hell happened to them both.'

As the day passed news came to me that Ann was no longer in St. Ives - she had been taken back to Manchester - by her fiancé.

"Fiancé? What bloody fiancé?" I asked.

"Well Gyp," said Beaky. "A bloke came for 'er in his car see. Took 'er from the 'ands of the police who were looking' for 'er - took her straight back to Manchester toot sweet he did - 'er bags were ready packed in his limo - nice car - nice looking fella as well," said Beaky. "They say 'is name was Peter - ring any bells Gyp?" Beaky concluded with a huge grin on her pretty face.

Ring bells? Ring bleedin' bells!!

My whole head was filled with 'em! Bloody Hell - I had been conned by Peter! Conned me good and proper the bugger had. Dono is going to laugh his head off," I thought. 'Bloody fiancés!'

I waited for Donovan to get in touch with me - all he had to do was get the word out when he returned, but I heard nothing as I waited with Natalie in our pub on the seafront. As the evening wore on I became involved in some serious talking with a very interesting girl. Her name was Rebecca and she had worked for over a year in a kibbutz in Israel. I hadn't heard of a kibbutz before, or the ideas behind them, but they seemed good to me.

"You don't have to be Jewish to join a kibbutz," Rebecca informed me. I tucked that information to the back of my brain.

Natalie was getting jealous, until she discovered Rebecca was engaged and that her boyfriend was returning to England from America the very next day. But Rebecca was broke; she didn't have the fare to Nottingham and was afraid to hitch hike alone, so she asked me if I would go with her. I was feeling the wanderlust myself so I thought, 'why not?' She was delighted by this and we arranged to meet the following morning at 5.30 on the main road, Natalie and I left the pub early and when we got to our kip that night she was even more passionate than usual - I guess she wanted me to return.

I was a little late at our rendezvous next morning but Rebecca was there waiting for me. Although only 19 she was very womanly with her natural wavy blonde hair and big hazel eyes. Looks made a hell of a difference to male drivers so I reckoned we would get to Nottingham in record time - but we ended up taking most of the day, mostly our own fault as we lingered too long in a transport café. In Nottingham she took me to her boyfriend's flat and made the introductions - Barry was very grateful to me for bringing his lady and I spent a pleasant enough night in their company. One thing stood out from that evening. Barry had brought some records back from the States and he was particularly keen to play one by a guy called Bob Dylan. I pricked up my ears in amazement at what I heard as he sounded very much like my old mate Donovan. 'Bloody hell', I thought, 'I must remember this bloke's name and let Dono know.'

Donovan had been practicing any song he could lay his ears on and we two were beginning to go out on the streets - Dono with his guitar and me with a paper and comb or a kazoo. I played the fool when passing the hat round and that helped a lot. It was handy if we were stony broke. I thought we were lucky that the audience paid good money just to hear Donovan sing - we had no idea then that the reason was some strange magic Donovan possessed, a spellbinding ingredient that was to turn him into a millionaire and one of the best known and influential artists of the mid-sixties.

But here was I, in a strange flat with perfect strangers, listening to a singer who was a dead ringer for my old mate Dono. We three were most probably the only three people in England who had ever heard of Bob Dylan - and a conversation with Joan Baez many years later proved that to be the fact. I said before, it's the little things that change the course of a life. This first visit to Nottingham was to change my life, and Dono's, irrevocably.

Of course I didn't know that as I climbed the high wire fence at the base of Nottingham Castle where Rebecca said I would get a kip in the caves for the night. We waved goodbye from opposite sides of the fence and I slept very well in those caves until I was woken by laughter and loud chatter. Then a voice said......'and this, class, must be one of Robin Hood's Merry Men.' I raised my head to see twenty or so girls dressed in school uniform and I bid them good morning from the confines of my sleeping bag. Their teacher laughed with his pupils and then led them off to see the real sights of the castle.

The journey back to St. Ives went well. I arrived late afternoon and immediately asked around for Donovan amongst the beatniks there. Within twenty minutes Don and I met up - though we had only a brief conversation as Dono was so pissed off about the way things had gone with Ann that he had decided to go home to Hatfield. As luck would have it he had met a man who was taking a shipment all the way to London who had plenty of room for Donovan and his battered guitar.

"OK mate, I understand how you feel - the season's nearly over anyway." I said. "I'll let you know where I settle for the winter - but it feels like Manchester to me."

"Don't mention Manchester," Donovan groaned.

"There is something I must mention though - it's really important. Listen man - Bob Dylan - he's a singer from America - you have to get hold of his album - I forget the name of it but yer gonna fall out of yer socks."

"Why Gypsy?" Dono asked.

"Because he sounds a bit like you or rather more like Woody Guthrie but he writes his own songs as well as singing other peoples. Could be you'll get inspired or something."

"Right - got it - Bob Dylan. Have a good journey Gyp - wherever you're headed - and have a ball when you get there."

"Sure will, and the same to you mate - be seeing you soon I hope."

"Yer, cool - keep on looking after yourself Gypsy."

"Love yer man," we said together as we hugged emotionally by the side of the road. I watched as he walked off. I could tell he was tired and a bit depressed because his limp was more pronounced - a sure sign of how he felt.

My heart went out to him.

We were not to see each other again for a few months - and what months they would be.

CHAPTER FOUR
<u>MANCHESTER</u>

Manchester was in my mind - and so was Annie.

The combination made me pack my few belongings into my doss bag a couple of weeks after Dono had left. I was sixteen years old and my thumb was in the air again as I set out to find Ann. I knew it wouldn't be easy - all I had to go on was her name - Ann Jones; no address; no telephone number; not even a photograph. Just how many Ann Jones's were living in the environs of Manchester was anybody's guess - probably hundreds.

Manchester in the early sixties was a great place to be. The Mancunians were a warm hearted and friendly people, generous to a fault. I liked their open-faced ways. Everything was *'love this'* or *'love that'*, *'How you doing love?'*, *'What can I get you sweetheart?'* *'Sure thing me darling'*. The two main remarkable things about the city was its all night bus service and its all night cafes.

In my time *The Sovereign* and *The Alcazar* were the best known, although *The Alcazar* bordered on being more of a club than a café. *The Sovereign* was the place - it was choc full of characters. Petty criminals, prostitutes, homosexuals, drag queens, alcoholics, upmarket bums and the occasional beatnik and Knight of the Road. Once in a while a normal person walked in. The atmosphere in this café was amazing.

It was situated on the second floor of a little square which had market stalls as a permanent fixture. You entered it by climbing up a steep narrow stairway to a heavy door, the wood panels of which had been replaced by thick glass. *The Sovereign* was always warm, noisy, smoky and full. Its coffee was thick and served in a mug - very unusual for the time. Its meals were homely and cheap.

When I began to be known in *The Sovereign* I was treated to the odd meal by the girl who worked behind the counter who was fascinated by the fact I came all the way from London. She was an angel and looked out for me as she knew I was all alone in the world and was living under a Privet Bush that grew to the right of the main entrance of Manchester Cathedral. Her motherly instincts came to the fore and if an order was wrong, or not to the customer's taste, she looked for me.

"Gypsy darling, your meal's ready!" she would call out in her loudest voice.

When you throw yourself on the good offices of the world you meet people like this - it's almost as if they were put there for any emergencies in the scheme of things to fill in the cracks in the unusual so to speak. I for one would like to thank the 'fillers' for being there.

Manchester Cathedral is in a very nice spot near the City Centre. The wild and wonderful Privet Bush near the main entrance was my doss. I had my sleeping bag wrapped up in two plastic bags to keep the rain out, tucked away deep inside it. On a clear night with the moon shining through silvered branches I was stared down on by the most remarkable of gargoyles. I remember vividly the first time I awoke to see these ghastly monsters leering down at me in the light of the full moon. It was quite an experience.

I met some interesting characters in the café. Frenchy, Pill Bill, Penguin, Diamond Liz, Stoned Stan, Fleet, Tex and many more. Frenchy and Stoned Stan were my closest friends as they were on the road proper. Pill Bill was about a lot but lived at home most of the time. He dossed down at his mother's house on Coronation Street whenever he wasn't too stoned. (Yes - there really is a Coronation Street in Manchester.)

It was a great age, an innocent age - an age when it was even cool to smoke dope. Why? Because very few people knew anything about cannabis , that's what kept it cool. If you were in the know you could buy it direct from several colourful folk in a pub on Moss Side. It wasn't a big deal then - there was very little profit in it. It was a little bit of sunshine for the rainy northern streets.

What was wrong with that I ask you? Cannabis is not remotely addictive. On the other hand the drugs that our society loves, alcohol and tobacco, really are addictive and very, very dangerous to our health. Believe me - I know - I went through hell to give up cigarettes, whereas I gave up smoking cannabis, when the time came ,with no trouble at all, though I had smoked a lot of the stuff for many years.

I guess I was a bit of a pillhead as well as a toker in Manchester at that time - mostly blues and amphetamines - which came via Pill Bill. Also we bought a thing called Nostralean from the chemist - it was in a plastic tube and made to put up your nose to relieve cold symptoms. For some unknown reason it contained some sort of speed. We would unroll the soaked paper inside, put half of it on a piece of bread and eat it. It tasted revolting and kept repeating on you all through the high. A cough medicine known as Dr. Collis Brown was another of our favourites. This cough bottle contained opium and must have been the nearest modern day recipe to laudanum, albeit weaker. Alcohol being out of our price range we'd buy a few bottles of Dr Collis and get the high we could afford.

Donovan had found his true soul in the creativity of his music. He was having a whale of time writing and learning new songs, wanderlust however was winding its spring in his young body. One evening a travelling Beat entered *The Cock Inn*. He ended up talking to Donovan about his new pal Gypsy Dave who was living in Manchester. Much to the Beat's surprise Dono told him I was his best pal and that we had left home together to travel the open road. This is how Donovan heard of my whereabouts and first heard of *The Sovereign*. Our young Beat gave Dono exact directions on how to find me and next morning Don set off on his journey, guitar in hand and sleeping bag tied to his back, hitchhiking to Manchester to join me. It was great to see him and out of the blue like that after our break of a couple of months. We sat together on a wooden bench catching up on our news and, dragging deeply on a joint. I related my search for Ann Jones.

For weeks on end I had been asking people in Manchester if they knew of an Ann Jones who had recently been in St. Ives. With each enquiry I left my address as *c/o The Sovereign*. Believe it or not I did find Annie. She got the message through the grapevine that I was looking for her and much to my joy and my friend's satisfaction, on a cold, wet windy evening Ann walked into *The Sovereign*.

Our reunion was short and sweet - Annie had changed - well, to be fair, we both had. She was living with her new boyfriend who sold pharmaceuticals. He was away that night and for the long weekend. She asked me to stay and so it was we experienced a sweet and sensitive come-down. My euphoria receding on the waves of each succeeding hour like so much honey dripping from a humming heated hive. Annie was wonderful and our time together was precious - but it was obvious to both of us that our paths in life went along different ways.

Within a few days of this meeting I found a fascinating beatnik girl called Lorna Smith. It seems funny that I went to Manchester in love and looking for a girl named Jones and fell madly in love with a girl named Smith. Lorna was the same age as me - sixteen. She had big, soulful eyes - dark and mysterious - eyes that carried at their centre a warmth and glow like a welcome home fire. Her long, lithe body was seduction itself to me. Somehow she held this sexuality in check with an innocent sincerity rare in such a young girl.

Together we moved into a room in Cheatham Hill, hoping against hope that we could pay the rent. We had to borrow a gold ring to put on Lorna's finger as in those days no one would rent a room to a couple they considered to be 'living in sin'. We were unbelievably happy in that small room and for weeks on end we lived on sex and joy and sliced bread. No marge, no jam, no eggs, no meat. Our love for each other was so great it overcame all objects put in its way whether it be fate, money or our landlord - Mr. Wiseman.

Mr. Wiseman was a kind hearted Jewish man who found my long hair and dark clothes quite normal. One day he said to Lorna, "My son too has long hair - he is studying to be a Rabbi. Is Gyp studying too?"

I told Dono the punch line as we walked side by side laughing our heads of at that thought in the warm hearted City Centre of Manchester.

"Well mate," I said, "there's one good thing and that's you don't have to kip too rough as you can come and doss on our floor for as long as you like. Lorna won't mind - of that I'm sure"

But Dono declined. He admitted that he might feel a bit jealous of my scene with Lorna.

"You could always get in touch with Annie," I told him.

"No man - I just had it in my mind that you'd be free to go off with me and have adventures like we did before. - but now there's another to bring into the equation. But it's cool Gypsy - I'm happy for yer - you old fucker."

He said this with a smile creasing the corners of his eyes as we climbed the stairs to *The Sovereign*. Seeing it, as it were, through the eyes of my mate I saw once again what a weird café it was.

"What do you think Dono?" I said proudly.

"Nothing like it in London Gyp - not even the *Two Eyes* has a patch on this place - not got the atmosphere."

"That's cos the owner's got another business - an antique shop. Any of the old chairs or couches he can't shift he brings 'em here for everyone to sit on."

The Sovereign was fast becoming the focal point of my life. I knew most of the regulars and most of them nodded and waved at me. Fleet was a tall, rather too neat, short-haired man who looked like the proverbial square peg in a round hole in *The Sovereign*. One evening he beckoned us over to his table.

"Hi Fleet, how you doin' man - Dono, this is Fleet - Fleet, this is Dono - an old friend of mine from near London."

"Yeah - you once told me when you was drunk that Donovan was yer best friend," said Fleet. "Look Gyp - this is urgent - so let's cut through the crap. I've got one question for yer - can you drive a van or car?"

"Yep - I sure can," I answered, wondering what he wanted from me. Dono looked on askance - he knew I couldn't drive.

"Well I need you to drive the Bedford for me," said Fleet, "only to Nottingham and only one way - I'll drive it back."

"What for?" I enquired.

"I found a scam to earn a little money - got to take a bloke's car back Gypsy. He got into a spot of bother over the engine and I got it fixed for him, didn't I?

Poor guy and his wife were going on holiday - thought I would 'elp 'em out."

"*I'll bet you did*" I thought to myself. " *- and put a few quid into yer own pocket along with it.*"

"OK, I said, "I'll do it - but only if Donovan can come along too."

"Got yourself a deal Gypsy my man - meet you both outside John's garage at 10 a.m. tomorrow."

"Who is that bloke?" asked Dono as Fleet ambled out the door.

"He's my old mate - craziest man in Manchester - used to be a policeman but he got drummed out the force for nicking what he should have been protecting. Has a heart of gold though. He let me use his van to kip down in whenever I had nowhere else to sleep. Drinks like a fish though and lives on runny eggs and tripe," I said grimacing. "So Dono - sorry I didn't ask you - are you up for the trip to Nottingham?"

"Are you kidding? I wouldn't miss it for the world - can't think of anyone more like Robin Hood than you Gypsy boy."

"More like Robin Hoodlum," I joked.

Little did we know that this was to be another mad adventure for us both. Fleet was the man and no mistake.

CHAPTER FIVE
<u>NOTTINGHAM</u>

Don spent the night on our floor as we needed to be up early the next morning. On the way to the garage he asked if I could really drive.

"I 'ad a couple of lessons from me Old Man," I said. "He reckoned I was a natural driver - and he was never one to give a compliment. Mind you, I can't remember much about it to tell you the truth - I guess it'll all come back and I'll take to it like a fish to water.

"For Christ's sake, I hope so," Dono muttered to himself.

Fleet was there before us with his red van parked by the side of the road.

"Right Gyp - let me show you the gears - all pretty normal though - here's 1st, 2nd, 3rd, 4th - and here's reverse. Right - I'll lead - if you get into any trouble I'll stop and come back for you. By the way - I'll be pulling into some pub car parks along the way. When you see me doing that pull the van nice and tight up next to the car."

"What for?" asked Dono.

"Well Don, it's like this - I've just got enough money to put petrol in this little bugger here, see? So we're going to siphon petrol out of other cars for the van - I've got the hose here - but you just leave that to me."

"How's he know those things Gyp - stuff like siphoning?" Don asked me incredulously.

"He used to be a copper - I suppose you learn all the dodges from the villains," I replied.

"Don't forget to go slow at first!" Dono shouted out the van window as Fleet pulled past us. Fleet put his thumb out and honked his horn as I pulled out behind him. I put the van through the gears smoothly enough and thought that although I was no Sterling Moss we would do OK. However, going back down the gears was a different matter and there were a few nasty crunching sounds which I didn't like at all. We nearly stalled.

"Shitting hell man! Do you think this is cool?" Dono asked, a little ruffled around the edges.

"Give me time to get used to the bloody thing and it'll be cool enough," I replied - a bit pissed off.

After some more mistakes, a lot of swear words, a near fatal encounter with a bus and a few stops for siphoning we finally reached the outskirts of Nottingham. Don thought I had achieved miracles and was very proud of me.

After asking directions Fleet stopped at the house of the car owner, knocked on the door and entered the bungalow like a returning hero. Twenty minutes later he reappeared grinning from ear to ear. I knew that grin. It meant he was drunk.

"Right you lot, that's that then," he said, patting his trouser pockets with great joy. "Time we were off to the pub."

"There's a great pub called *Ye Last Trip To Jerusalem*," I offered.

"Been here before have you Gypsy?" Fleet asked.

"As it happens I have. I brought a lassie here who was scared of being on the road alone - brought her to her boyfriend - the bloke that had the Dylan album. Did you find that album Don? Was I right? Sounds a lot like you on a bad day when you've smoked too much dope."

"Fuck all that lads", Fleet said impatiently, "let's find the pub."

"Sounds a bit snobby to me," Donovan intoned, raising his eyes.

"It's supposed to be the oldest pub in the world, " I said proudly. "Goes back to the days of the Crusades."

"Well I hope they've changed the bleedin' barrels since then," said Fleet.

The pub was seemingly stuck to the cliffs just below Nottingham Castle. Inside it was snug and warm with a huge Inglenook fireplace. Old dark beams contrasted with the ivory coloured walls and ceiling and the deep red wine coloured velvet curtains gave a rosy glow to the interior lighting.

Fleet - the only one in our company who had any money - bought the drinks. It was good beer and we drank in silence. The landlord looked askance at us, especially at Donovan. Maybe it was his guitar or maybe he was wondering if he was eighteen. Yer, well we were sixteen going on sixty.

Fleet was a great bloke, but if you looked at him long a shudder would run down your spine. That was your instincts telling you to be careful. As for me, well I had a devil-may-care attitude and a twinkle in my eye that usually showed kindness - but it could just as easily show trouble if it was upset. Donovan was as cute as a button, but well able to look after himself if push came to shove.

The night went by and the pints were downed. Out came Dono's guitar and a few songs were sung. From the corner of my eye I noticed a youngish, well dressed man watching the performance intently.

"Fleet, see that young chap by the bar? He's been clockin' our man here with gusto - what do you think his game is?"

"Can't tell yer - but he don't look queer to me and he's got plenty of the green stuff. Nice suit and smoking Turkish cigarettes, but what really gives it away is that he's been drinkin' shorts all evening - whisky mostly."

"You don't say - well I'm going to have a word in his royal ear and see what it is he has to say."

Dono continued to strum his guitar and watched as I walked casually up to the stranger whom I soon had deep in conversation. Ten minutes later, three pints in hand, I brought the wealthy stranger to our table.

"This is Roy - Roy this is Dono - and this very fine gentleman is the one and only Fleet."

"Pleased I'm sure," said our benefactor coyly.

Fleet eyed Roy with disdain. He didn't like rich boys as a rule

"What's the score Gypsy my old Arab?" said Don.

I smiled down at him. "Great news Dono, great news. It appears Roy here is a bit of a musical buff - likes your music man. He wants to know if he can record your live performance - says he has a recording studio with all the latest gadgets and that we can go there when we finish up here. So, what do you say - in or not?"

"What's the catch mate?" Fleet asked nastily.

"No catch my man," said Roy. "I'll buy some beers and a bottle of whisky from the off licence and we'll drive up to my home - it's not far from here. You do have a car don't you?" he ended, looking down his nose at Fleet.

"We 'ave a van," I said. "We're on the road - in between gigs as it 'appens." I winked at Fleet.

The beer and whisky was too good an offer to turn down

"OK lads, let's do it," said Fleet, " but you listen to me Roy and listen good - if you ain't on the level I'll have yer balls for dinner."

"As I am on the level, that is one culinary delight you will have to forego my good man," Roy replied, holding his own quite nicely.

"We'll follow you pretty boy," said Fleet as we tumbled into the van.

My head was beginning to spin - thankfully I wasn't driving - but Fleet was and he had taken about six times the amount of booze I had! Pulling away drunkenly we were soon headed uphill to the more elite parts of Nottingham.

"Bloomin' hell, this is a posh area," called out Donovan.

The houses got bigger and bigger until our new acquaintance pulled up at a six bar gate behind which were strewn small pebbles.

"That's a gate and no mistake," I said. "Looks like it was made by Leonardo and painted by Michelangelo."

As we passed on through, the grandeur made us feel like the poor relatives and that's no lie. Roy closed the gate carefully behind us and putting his finger to his lips he admonished us to be quiet.

"See you two - I told you he was just the bloody butler," Fleet chuckled.

The magnificent doorway to the house led to an entrance hall that was bigger than the room Lorna and I lived in. Cut glass vases full of brightly coloured and freshly cut and scented flowers stood on small antique tables. The carpets went up to our knees and the high walls were hung with tapestries.

"Jesus, Joseph and all the saints - these must be William Morris's!" I cried.

"Sure as eggs is eggs they ain't yours Gypo," chortled Fleet.

"Shush! Shush!" Roy said impatiently as he showed us to a door that led down to the basement. There before us stood an Aladdin's Cave of the latest technology in sound recording. Roy was so definitely on the level he could have re-invented The Flat Earth Society.

He hustled Donovan to a swivel chair that sat squarely in the centre of the room and placed a microphone near his face and another near his guitar. Roy was so excited it was infectious. He brought three tumblers from a nearby cupboard and poured us all an oversized whisky, much to Fleet's enjoyment.

"Now Donovan, I want you to sing into that mic softly - don't swallow it, if you know what I mean."

Dono was beginning to enjoy himself immensely. He felt quite like the star.

"When you need a roadie, I'm yer man," I said laughing uproariously as I trailed my feet through the spaghetti of cables that littered the floor.

"Alright my man," said Roy, "give me that last song you were singing just before we left The Trip."

This was fantastic. Me and Fleet were soon drunkenly banging away at anything that would make a decent sound. The Devil Drink made us ever more boisterous and louder. Roy, forgetting everything in his enthusiasm, didn't see the door behind him open slowly on its well-oiled and expensive hinges. Neither did he see the look of horror on the expression of the woman, draped in a feather boa over silk lingerie of exquisite taste that whispered 'money' with every rustle of its audacious movement, as she looked into the Den of her inebriate son. She took in at a glance the upturned bottles of beer, the nearly empty whisky bottle and the decrepit and drunken state of her darling son's companions. Ruffians of the highest order - of that no doubt. From my vantage point I could see behind her a much younger man dressed in a silk paisley patterned dressing gown - obviously her lover. He was very put out. His young face told us we were well below his high stratosphere and what's more, we had deigned to disturb his lovemaking - a capital offence at the very least. I couldn't help it. The expression on Roy's mug as he caught sight of his Mater made me fall from my chair in laughing delight.

"Mother!" he squeaked, mouse-like.

His mother's eyes were burning scorching holes in his deflating ego.

"Get these disgusting people out of my house," she screamed at the top of her lungs. "Are you deranged? Did I not send you to the finest schools in England? Were you not educated at Westminster? Is this where your education has taken you - to associate with riff-raff of this calibre?"

"Diabolical!" was the comment from the young lover as he looked down his nose at us over the shoulder of his older patron.

This was the straw that broke the camel's back for Fleet, he stood up to his full six feet one, legs apart, swaying slightly from side to side and with as much dignity as he could muster he stood his ground.

"Madam, you are speaking to a policeman of long standing. I will have you know that in my entire life I have never been so insulted. Do you believe I will stay for one minute longer in a place where I am not welcome? If you do Madam then you have another thing coming. Come gentlemen, we shall depart," he said, scooping up the nearly empty whisky bottle.

I sobered up as quickly as I could. Shit - I knew Fleet very well and I knew in this mood he was capable of nearly anything. In this mood I had seen him single-handedly demolish a Night Club for the simple act of being refused entry for seeming too drunk. That time I had been violently thrown down a fifteen foot stairway by a recovering bouncer whom Fleet had scarred for life that night. - it should have taught me to mind my own business - but it hadn't. Dono was really pissed off with the way things were turning out. This meant he would never get to hear his session and he, as we all were, was very pleased with his performance.

"Out! Out! Out!" was the command on the lips of Roy's suppurating mother. Poor Roy was as disappointed as the rest of us but he couldn't do anything to help us - obviously mummy held the purse strings.

We filed through the mansion's portals like shorn sheep. Donovan, with as much bravado as he could muster, climbed into the back of the van and I jumped in the front as Fleet gunned the engine. He drew up slowly to the magnificent gates - I could see from his florid face that he was about to blow.

"Well Gypsy, what the fuck are you waiting for - the pissing manservant?" he shouted to me sarcastically

'Here it comes,' I thought to myself as I scrambled from the van and endeavoured to open the Six Bar Gate.

It wouldn't budge, no matter what I did.

"What's the bleedin' matter with the fucking gate Gypsy - can't you shift the thing?" Fleet intoned with pent up anger. I looked at his face and knew it was over. "Get the fuck back in this van man. I've just about taken all the shit I'm gonna take for one day." I knew better than to refuse.

Fleet brought the front of the van very slowly, even lovingly, up to the painted wooden bars of the gate and then began to edge forward. The gate began to bow. I threw myself on the floor of the van and saw Fleet had an expression on his face that would have won him a prize in Hell. He pushed his foot down hard on the accelerator.

The van shot forward and the beautiful gate was no more. It was hanging in parts on the front of our van and on the bumper, making the sound of a scalded cat as Fleet dragged it with us to the bottom of the road.

"Mary, mother of all nutters! What did you want to do that for?" cried out Donovan. I jumped out the van and threw what was left of the gate onto the grassy pavement, trying not to make too much noise - which was a joke, as we'd sounded like a Banshee on fire coming down the hill.

"Her Ladyship wanted us off her property as soon as possible Donovan, so I obliged the good woman forthwith," laughed Fleet.

"Can't keep a good woman waiting now can we?" I quipped.

"I think we should get the hell out of here before the coppers arrive," said Dono realizing the trouble we would be in.

"Too late," I said seriously, "they're already here." Then with a smile I pointed at Fleet. There was silence for a second then we all three collapsed into fits of laughter. Fleet recovered his composure and was soon ready for the return journey to Manchester. *'Thank God for that,'* I thought, *'that's that adventure over and done with.'* But I was to be proved wrong.....very wrong.

CHAPTER SIX
<u>SMALL CHANGE</u>

We were back on the road again and soon saw a couple of young hitch-hikers. Fleet would have passed them bye but I, like an idiot, I persuaded him to pick them up. They were extremely thankful as they climbed into the back beside Dono and gave their names as Michael and Nancy. Nancy was fantastically pretty, so Don played up to her over the neck of his guitar every time the street lights lit up the interior of the van.

"You're bloody quiet Dono. What's the matter, cat got yer tongue?" I said teasing him.

"Are you kidding, the scenery's just got better, that's all," he said eyeing the chick with intent.

I noticed she gave him a tentative little smile.

"Give us me favourite song Donovan - you know, the one you sang first in The Trip - the one with the fast tempo," Fleet called out over his shoulder. Dono knew what song Fleet meant and began giving it all he's got to impress the lassie. It was a great song and he played it with feeling, making us all feel light-hearted and free. Nancy was looking at him wide eyed now. Her boyfriend, if that's what he was, wisely took a back seat during this performance.

Nancy's eyes widened even more as Fleet caught up the rhythm, leaned out of the side of the van and started hitting his right hand on the roof while gunning the van to the off-beats with his right foot hitting the accelerator which made us bounce up and down like a demented kangaroo. It wasn't so bad for him - at least he had a steering wheel to hang on to. I suppose it wasn't too bad for Dono or me either after our experiences of my drive down but our new passengers, poor souls, were starting to think they had been picked up by three escapees from the local Insane Asylum.

Nancy was very frightened, I could see this even in the very dark interior of the van. I tried winking at her, trying to get her to see the funny side of things. Suddenly we swerved violently to the right - Fleet had nearly fallen out, catching onto the side of the van with his left hand in the nick of time.

"Fucking hell Fleet!" I cried. "You're going to kill us all if you keep going on like this. For Christ's sake Dono, stop singing that bloody song - you'll drive him mad," I shouted as I hung onto the back of the seat for dear life. Fleet slowed right down and turned to me, sober as a judge.

"What's drivin' me mad Gypo is the need for a bloody cigarette - 'ave you got one for yer old mate me Gypsy Boy?"

"Jesus Fleet, if I'd got one I'd give you one and that's no lie, but I got nix.

How about you two lovelies?" I enquired of our new friends.

"Sorry, we don't smoke, either of us," piped up Nancy

"Don't tell me we have no bloomin' cigarettes," said Fleet. "Dono - you got any mate?" Dono shook his head sideways.

"For fuck's sake Gypsy, that's diabolical - a real waste of space. We'll have to do something about it," he ended in a quiet voice.

Two minutes later, in a quaint little village, we pulled up at a cigarette machine.

"Anyone got any small change?" I asked

"Come on, get it out if you have," Fleet said, looking hard at Michael.

Michael looked scared but said nothing. "OK - come with me young man, I have something of interest to show you. It might just come in handy for the rest of your life."

He grabbed the hat off Don's head then took the crowbar he always carried under the front seat of his van.

"Come on you little fucker - I won't tell you again!" Fleet told Michael in a nasty tone.

"You better do as you're told," I whispered to Michael. "I think my mate Fleet thinks you're hiding your money and won't buy the cigs."

Michael traipsed after Fleet and stood like one entranced by the sight of the cigarette machine. Fleet acted like Houdini about to perform one of his famous illusions.

"Now Michael, me old mucker, I want you to concentrate. Look carefully at what I do," he lectured Michael, like a crazy Professor explaining algebra to a wayward student. "Now, first you take this crowbar and catch it under the lip of the first drawer of this wonderful dispenser - then, my little friend, you give it a sharp yank down - like this!."

The handle of the drawer flew off and landed at their feet with one packet of cigarettes. Dono and I felt like applauding, until we fully realized what Fleet was getting us into.

"For God's sake stop it Fleet!" I called out. "We can get some fags at the next garage."

Poor Michael was a second away from fleeing when a heavy hand fell on his shoulder.

"No you don't me old sport - you look carefully now me lad, this is very important. First you hold Don's cap at the bottom of the drawer - like this. Stop shaking lad - now watch. With your third finger on both hands, you catch the corners of the packets - just so. Then, with a quick flick, you send the packets cascading out as fast as they will come, see? *flick...flick...flick"*

Before we knew it all the cigarettes from the first drawer were sitting in Don's old hat. This time Donovan and I did clap. Michael however was looking as if he would pass out from fear at any moment.

"Now my boy, your turn," Fleet said with joy as he snapped off the second drawer. "Let's see what sort of student you are, shall we? Quick me old son, or we'll have every copper in the district breathing down our necks."

Michael was petrified but mastered his fear and did as he was told. He managed extremely well - considering. The packets were thrown unceremoniously into the back of the van where Dono sat in tears of laughter.

"Let's get out of here, Fleet" he said. "We've got enough fags to last us ten journeys."

"That's not the point - you don't understand Donovan - it's not the spoils we're after - it's the Art man - it's what you can learn from a beating heart and a mind that wants to run the body royal - it's how you discipline the soul to stay put when you want to get the hell away from the situation you've put yourself in. It puts you in touch with Risk man - the only drug worth having."

Fleet stood there on the street, the cold air passing on his unshaven chin and I swear at that moment in time he looked like a hero of past times. It was almost as if the spirit of Robin Hood himself had taken over his body. What chance have the villains got I thought, when this was an ex-policeman talking? Nancy put her arms around Michael protectively. They had never met anyone like Fleet before.

Unfortunately for Michael, Fleet had heard the tinkle of small change in his pocket. Twice more on the journey home Fleet made him run the gauntlet of the cigarette machines. Finally I stepped in.

"Come on Fleet, let the man off the hook for pity's sake. His little lady here is in tears. Be kind man - let's drop them off at the Transport Café coming up."

"You're getting soft Gypo, real soft," Fleet laughed back at me.

"OK - get your arses out of here you two - and Michael....you owe Gypsy one - you owe him one fucking great big one - and next time pay your way.'

Nancy held on tightly to her man as they ran into the lights of the café. It was almost as if they had been released from a spider's web. They appeared like children compared to Dono and myself but I bet they were a good three years our senior. Fleet drove us all back to the street where Lorna and I lived. It wasn't much, but as I looked up at our room in those dawn hours and saw Lorna's shadowy figure it felt a lot like home. She pulled the thin curtains slightly apart and gave a wave.

"You two want any of the fags?" asked Fleet.

I looked at Dono who shook his head in the negative. We were all smoked out, wheezy and ready for a kip.

"No thanks mate, you worked hard for 'em - you keep 'em," I said, yawning into my open hand.

My back was turned giving the thumbs up to my darling Lorna when unbeknown to me Fleet handed Dono a fiver. It was part of the profit from the car deal. He told Don to give it to me to help pay the rent, "but not till after I've left," was his last command. Just as I always said, Fleet had a heart of gold. He didn't even want thanks for his generosity, good soul that he was. But he was trouble was our Fleet and no mistake. Little did we know just how much trouble he had in store for our untroubled Donovan. We were soon to find out.

Fleet was a good guy - he had his problems, that's all - one of them being his wife. She was Swiss - not that anyone held that against her by any means. The trouble was she hated alcoholics and with a vengeance - unfortunately Fleet had become one. Fleet had a business of sorts - what it was I never found out. In my time in his company I never saw him do a single day's work. What I did know though was that the van he was driving around was supposed to be for work, but there was never much in it and he had told me that whenever I needed a dry place to sleep I could use the van to doss down. He even showed me the way to break in without a key. It saved my life on occasions.

If I slept in the van I was usually rudely awakened by being rolled from side to side in my sleeping bag as Fleet rushed off at top speed to get to the Pub at the precise moment of opening time. It was a matter of honour with him.

"That you Gypo?" he would say good heartedly as he heard my groans in the back. "Come on in when you're up and I'll buy you a half pint and some crisps for breakfast - then at closing time we can have eggs and tripe together."

Fleet swore by tripe - and I swore at it. He maintained it was the best thing for the stomach if you'd swilled a lot of booze.

Despite his drinking, Fleet was loved by everyone - apart from his wife - wherever he ventured to pour a pint down his throat He was always giving friends a helping hand, but if he thought you were taking the piss out of his good heart he'd come down on you like a ton of bricks. His biggest bugbear was himself. Deep down in his psyche he was disappointed in himself. Why? God only knows.

A couple of weeks after our return from Nottingham, after one drunken bad-tempered evening too many, his wife filed for divorce and he was thrown out of the house he jointly owned with her. She also obtained a Court Order banning him from coming within two blocks of his own home. Poor bastard, he was stymied good and proper. In desperation he looked around for a big enough scam to keep his tonsils permanently saturated in alcohol - and he found it. Unbeknown to Donovan, he was to be involved in the plot.

It was the Mother of all cinema break ins.

Two small time gangsters by the names of Tex and Taffy saw a golden opportunity to break into a cinema through a small back window conveniently placed at pavement height in a deserted back street. Once in through the broken window, Tex would tackle the safe (he claimed to be an expert safecracker). Fleet's task was to be the getaway man and he was to take the safe in his van in the unlikely event of Tex not being able to open it then and there. Dono was to be lookout - though he had no idea of what was actually going down as Fleet had told him a whole other story. Fleet, working on the theory *'least known, soonest mended'* told Dono to stand in the cinema entrance way and to sing his heart out if anyone should come along and then to whistle when it was all clear again.

"If anyone comes along just play your guitar like a maniac," Fleet laughed, grinning from ear to ear.

"But what for Fleet?" Donovan wisely asked.

"Well Donovan, it's like this......You know me missus has thrown me out - well, I've got a new girl - she's incredible and wants to move in with me in my new flat. What's more, she's filthy rich - got loads of the old spondulies - her folks are rich because they own a big shop near to the cinema - they live above it in a grand flat. Now here's the problem - if they catch her movin' out then there's goin' to be hell to pay. They hate me with a vengeance and Eleanor would never get to leave if they caught us."

"Jesus Fleet - Eleanor?" joked Dono.

"I know - I calls her Ellie for short. Anyway, I'll have to get her out of there like she was sittin' on soft boiled eggs, if you know what I mean. We don't even want the neighbours to know about me or the van - so we need to know the coast is clear when we run out with her belongings - that's where you and your guitar come in Donovan. I've arranged for a couple of buddies to help with the heavy stuff, so when you see me van go by you just walk off as if nothing had happened. If it all goes well me girlfriend and I are going to treat you to a couple of tickets to Tangier. I know it's what you would like, cause I hear you and Gypsy talking about it all the time."

"Two tickets to Tangier?" Don asked incredulously.

"Well it would be as a 'Thank You' - how about that mate?"

"Fucking fantastic! You're on man - got yourself a shooting match," Donovan laughed loudly, excited by the prospects.

"But we mustn't get caught, see, or the whole fucking match goes up in smoke," Fleet answered seriously.

Donovan did indeed 'see' - but I'm damned if I did when Dono told me his news later that evening. I hadn't seen Fleet for a few weeks - then I saw him in *The Sovereign*, huddled in a corner talking intently to a couple of dodgy characters. He had given me one of his devil-may-care grins and a wave, but he hadn't asked me to join him. *'Friendly enough,'* I thought *' but up to something'*. Now, after listening to Dono, I was sure he was cooking up some scam.

"Look Don, it sounds too pat to me. Fleet's got some plan hid up his sleeve. Why are you singing for instance? It don't make sense - you could just go up and tell him if anyone's coming."

"I've thought that out Gypsy - you see the singing voice carries further than even a shouted voice - and no one would be alerted by singing, would they? It's very clever of Fleet to have thought of that Gyp," Dono explained to me.

"Well - you could be right," I mused, "but if you take my advice you won't do it. If I were you I'd drop it like a ton of dog shit."

"Come on Gyp - for a song we could be in Tangier. Think of that mate - all that lovely marijuana going for nix legal too - and the sun Gypo - the sun."

Donovan's enthusiasm was catching. "OK mate, let's try for the sun - I suppose stranger things have happened," I said wearily. "When is he wanting you to perform?"

"Tomorrow night - about elevenish. - but I kind of think he don't want to hear me vocals."

"Alright then Don, Lorna and I will meet you here after your non-performance - but for Christ's sake take care."

We hugged as we parted. It would be many a dark week before we saw each other again - hard and weary weeks for Donovan; weeks you don't want to repeat in a lifetime; weeks that build character in the hardest possible ways.

As Lorna and I weaved our way home that night, the conversation with Dono still uppermost in my mind, I was not feeling comfortable. OK - what did I know? Let him have his plans - Donovan was so enthusiastic there was no way I wanted to dampen his spirits.

Lorna and I left our room late on Sunday evening and sat in *The Sovereign* awaiting the outcome of Don's adventure. Slowly the evening went by - midnight - one - where was he? Then I saw Fleet waving at me from the door - his face told me all I needed to know.

"For fuck's sake, what's happened now?" I mumbled to Lorna as I got up from my seat. I ambled over to the door and Fleet and I lumbered down the stairs and out into the darkened streets below. It was drizzly. We sat on the empty market stalls as the canvas topped trestle tables were dry and deserted.

"Sorry Gypsy, but Donovan won't be coming - he's been arrested," Fleet said sadly.

"Oh shit man! What have you got him into?"

"Strangeways Prison I'm afraid."

"Oh for God's sake Fleet - Strangeways - that rundown piece of Victorian shit!"

"It's only for a while Gypsy. We had a back up plan - just in case anything went wrong. Tex and Taffy agreed to tell the truth about Donovan and say he had nothing to do with the break in. I'm sorry Gypo - I used Donovan and for that I'm sorely repentant. But listen, the boys will get him out of the trouble we put him in - it'll just take a bit of time, that's all."

"Time my friend is a bad time in that fucking excuse for a prison. Strangeways is a God forsaken piss-hole of a prison!" I shouted at Fleet.

"Funny enough, it's not so bad on the inside Gypsy. The Prison Staff are the best in the business. I've taken many a prisoner there in the old days," he said, trying like mad to placate me.

"Thanks a lot Fleet - I'm sure Donovan is appreciating that right now - you bastard! Shit man, come on - tell me the truth. What did you get Dono into," I demanded forcefully.

"Calm down Gypo - then I'll tell yer….I've never seen you so upset - I'm not saying that you shouldn't be upset - I'm just asking yer to be cool."

"OK - I'm calm - now tell me what happened," I said, getting hold of my temper with extreme difficulty.

"Look, it was a simple break in - in through the window, find the safe, open it, take the money, out through the window again and into my van and away - no problems."

"No problems?" I echoed in disbelief.

"Gypsy - keep cool now," Fleet intoned. "Don's part of the tale is simple. I asked him to play his loudest song if anyone approached the street."

"Yeah - I know all this - Donovan told me. He thought it was something to do with your girlfriend leaving home," I said impatiently.

"Yep - we tricked him. Anyway Gypsy, for fuck's sake keep quiet for a minute and you'll know all there is to know."

I looked at Fleet open mouthed but decided it would be quicker if I did keep quiet.

"Well it all went wrong, didn't it? Blew the whole fucking shooting match. That street is usually deserted at that time of night - not a soul on the pavement on a Sunday evening an hour after the show - Manager and staff nicely tucked up in their beds by midnight. We cased it for three weeks to find the best time to do the heist."

"Three bloody wasted weeks," I said.

"Yep - you're right Gypsy - three fucking wasted weeks. It was just bad luck, that's all - luck like you wouldn't believe. Tex and Taff got in as smooth as silk, hardly a sound breaking the glass - cleaned up the glass quick too - just like Pros - I was very impressed.,"

"Fucking good for you," I said sarcastically.

"Now Gypsy shut the fuck up and listen will you?"

Well it all was as good as gold till I reckoned it was time for them to come out with the money. I was circling in me van ready to pick 'em up when I sees this copper. As quick as a flash he dodged down our street.

'Why?' I asked myself, knowing that this wasn't his beat - then I sees the reason - a bloody cigarette.

"He wanted a bloomin' fag and he wasn't taking any chances with getting caught smoking on duty, so he ducks down this side street to have his puff. Well, I thinks to myself, he won't see anything - Donovan will distract his gaze from the empty glass of the window and we might just get away with it if everyone keeps their cool. Sure enough Donovan started singing as soon as he saw the copper. The policeman most probably thought he was an idiot, singing at the top of his voice to an empty street. The trouble was Donovan was too good - the bloody copper stood and listened to his song! I believe he was thinking of giving him some small change when right onto his big black shiny service boots went a pile of cigarettes, chocolates and sweets which poured out of the broken window. I was sitting in me van watching it happen! I saw him collar Donovan in a second then he blew his whistle and suddenly there were coppers everywhere so I took off in the opposite direction - there was nothing I could do."

"Why the hell didn't Donovan make a run for it?" I asked Fleet.

"Because he had no idea of what was going on - he knew he was innocent so he wasn't concerned at all. Thought he could explain his way out of trouble with no fear."

"You bastard Fleet! You absolute bastard!" I said with real feeling.

"You're right Gypsy, there's nothing I can say in my defence - guilty as charged."

"What happened to the money in the safe? Surely Tex and Taffy didn't go to all that fuss just to rip off a few sweets and cigs?"

"Dunno, but I'm going to find out. I'll try and see the boys tomorrow and let you know how it stands with Donovan."

Lorna came out of *The Sovereign*, concern written all over her lovely face. "Not good?" she enquired looking me deeply in the eyes.

"Not good at all," I said ,walking her away from Fleet and *The Sovereign*.

One thing I can say though - as I glanced back in Fleet's direction I had never seen a man more folded into himself with remorse and blame. Even so, I couldn't find it in me to lighten his burden by calling 'goodbye'.

It was a week later that he found me. It had taken him that long to get permission to see the boys. He sat me down, bought me a cup of coffee and a chip buttie and started his tale. It appeared that the cinema they broke into had a very old safe - a huge monster of a thing that wouldn't pass through the window and too old by far to be within the expertise of Tex, whose knowledge of safes was a lot more modern. Beaten by antiquity they decided they weren't leaving without taking something for their trouble so they took the float out of the till and grabbed some packets of cigarettes, chocolate and sweets.

"The good news Gypsy is that the boys both kept to our agreement and told the truth to the coppers. Donovan also protested his innocence."

Weeks passed until the trial. The Judge found Donovan 'not guilty' - though he didn't seem to have any great confidence in that belief. He told Don he would not be welcome in the environs of Manchester. There was no protest from Donovan - as he'd had just about enough of Manchester as he could take. He was deliriously happy to be out of Strangeways Prison.

Lorna and I said our goodbyes at the station as Dono and his father Donald waited for the train back to Hatfield. It was the first time I had met his father - he seemed cool with his heavy Glasgow accent and reminded me of a poet or 'back stage Johnny', yet had the air of having been abandoned in the Thirties and being unable to find the stage door he had once passed through. We were to work together in the future and my first impressions of him turned out to be strangely prophetic.

The train started to build up a head of steam as we hugged our goodbyes.

"Well, there's one good thing come out of all this Dono - you should have plenty of things to sing about now you've experienced prison life," I joked.

"All that rubbish about breaking stones on the chain gang you mean?" he laughed.

"Something like that."

"Gypsy, I will have great pleasure in forgetting the whole bloody incident. I learned one thing inside - and that is that there's nothing romantic about spending time in prison mate - nothing at all. It's just a bloody waste of time and youth and life," he told me.

"Better to be on the road and free," I said.

"You got that right Gypsy - nothing compares to that freedom. See yer later man. Stay free Gypsy - stay free man," Donovan said, leaning out of the open carriage window as the train pulled away.

CHAPTER SEVEN
<u>FINDING THE BREAD</u>

Spring was beginning to be felt, even in the grey and red tenements of Manchester's inner city. My mind was returning to the coasts of Devon and Cornwall. I praised Cornwall for all it was worth to Lorna in the hope of persuading her to come with me on the road.

If we go down early we can take our pick of any jobs on offer," I told her. "We can live in the beach huts till we've got enough cash to get a room."

"How about a tent Gyp? I've got one you know. It's in the loft but still in good condition, I saw it only the other day." Lorna asked

"Alright, why not - as long as it's not too big and bulky it should do the job," I said, pleased that she was contemplating coming with me.

"But I insist we spend a few nights in a beach hut - it's so lovely with the sound of the waves lapping the beach, the moon shining on the sea and the gentle warm air slipping its way under the door flap like a warm blanket."

"Jesus Gypsy Boy, I've never heard you so lyrically poetic," laughed Lorna.

We were still in the little one room flat in Cheatham Hill and lived on next to nothing like a couple of church mice, yet still we owed a couple of months rent. We were going nowhere fast and achieving nothing of any importance, except we were getting to know and love each other. Mr. Wiseman was living up to his name and being very patient with his two young renters. One morning he knocked on our door and I jumped to the conclusion that his patience had run out, but I was wrong - he had come to offer us a very generous deal. He had got wind of a proposed change in the law that was going to give more rights to tenants and was going to make it harder to remove renters from landlord's property, so it was sensible to reduce his renters and make his rooms into flats. Would Lorna and I be happy to move out after two weeks? he asked persuasively As compensation he would waive the money we owed and give us the next two weeks rent free until we moved out. Would we be happy? We would be over the moon, thank you very much!

For us it was perfect timing as it gave us enough time to get our things in order and prepare ourselves for the journey to Cornwall. Someone even gave us a double sleeping bag. It was a good one and rolled up small even with the few clothes we possessed wrapped up inside. It was important on the road to give the impression that we weren't burdened down - it made it much easier to get lifts. Simplicity in all things.

Our goodbyes said to Mr. Wiseman we two lone figures headed off for the highway. We were moving on, moving to a natural rhythm that sings to the musical heart of a voyager who knows only the instinctual melody of the Open Road. *'Keep on truckin' mama, truckin' yer blues away.'*

The lifts came fast and furious.

"Wow! This is easier than I thought love," Lorna said to me, a pleasant warm smile on her lips.

"It can be a bastard too, believe me, but you've brought us luck," I replied.

"We'll be in St Ives in ten minutes," our driver informed us after several hours in his company. "Where can I drop you?"

"By the Ice Cream Parlour on the Front, thanks - if you're going that far," I answered.

"Very near it," he said with his pleasing Cornish accent.

"It's all so beautiful," Lorna declared.

"Wait till you've tasted their ice cream, it's gotta be the best in the world," I said, my mouth watering.

There was a magic in St. Ives that made it timeless.

The seagulls still sat on the railings now that the original wall had been knocked down and screamed out at the warm sea breeze that brought the slight metal tang of fresh fish on its tender breath. Lorna was exquisitely happy.

"How can I have spent my whole life in a city when there was all this out here?" she marveled

"Easy love - you didn't have me to show you the wonders of the world," I laughed.

"I don't know how you do it Gypsy my love, but your interest in all things beautiful somehow rubs off on other people and makes them see the world in a new, cleaner, brighter way."

"Jesus Lorna! And all that before we've tasted the ice cream!"

There was that smell again - it permeated your entire being with wellness. We ate our ice creams with silent glances at each other. God it was good - *'And so are you my little love Lorna,'* I thought while savouring the heavenly taste of that Cornish ice cream.

The evening wore on as we walked around the little town and shared half a pint of beer in the pub Donovan and I used to drink in, then I showed her the restaurant where our friend Dominic, in desperation and hunger, had snatched a crab from the main display and then ran like a demented dwarf, swaddled in his duffle coat and falling out of his torn plimsolls, trying to look innocent with a cooked crab stuffed down his trousers.

"Well my love, what's it to be - tent or beach hut?" I asked her.

"Ah my Prince, beach hut I believe," she whispered sexily.

"Tent tomorrow when I get the white stallion back," I joked.

"All you Arabs are the same - promises, promises," she sighed in mock regret.

We walked slowly arm in arm to The Island. Only the best for my love - and these huts were the best. There was no wind that night, just the gentle warm breeze I had predicted. She opened to me like a flower and her scent was of the sea winds touched by Patchouli.

We awoke early enough to walk the star strung beach, threw ourselves naked into the crisp cold sea and held each other close for the eternity of that moment, the slowly melting heat of our young bodies moulding us into a unity of oneness seldom realized in this poor mistreated world.

That first morning as we sat with a cup tea and a roll and butter in the Tea House - where the proprietor remembered me - we asked after our first job.

"You're a bit early Gypsy. Most of us that are open now work our own places till the season's properly upon us. We wouldn't make enough money now to take on help. Still, I'll keep my ears and eyes open for you both - seeing as you helped me out with your chums last year."

"What help was that?" Lorna asked me.

I'd forgotten all about it but with his reminder it came back to my memory. What the owner was referring to was the time he had asked me to tell the beatniks not to come to his Tea House all at once as it scared away the ordinary customers who spent a lot more money than we did. I had it out with our young Knights of the Road on the beach and nearly everyone understood. From that day on no more than two tables at a time were taken up by our young beatniks.

We left the Tea House and rambled the streets looking for a job but I had miscalculated. Instead of the surfeit of work I was expecting there was nothing.

"Oh well," Lorna said, "not to worry Gypsy my darling, you're always telling me it takes at least fifty one days before you die of hunger. That gives us roughly two months to find a job, so let's have a holiday before we die."

She was a great chick to be on the road with. We walked the half mile to a field where the farmer let campers put tents up. The site was perfect, pitched as it was near to the sea and up a winding road from the rocky beach.

Ours was the only tent there. After a few days we received a wave from the farmer, but he never bothered to come over for any rent money. What he did do though was send someone over to keep the toilets and the small showers clean. He was a real gentleman of the old school.

Lorna soon learned to cook simple meals over an open fire and we lived well enough on boiled potatoes, baked beans and any tinned product we could afford. I found a two day job painting some toilets for a pub and returned each day with more and more white spots on the only clothes I had - it made me feel like an artist. Lorna called me Rembrandt.

We lazed around the beach and went for long walks in the countryside and each day we walked the half mile to St. Ives town centre to see if notices had been hung up advertising employment, but there was nothing doing. I helped out on a dustcart for three days while the usual man was off sick - horrible work, but it paid well. It was our friend from the Tea House who told me about that.

Lorna heard about a little job helping with the small change in an Amusement

Arcade but when she arrived there the job had already been taken.

"Never mind dear, have a cup of tea on the house while you're here," the owner said.

As she sat drinking her tea she couldn't help but notice a young man in a neat sports jacket and polo necked jumper who was throwing pennies into the machines like confetti. He eyed Lorna with a cocky glance.

"Want a scone luv? He asked

"I should take one from you just to save you losing all your money," Lorna piped up.

"Scone for the lassie mate, make it snappy - lots of butter and jam. Some you win, some you lose," he said, nodding at the one armed bandits. There was a big noise as lots of pennies hit the drawer. "See?" he said. "You brings me luck you do. What yer doin' later?"

"Going home to my boyfriend."

"Bet he hasn't got two of these pennies to rub together, bet he's not got a penny to his name, has he? You're a bloody Beatnik, aren't you? Pretty little thing for all of that though."

"You watch it! My boyfriend's over six feet tall and built like a barn," Lorna said

"Bloody looks like a scarecrow I dare say if your looks got anything to do with it. Can't you afford to eat?" he said in a softer more concerned way.

"We eat plenty. I'm just on my way now to cook us a meal."

"Are you indeed. Well let me chip in and we can all eat together - I haven't had a homemade meal in ages."

"Don't know if Gyp would like that," Lorna said quietly.

"Gypo is he? Well I'm sure he will - cos I'm going to throw in two bottles of wine and a bottle of spirits just for good measure, see?"

"Jesus! You must be rich!"

"Just like Croesus, ain't I?"

"What's your name?"

"Me name's Brian from the Midlands."

"Nice to meet you, Brian from the Midlands," Lorna smiled up at him.

"Well, if we're going to eat this afternoon let's go - we can call into the shops on the way back and buy what we need."

Brian was very cool and paid for all that was needed for a simple meal - he also brought along plenty booze, as he had promised. When I met him I liked him immediately. He was very civil and a lot less Bolshie than he had been in the Arcade - so Lorna told me anyway. We ate a little and we drank a lot; not a good thing to do at the age of sixteen. I don't think Brian, for all his swagger, was much older than us, maybe a year or two at the most. He liked the idea of a tent a lot.

"I might price one up in the evening - see if I can't buy one in St. Ives. What do you think Gypo?"

"What's wrong with where yer staying now?" I asked him

"Just got in really," he said. "Still got me clothes in a bag at the Railway Station. The place I got's not much, I only put a couple of quid down. Made no commitment - so I can move out anytime I like. I think I likes this tent business. Don't see why I shouldn't pitch up right here. What will I need Gypo?"

"You'll need a sleeping bag, as it gets bloody cold at night. If you've got the bread you should buy a good torch and some pots and pans. The most important things really are a good sized frying pan and a half decent knife. It's a great pleasure to have breakfast made around the fire first thing in the morning. The smell of bacon's enough to drive a man mad," I said, dreaming of things Lorna and I didn't have.

We were awaiting Lorna during this conversation. She had bought a steamed treacle pudding and was boiling it in our one big pot. We didn't mind the wait as we were now getting through the tequila. I'd never heard of the stuff but after a couple of bottles of red wine, who cared. Lorna hadn't had a lot to drink because she was cooking and looking after us like we were kings. She gave us our pudding on paper plates and we drank on. Wanting, as all boozers do, to have those around them in the same state of mind as they are, I pressed Lorna to drink some tequila. She slugged away at the bottle, squeezing her nose.

"Come off it love, it's not medicine," I said taking the bottle away from her.

"Not a lot of difference, is there? It tastes terrible. Brian, throw me over the water."

Brian did exactly that; as a joke he emptied his glass full of water over Lorna, but before he knew what had hit him Lorna had slung the whole of the washing up bowl of water on him. She had got her revenge and no mistake. He was soaked to the skin in one drenching downpour. Bloody hell, did we laugh. Brian was really a good sport and laughed as much as us.

The only problem was that the warmth of the day was fast becoming the cold of the night. Brian was drunk and his teeth were beginning to chatter due to the strong cold winds coming off the sea. He couldn't stay in those wet clothes. Lorna went into the tent and pulling out our sleeping bag she wrapped it around his shoulders - but Brian still appeared to be turning blue.

"Fuck man, where's your digs? I can run there and get you some warm clothing," I said.

"It's OK, you don't 'ave to go there. I got me bag at the station - that's a lot nearer," said Brian.

Here's me key to the locker in the Left Luggage Department - it's number nine. Get me the big wool jumper - the navy blue one - my brown corduroys and a tweed jacket is inside the bag somewhere - oh and me thick black socks."

"Anything else your Lordship?" I laughed, somewhat relieved, as the train station was a lot nearer than his rooms. "Get a good blaze going Lorna and Brian will be halfway to being human again by the time I get back."

It only took me ten minutes to get to the station. The uniformed man at the Left Luggage was very pleasant.

"What can I do for you sir?" he asked.

"I want to get something out of the bag in this locker," I said, holding up the key. "Number nine." He walked me over to the big locker. "Got to watch you open it," he explained.

I turned the key in the lock, opened the door and pulled out the bag. Christ, it was heavy! I went for the zip.

"No you don't young fella," said our man putting a hand on my shoulder. "You don't open it here - not allowed. You could 'ave explosives in there for all we know - it's more than me jobs worth to let you open yer bag here. We got a nice big room for that kind of business."

"OK - lead on McDuff."

When I was inside with the door closed I opened the bag on the long trestle table. For the life of me I couldn't remember what clothes Brian wanted. "Fuck it," I said, tipping the contents of the bag onto the table - things falling everywhere. "That's it - black socks, blue jumper, brown trousers and tweed jacket. Great! Got' em!" I threw everything else into the bag again and zipped it up and took it back to the attendant.

"Be careful you haven't left anything in the room - Finders Keepers you know," he said giving me a wink.

I knew I was still a bit pissed - there was maybe the chance that I had overlooked something - so I popped my head back in again. Nothing on the table. I bent down to check the floor and in the corner where two tables met I saw a bundle of coloured paper. It was pushed right to the back as if kicked there or hidden by someone.I bent low and hit me head a right good smack on the wooden counter as I retrieved the loosely bundled paper.

Jesus, Joseph and half the Saintly crew - it was money! And a lot of it!

It was just like all those books I had read as a kid - the Famous Five down on the beach for their holidays finding a secret stash of money, obviously dropped by the long coated, dark complexioned, squint-eyed villain with a black hat and a strange accent.

I counted the money quickly - 150 quid! An absolute fortune!

"You alright in there?" the attendant shouted.

"You fucking bet I'm alright!" I mumbled. "What time's the next train to London? I asked, much to his surprise.

"Goes in three-quarters of an hour."

"Right you are - I want two singles for it - all the way to London."

My first thought had been to get as far away as fast as possible from whoever had lost, or hidden the money. But now visions of Tangier began to float through my intoxicated brain.

That's what Lorna and I would do - we'd go to North Africa! I suddenly became paranoid that whoever had lost the money would return for it.

"Been busy tonight 'ave yer?" I asked the attendant.

"Funny you should ask that," he said, "I had a couple of so called 'gentlemen' to help not more than an hour ago - big guys with dark moustaches and dirty suits - spent a long time in the room you was in. Didn't like 'em at all - seemed shifty to me."

Shitting hell! I thought - it's them! Maybe a big drugs deal or something. Time was wasting, I had to get back to Lorna, tuck away our few things and head back to the station. I got the tickets and ran off like the wind.

When I arrived at our campsite Brian was getting drier by the fire and was grateful for the warmer clothes. I hustled Lorna into our tent and told her to pack up as quickly as possible.

"What's wrong love?" she asked

"Wrong?" I said, smiling fit to burst. "Nothing's wrong my flower - in fact things couldn't be better. You and me is off to Tangiers, that's all," I said beaming at her like a light bulb.

"Tangier! But - "

"Lorna - shut up and pack up," I said laughing.

"What about the tent?"

"Forget the tent - and hurry, we've got a train to catch."

She looked at me for a second, knew I wasn't kidding and decided to trust me.

"We're off Brian," I said.

"Eh? Off where?"

"I've been offered a job and me and Lorna's got to go straight away - it's a live-in, so we got to be quick. We start work tonight," I lied.

"You can have the tent if you like Brian." Lorna said.

"You two are off in a hurry ain't yer? Here, where's my key?" Brian asked nastily. "Give me that fucking key you Gypo! Fucking thieving lot of bastards, all of yer."

"Fuck you Brian," I said in sudden anger. "What? You think I stole a pair of your sexy socks, you twat? Here's your precious key you fucking arsehole," I said, throwing it as far as I could into the long grass behind him. "Have the bloody thing and stick it up yer kybosh!"

"Gypsy my love, you said we was in a hurry," said Lorna, wisely interrupting me.

"Right you are, give me the sleeping bag and let's run."

We just made it - as the train pulled out we were sitting in our compartment panting our hearts and lungs out from running. Never again would I drink tequila, I said to myself. What with all the booze and excitement I fell asleep on Lorna's shoulder. I awoke to find her looking at me.

"Well? Aren't you going to tell me what this is all about? A girl's only got so much patience you know. Where the hell did you get the money for the tickets for a start?" I said nothing but pulled out the pound notes.

"My God! Did you kill someone Gypsy?" was Lorna's astonished squeal.

"I found it, didn't I?"

"Tell me what happened."

I told her the story of what went down in the Left Luggage room.

"I wouldn't believe any of it if it had been anyone else but you telling me this tale Gypsy. Did you ever think that it might be Brian's money?"

"Brian's? Brian's never had more than 30 quid in his hand at one time in his whole life," I said with conviction. "Believe me, all his flash was just that - flash.."

"I'd say you were right - if it wasn't for one thing Gypsy my darling."

"What's that then me love?"

Something a little bird whispered in my ear when I was in the Arcade and Brian went for a pee. There was a girl there who told me to stay away from Brian - she told me the police were looking for him - not in St. Ives, in the Midlands."

"You're joking aren't you?" I said in amazement.

"Not according to Beanie I'm not."

"Beanie? Christ, Beanie's as reliable as Big Ben on a good day," I said.

"Well she told me that Brian had tried to come on to her the previous night when he was drunk and he spilled the beans to her."

"So what's he wanted for then?"

"Stole money from where he worked - stole it instead of taking it to the bank as he did every Friday."

"Then decided to take it for a nice holiday in Cornwall," I finished for her.

"Yeah - that's about it."

"And he had the balls to call me a Gypo and a thief! Bloody liberty! Me has never stolen a thing in me life worth stealing."

"Well it might be that you have now love," was Lorna's reply.

"Shit - that's a drag that is," I said with deep regret.

"What you going to do about it Gyp?"

"Don't know - haven't had time to think about it yet with that sodding tequila mucking up me mind. When we arrived in London we sat in one of the big station cafes drinking tea, eating pies and thinking. I saw the word 'Brighton' come up on one of the boards. The name felt good.

"Alright love, let's get out of here - we're off to Brighton till I figure out what I'm going to do about this here bread situation."

"Is there that much to work out Gypsy?" Lorna asked in surprise.

"Well I didn't mind if it was just some scam going down and I ended up the beneficiary by finding the money but this new scenario of yours has got me a bit mixed up to tell you the truth."

"Wish I had kept me mouth shut Gypsy my sweetheart - you were a lot happier before I said anything. Look, you have no idea if the money's been stolen by Brian or left you by Fairies," she said sensibly.

"The only Fairies I know who would leave me that sort of money would want something I wouldn't want to give 'em," I joked, lightening up my mood.

"That's better Gyp - come on - train's leaving."

"Now I think on it - there was a sort of wallet you know," I said, my mind beginning to clear from the tequila. "I remember now - I picked it up from the floor after it must have come out when I up-ended the bag. I threw it back in the bag after I found his clothes. It flipped open - but there was nothing in it as far as I could see - certainly no money - me eye would have caught that. Shit, I don't like this. He turned out to be a bit of a fucker but I still wouldn't want to rip him off."

"If it was his money, then he ripped it off himself Gypsy," said Lorna. "Think about it like that and you should feel better."

I didn't take the decision lightly - but I decided to keep the money. Fuck it, worse things happened at sea.

"Right love, we spend one night here then in the morning we hitch to St. Albans - or takes the coach," I said.

"Coach would be nice," she purred.

"What do you think of the idea of taking Dono along with us to Tangier," I said, testing the waters.

"Alright with me Gypsy, but I insist on us getting one room and Don getting his own. It's a bit embarrassing otherwise," Lorna said coyly.

"Well you shouldn't be so bleedin' randy all the time Lorna."

"Me?" she exclaimed in disbelief.

We were both laughing as we entered the station at Brighton. She was such a gas was Lorna. Total strangers would look at her and just have to smile. She made the heart sing just to look at her because she had such a clear spirit. I was beginning to feel light hearted about our future now. Life is what you make it. Opportunities come along to do the things you're dreaming off - but not every day.

Yesterday Fate took my hand and showed me my future with a bloody great grin on its face like a cobra transfixing its prey.

"I could kill for a pint," I said.

"I'm getting worried about you," Lorna said simply, "yesterday morning you would have killed for a half pint."

"You see how money corrupts my love?" I replied.

A little later we found ourselves in another Arcade. Right at the end there was a sparkly curtain with a sign above it advertising:

Bill the Tattoo Artist.

We could hear a high pitched hum and a voice saying, "That don't hurt much Bill."

"I can make it hurt if that's what you want mate," Bill laughed

"No - that's alright - it's just that yer new machine's a lot less painful."

Here I pulled the curtain back to see an arm covered in blood. Lorna screamed but Bill just looked up as cool as a cucumber and with his left hand holding some cotton wool he wiped away the blood to reveal the most exquisite tattoo I had ever seen, in colours I found almost impossible to comprehend.

"Shit! That's beautiful!" I exclaimed.

"Got the balls for one?" Bill asked looking up at me. I had never thought of having a tattoo in my life.

"Me books in the corner - see if anything takes yer fancy."

I flipped the pages and a green dragon with red, brown and yellow wings fell out. It was love at first sight. Lorna knew I would have it done before I did.

"How much is this one Bill?" I asked

"Couple of quid to you son."

"Ah - it's not for me - I was thinking of having it tattooed on her bum," I said pointing at Lorna.

"In that case it's free," Bill laughed.

Lorna's face was a treat to see.

"I likes you son - for you it's only one pound ten shillings - how about that for a bargain?"

Watching the raised outlines of the tattoo swell up I wasn't so sure it had been a good move, as we planned to spend the night on the assorted sized stones under Brighton Pier, but Lorna wrapped my arm in a couple of extra tucks of the blanket before we turned in.

The stones weren't too bad to sleep on - if you wriggled your body in them they took on the shape of your form.

At six o' clock the next morning we were in the Coach Terminal buying tickets to St. Albans via St. Pancreas. There were so many saints in our lives - it had to be a good sign. Not having had a great kip the previous night we both fell asleep almost as soon as the coach engine started. Suddenly Lorna woke up and said "Passport" loudly.

"What are you talking about love - we don't need passports to go to St. Albans."

"No, but you will for Tangiers - not to mention France and Spain. For your information Gypsy I have a passport."

"With you? Here and now?" I asked in astonishment.

"Yep - I had an idea I might need it - and I wasn't far wrong, was I?" she said proudly.

"How the hell did you know to bring your passport?" I said amazed.

"Gypsy my love, you men are so silly - you forget I know you very well. You were always dreaming of Tangier and I knew determination would get you there some day soon. Do you think I was going to let you go off on your own without me? No way darling - not with all those fantastically beautiful Arab girls just waiting to get their scented claws into you - and every other Englishman. So I thought, Lorna you'll need your passport so you can go with Gypo when he's good and ready to go."

"You clever soul," I said, bowing my head to kiss her hand that was held tightly in mine as she spoke.

She sighed with relief. "I was afraid you might not like me being so pushy Gypsy my darling. I know how important for you your freedom is."

"Lorna my soul - you are my freedom," I said with passion.

She burst into fits of sobbing fit to bust her drawers and I laughed my socks off as people turned their heads to see what all the excitement was about. What a woman! She dried her eyes on my shirt tails, pulling them out of my paint speckled jeans. We were pulling into St. Pancreas by now.

"What are we going to do about your passport Gypsy?" Lorna asked seriously as we changed coaches.

"Don't worry - we'll work it out," I replied, sitting down heavily on the upholstered seat.

CHAPTER EIGHT
TANGIER ON THE HORIZON

St. Albans was associated in my mind with being young and a deep deep calm. My grandparents on my mother's side lived in a council house 20 minutes walk from the town centre. My grandfather was a wonderful old codger who was a train driver by profession. He loved nothing better at weekends than watching the horseracing on TV with a bottle of stout at his side. His spare cash went on the horses and his spare time went on his garden where he grew prize dahlias and chrysanthemums. He was one of six brothers, four of whom were killed fighting in the First World War, including his twin brother. My grandmother on the other hand loved a good gossip and church on Sunday - if the two were combined she was in heaven.

I spent a month of my school holidays each summer living with them in their house and being treated like royalty. I loved it - and in this way I got to know St. Albans very well, so when Lorna and I disembarked in the town centre I had no trouble showing her around. We went to Christopher's Bookshop and Café which was situated on a small street leading to the Cathedral. Above it there was a row of small flats where my good friends Mac Macloed and Stella lived.

We were just about to go and see them when into the café came Bomber. He let us know that Mac and Stella were away - he also let me know about a derelict house he had discovered.

"You go and look at it Gypo - you're going to love it," he said, mouth full of rich apple crumble. This was good news for sure - but he had some bad news for us too. "Donovan? Don's gone mate - left two days ago - went with Dippy - to Cornwall I think - or was it Devon?"

"We came to take Donovan to Tangiers," I said to Bomber.

"Jesus - Tangiers! Well - cor blimey! I'll let you take me if you like - won't charge you much either - in fact you can have me almost for free," Bomber joked.

That night we slept in the derelict house Bomber had mentioned. It was indeed a good house on a posh road and we soon made ourselves comfortable in one of the top rooms overlooking the overgrown garden.

"This is great," said Lorna, laying out our sleeping bag in a corner near the window.

"Let's go and get some clothes for the journey tomorrow - we can buy a bag too so that we look like normal travellers," I said

"Gyp, I got news for you - you could never look normal whatever you did," said Lorna.

It was while we were shopping that we met Peter on his big motorbike. Peter was a very young man but he had already made good. He was even in the *Guinness Book of Records* for attaining 9 A levels at the age of eleven. He worked for ICI and was paid a fortune compared to ordinary mortals. Unfortunately he was also hooked on cocaine.

Funny thing was you never knew he was stoned, whereas when he drank alcohol - which he often did - he was a positive danger to himself and to others. He was always a mine of information, so he told me exactly where to go for my passport and informed me that as I wasn't 18 - Jesus I wasn't even 17! - I would have to get my parents to sign the form.

"The easiest way Gyp is to get a six month passport because no one checks up on them," Peter told me.

"That means you'll get to meet my parents Lorna," I said after Peter had roared away on his motorbike. "They live about seven miles from here."

How and where I got the form to fill in I can't remember now, but by the next afternoon we were outside my folks house in Welwyn Garden City - shouting our heads off, but to no avail. Mrs. Morris from next door popped her head out to see what all the racket was.

"Ah, it's you David - I thought it was. Yer mum would have loved to have seen yer but yer too late. They've gone on holiday - left two days ago for Austria - or was it Australia? All the same to me them foreign places. Never been further than London meself - and very proud of the fact to tell yer the truth. All this wandering the world's going to get us all into trouble one day, you mark my words David."

"Marked with a dirty great red line Mrs. Morris," I said, winking at Lorna.

"Good boy you is - I always said so," she replied as we waved to her and got on the road heading back to St. Albans.

"So what you going to do about your passport now?" Lorna asked, a little worried.

"Not a problem - I'll sign the bloody thing myself - you remember Peter saying they never check a six month passport."

"But that's against the law," Lorna whispered in mock fright.

"So are half the bloody things done in the world love - so I wouldn't worry too much about that."

We got the passport with no trouble and we were soon in London buying two single tickets for Algeciras in Spain. The train left at 6 p.m. and we would arrive two nights and a day later. The first night we spent on the ferry. I found the film room and behind the rows of seats there was a darkened area where the carpet was thick. Here we put down the sleeping bag and, clasped in each others arms, we fell asleep. It was the first time I had left England. Lorna had once been on a weekend trip with her school to Paris - hence her passport.

On the train journey everything went well until we were halfway across Spain, when an announcement was made in broken English that we'd be having a 15 minute stop at the next station.

"Right Lorna, you sit tight and look after our gear and I'll go get us some pinsetters to spend."

"Pesetas Gypsy my love - pinsetters are flowers."

"All right, I'll bring you a bunch of them too," I said smiling at her.

It took longer than I thought to get the pesetas, but I was back on the train with some snacks just in the nick of time.

"Where's my flowers?" Lorna demanded, a smile on her elfin face.

"I gave 'em to the Spanish girl in the next carriage - she's much more beautiful than you."

Lorna jumped on me, her fists raised in play. "You just keep your eyes off them Spanish girls my Gypsy boy, or I'm going to flatten you," she said cutely

Our snacks eaten and soft drinks drunk we settled down for the night. We could turn the lights off inside the compartment but the outside corridor light was still shining. On Lorna's advice I drew the curtain that was on a pulley against the sliding door and it shut out the light nicely.

We were tired - it had been a long journey. We were just succumbing to that wonderful feeling that plays melodies with the mind before sleep when the door was thrown violently open and the curtain rudely whisked aside. I sat up instantly, thinking a couple of late passengers were needing to sit down. I looked up to the doorway and there stood a young Spanish man, he stood stock still in the doorway, taking me in first and then Lorna - confusion written on his face. Then, as if the penny dropped, he turned arse about face and ran off down the corridor without closing the curtain or the door.

"What was that all about?" I asked Lorna.

"Not got the faintest," she replied sleepily, rolling over to face the back of the couch. I got up, slid the carriage door to and pulled the curtain shut hoping soon to be dreaming of nicer things. Five minutes later I had a *déjà vu*. The same screaming door, the same rudely pulled aside curtain. I came out of a light sleep to find the fella standing transfixed as before. As my eyes got used to the light I realized it was not the same man. He re-enacted the same scene, but stared longer at me - as if I had insulted him. His eyes slid over Lorna's reclining figure in a way I did not like at all. Then, as if on elastic bands, he sprang back down the corridor in the same fashion as the other character.

"What the fuck's going on with these people? Lorna? Have you got any idea?"

"Sorry - not one idea in a hell of a lot of ideas - but I don't like it Gypsy. If you weren't here with me I'd be scared to death right now."

As Lorna said this a shiver ran down my spine. Now I know this shiver - it's a sure sign of danger, but like a young idiot I chose to ignore it. I arose slowly, tired as a young man can be, and closed the door and the heavy curtain, swearing under my breath.

"Let the fuckers do it again and I'll slaughter 'em," I mumbled to myself.

"Patience Gypsy, patience my love," intoned Lorna half asleep.

I settled down again - ah, that felt so good, body slowly getting lighter, floating, flying, disappearing.

Crash! The door hit the metal frame like an explosion and the curtain was pulled back with such unnecessary violence and uncaring disrespect for us within that even Lorna looked up in horror. I jumped up in one smooth movement to get my mitts on the bastard but he slipped through my outstretched hands and fled as fast as his legs would carry him in the same direction the other men had gone. Lorna was laughing at my expression - and my jeans, which had fallen and wound up around my ankles.

"Fuck You!" I screamed down the corridor before going through the same procedure for the fourth time that night. Lorna had recognized the third man. While I had been off the train changing our money he had poked his head into her carriage, gave her the once over and left. He saw she was alone and vulnerable. Obviously they had been discussing this in their carriage and had come to investigate.

"OK Lorna - that's it - one more visitation and I'm going to smack 'em!"

We slept - the shutters of our minds closed down with a snicker of exhaustion - but it was the snicker of the door handle being prized down quietly and the door slowly sliding open that woke me up once more.

'Right you bastards - got you now', I thought, the vision floating before me of pulling the curtain back sharply and hitting whoever was there smack on the end of their nose. They would get the surprise of their life - nothing like a bleeding nose to make sure they knew you meant business. This thought was going through my head as I whisked the curtain back quickly, my fist already slamming out into the train corridor. What I saw was the nearest thing to aliens I had ever come across - but aliens they were not, they were the feared Spanish Guardia Police. I had no idea then but they were on the train to check up on smugglers - there was a roaring trade in illegal contraband going to Spain from Morocco and vice versa. I suddenly remembered that Spain was still a fascist state, as time stood still and the guy was bracing himself for my punch. His partner, standing behind him, was already prepared for the assault, his finger cocked on his machine pistol and murder in his eyes as he brought the gun up to my chest.

With a supreme effort I pulled my fist backwards and managed by the will of all the saints to drop my arm, saying as calmly as I could that we were having trouble with some lads in the other carriage. I saw my terrified face reflected in the sheen of their strange hats of gleaming polished leather as the two machine pistols lowered slowly.

"Ah, the mad English," one laughed at his friend and without even demanding to see our passports they ambled on their way down the corridor as if this had been a bit of fun for them. I slumped onto the seat, the blood draining from my face.

"You look like you seen a ghost Gypsy - are you alright?" Lorna asked, not quite understanding the horror we had just escaped from.

"Yes my love - I just saw our own two ghosts, wandering on this bleedin' train forever," I said, exhausted by the experience.

We arrived at the station in Algeciras just two hours late and followed a few youngsters who were intent on going to Tangiers down to the harbour. Here we hit a snag. There was a table set up near to the embarkation ladders and around it were six soldiers and an officer who looked up at us as we approached. I noticed there was a rope draped so as to keep people out - with two or three anguished looking people behind it.

In very good English the officer said, "Go behind the rope please,"

"And why is that my good man?" I said, putting on as high a class accent as I was able.

"Because you youngsters have no money and just cause trouble on the streets of Tangier, that is why."

"Well I will have you know that my stepfather, Lord Sparkington, will have your epaulettes if I don't get to his office in Tangiers," I said - at the same time pulling out my wallet and letting him see the notes bulging out. He called two soldiers over, scribbled a note and told the men to escort Lorna and I onto the boat personally and give the note to the Captain.

The look of disbelief on the faces of the growing crowd of beatniks was amazing to see as we were escorted onto the boat by the soldiers who saluted first myself then Lorna.

"Jesus! How did you do that and keep a straight face?" said Lorna. "That was the funniest thing I've ever seen - Lord Sparkington indeed! I nearly peed myself!"

"It was the first thing that came into my head love. I wasn't coming all this way to be turned back."

"You must have some Irish in you - the way you can Blarney the knickers off a virgin."

"Didn't take too much Blarney to get yours off, did it?" I laughed.

"Well that's because I was no virgin my love."

"What? And all this time I was under the misapprehension that it was me wonderful style that made it so easy to enter your holy portals," I said, giving Lorna the biggest wink.

"No, that wasn't it Gypo - I only let you have your dastardly way cos I knew deep down inside you was the stepson of Royalty."

We laughed fit to die. "Next stop Tangiers," I said theatrically with a wave of my arm. We looked - and it was indeed Tangiers on the horizon.

CHAPTER NINE
DROWNING MAN

The first thing that hit you - before even landing - was the noise. It rolled out to sea like a thunderstorm's progeny. Voices, music, chanted prayers, bangings, bashings, a human humming bee's nest of activity and sound, all mixed up in a colourful display of striped robes with long hoods suspended at their backs like old emaciated bitches tits. The hustle began as soon as your feet hit the concrete shell of the harbour.

'Here you are my brother, here is the best hotel in the whole of Morocco.....let me show you the best place to eat Sahib, you must be hungry from the sea.....come to my place sir, I can show you the best leather there is, not the elephant dung they say is cured properly but is only pissed on by the relatives of thieves.....'

"Best hashish in town sir, only the very finest pollen used - dust caught on the purest of suede aprons by nubile virgins running naked through the fields."

"I'll take three of the nubile virgins," I said.

"I can get you lovely ladies sir," another man piped up from behind the crowd, "or the very prettiest dancing boys if that's your choice," said another man smiling with his gold teeth reflecting in the sun high in the blue sky.

The heat was like a snake wrapping its body around you. The smell was wonderful - sweet aromatic tobacco stole its way into your being like a con man giving you something instead of taking something. The smell of roasting meat, sweet pastries, mint tea and honey coated biscuits with the dark backdrop of herbal kif singing to the soul in scented whirls of wonderment that made the head spin - and that was just in the harbour.

When the crowd eventually parted to let you through to the city of Tangiers your senses were assaulted by colours, shapes and metallic objects reflecting surfaces embossed and artistic. The smell of leather was everywhere and their glowing colours of green, red, yellow and brown were the same colours as my tattoo. Indeed the Dragon of the East. Metal was everywhere, made into plates, bottles, lamps, swords, knives and guns. Hanging lamps, huge and old, threatened to decapitate a tall man like myself when you walked into a shop, the owner ushering you into his humble premises with bobs and scrapes, putting into your fingers hand-painted cups of clay filled to the brim with sweet, warm mint tea.

Gold dripped from outstretched hands - silver bracelets of exquisite workmanship were clasped onto Lorna's arms - and removed just as quickly - she was Cleopatra for a second - rolls of silk shining as though straight from the waters of the weaver's cocoon - linens dyed to shades of colour so subtle as to make the heart break open with passion - cottons hanging in wide swathes, making a patterned doorway fit for a Prince to pass through. And wool, striped and plain, thick and thin, lumpy or as smooth as cashmere can be made - water sellers with their cups of metal cleaned to make your face reflect in them as the water comes pouring like crystal tumbling down a mountainside from their long stemmed bottles - Then you realize swimming from every doorway crack and crevice, winding its way through every alley ,just like a dragon of sound - their wonderful music - Music that seemed to be written by a musical poet whilst on horseback or camelback, the pure joy suffusing his soul at the beauty in the world - The shining eyes and dark skin of the people, like chestnuts roasted gently, curly haired or straight of comb - clean as their prayers could make them, they had pleasure in talking, cajoling or just passing time of day with a stranger - The Moroccan marijuana, known as Kif, - kif, kif and more kif, usually smoked by the locals without tobacco, or just miniscule amounts to give a good burn in a small bowl of clay pushed onto turned wooden stems - Then there was the sweet mint tea given to relieve any headaches that smoking too much kif can sometimes bring on.

There were, I suppose still are, three main sections of Tangier, as our Arab friend told us. The European sector - one death per year by murder. The Spanish sector - two deaths per month. The Arab or Moroccan sector - one murderous death per night. Prices rose and fell depending on which sector you were in.

We were taken to the Spanish sector by a very nice young Moroccan who assured us of a lovely big room in the home of a Spanish family. It was large, clean and had a high ceiling with embossed patterns in it, it also had a wrought iron and marble balcony with a view to the window of the house opposite and the alleyway below. Thick brocaded curtains covered up the sun's brightness. You could have lived in the double bed - the clean white scrubbed sheets of which would have made a covering for a tent made for ten, or so it seemed to me. Outside to the right was a set of clean, though crude, squat down toilets.

We were told by our Spanish host, on no account to go out without locking our room, for this purpose he handed me a huge key telling me at the same time to never sleep in the room without slamming home the big sliding bolt on the inside of the door. We lay on the big bed having indeed landed in Tangier. The room was a bit fuzzy around the edges, as somewhere on our journey I had purchased two sticks of Maajun, a sweet and not nice tasting bar of mixed kif and honey or treacle. I ate mine like a Mars Bar, swallowing it quickly because Lorna had also given me hers, screwing up her face at the taste of it.

I had eaten the second bar before being told that one ate a Maajun Bar in small nibbles over maybe three or four days. Oh well, I had eaten a week's supply in six minutes - definitely a sign of things to come.

We were waiting in our room for the Arab, Abdul, who had introduced us to

Maajun. Soon he appeared with our first kilo of uncut grass.

"The best kif in the kingdom." he assured me.

He would teach me how to remove the seeds and thick stems, which caused headaches, and he would also show me how to refine what was left with the use of only a sharp knife.

"Do you have a sharp knife?" he asked.

"No," I replied.

"Then I will purchase one for you - only the very finest metals used. Steel that will hold an edge after cutting the throats of two thieves in one plunge."

I was very stoned by the time Abdul arrived. I don't know how I got off the bed to tell you the truth - as it had taken on the dimensions of Waterloo Station. But even so we sat at the old wooden table, scored by eons of the same knife damage, and here I learned to chop kif to perfection by the finest of movements of the knife and the pressed fingertips of the left hand. My teacher was a master. The knife he brought for me was a simple wooden handled affair but its blade had a bluish sheen and it cut paper held in the hand with one stroke. *'Bring on the throats,'* I thought, *'I'm ready for 'em now.'*

The grand total for the lessons, the knife and the kilo of best Kif was the princely sum of one pound and ten shillings - thank you very much. We had cut the kilo up in about half an hour and our friend brought out three pipes of clay and three turned wooden stems. He gave us two pipes as a present and showed us the correct way to fill them. Soon we were dragging away, filling the room with the pungent herbal aroma.

After two or three pipefuls we went out to the big café in the main square where we treated Abdul to pastries and sweet coffee. You're either sweet or savoury when stoned on Kif - all three of us were sweet. The Kif I had smoked seemed to be evening out the Kif I had ingested. The rushes were coming less and less and I was feeling that all over glow of contentment . Like a good sun tan gives the body and a day of swimming and relaxing. I looked at Lorna and the smile and the look in her eye said it all. We had indeed arrived at the entranceway to the world - it was at our feet.

We were in Heaven during the day and Paradise at night. Rarely did we go to the beach, though it was good sand and the sea was clean. We spent a lot of time in the big square drinking cold beverages and playing 'Patchy' - a board game played five different ways by the Moroccans.

As time wore on and the locals got used to us they hustled less - all except the children, they never stopped hassling you for a little money. I didn't blame them when I saw the remnants of their poor families, shuffling about in the back streets trying to make ends meet.

But now picture a drunk young man celebrating his 17th birthday on the beach of Tangier with his friend Abdul and love Lorna. Abdul has paid for the wine but dare not carry it to the beach for fear of reprisals - it was against his religion to drink alcohol - he could be flogged for it actually. Still, Abdul loved his wine once in a while, he loved the taste as much as what it did to him.

I had rolled five three paper joints for our stay on the beach and had carried the wine openly, as I was a foreigner allowed the privilege of indulging my illegal alcohol habit on holiday. Abdul had my spliffs tucked into his jacket, neatly displayed in the top pocket for all to see.

First joint smoked, we headed out to sea for a swim. Abdul wouldn't come because Lorna looked almost naked to him - even in her swimsuit. We respected his customs and his sensibilities.

On our return to the beach we opened the wine and I poured two large glasses.

Abdul drank from the one nearest to him - whenever he deemed it safe enough to do so. Lorna drank from my glass while we passed the second joint around.

Abdul so rarely had the time to sit and gossip in a relaxed atmosphere. He was a hustler of many different and varied goods and an opportunist of the highest calibre, but when he was relaxed his face took on a kindly honest expression and you could see the young Abdul shining through as pure as glass.

Two more joints and a second bottle of wine later our friend was loose of tongue enough to tell me something he had been meaning to say for some time.

"Gypsy my brother, with deep respect can I ask you how much of that kilo of Kif you have left?"

"Why - want to buy some?" I laughed, worried by his seriousness.

"Well Abdul, you're too late because there's so little left that I was going to use your good and gracious services to get me another kilo."

"With pleasure Gypsy, but you must forgive me for what I now say - and I only say it my dear friend because you *are* my dear friend - you smoke too much Kif my esteemed brother. Please forgive me this intrusion on your private life - but I just thought you should know. I mean you no disrespect my dearest brother."

"You're a good friend for speaking your mind Abdul - and a good brother to show such brotherly care, for which I thank you and I will think very seriously on what you have just told me. Already I will promise you the next kilo will be smoked much slower for sure - in fact I might just stop Lorna smoking - that would do the job," I joked to cut the atmosphere.

The expression on Lorna's face was comical. We all cracked up with laughter. But I should have listened and slowed down on my smoking then and there - though it was probably too late by then anyway - the bug was coursing through my body even as Abdul spoke and it was about to flatten me good and proper.

There is a disease that Kif can get while growing in the wild which can, on rare and misused occasions, get into the human body where it produces very strange and unforeseen results. Unforeseen by me - but not by my friend Abdul.

A few days after my 17th birthday I could not get out of bed, there was no will to do so. Bed was the only place worth being in in the whole world. I told Lorna to leave me alone and not to fuss.

"No I don't want to eat, don't even want to have a smoke - just give me water love please, just water."

After two days of this Lorna could see me getting thinner than I should have been after such a short time of not eating. She managed to get some soup ladled down my throat from time to time but by the third day my eyes had turned into piss-holes in the snow of my whitening face. Lorna was petrified because I refused to get up except when I had to go to the toilet - and I could only walk there on my rubbery legs with her help.

The impression I had was of a permanently floating brain going here and there as it chose, like a deserted boat through the canals of Venice, bumping here and there into an idea or two. My mind was seeing things, but as if held before it on a sheet those images would bend and buckle as soon as concentration was focused upon them.

It would itch at the edges of your very soul with its undulating edges.

It's impossible to scratch the brain with your mind and the need to do so is excruciating.

Every time Lorna tried to move me the feeling was so alien that I would have felt more at home having little green men lift me by levitation. When I did move, even my hand, it was as if each knuckle and joint was a tin with a lid, half filled with thick, syrupy liquid. Each joint was the same, from the wrist to the elbow, from the elbow to the shoulder, from the shoulder to the belly and so on throughout the body's landscape.

I truly felt like a knight in armour, but half filled with thick liquid splashing around when I tried to move. It was so impossible to be in motion I just didn't have the energy or will to try. I just wanted to drift on into nothingness.

I have felt that sensation since whist laying stretched out in a cooling sea, eyes closed but headed towards the sun. The mind elasticises to the horizon in a golden haze of self-realized oneness with the sea. Or is it a realization of you yourself as one tiny drop of light in a wondrous sunset?

On that bed in Tangier I was indeed wandering off into that one drop of light that makes the sunset. Another few days of this and I would die. Lorna was so worried she searched the casbah for Abdul, a very unwise thing for a girl to do unescorted. She eventually found him in the *Dancing Boy*, which was an Arab equivalent of a European Club Bar. They wouldn't let Lorna in, even though it was open for the evening, but one of the waiters who recognized Lorna did call for Abdul.

"It must be something very important for you to come and find me Lorna. Where is my brother Gypsy? What has happened to him?" asked Abdul, shocked at the look on Lorna's face.

"Will you come with me Abdul? Gypsy needs your help," Lorna pleaded with him.

"We will fly on the wings of an eagle Lorna."

Bowing to the men he had been talking to Abdul left with Lorna.
On the way back to our room Lorna told him my symptoms and how long I had had them.

"Four Days! Four days is very long Lorna.
We might not be able to bring him out of it, that depends upon Gypsy's inner strength," he said.

"Run quickly Lorna - every minute counts now."

They were both a red and blue blur to me as they entered our room. I had fallen out of the bed and was on the floor naked - trying to swim Lorna thought.

"Quickly, get him dressed, we have to take him outside - we have to walk and walk and walk him till he is fit to drop. Movement is the only way to remove the poison in his body Lorna, do you understand?"

It was agony as they got me to move but I was determined not to cry out. At first there was no voluntary movement in my body. Abdul took most of my weight but my love Lorna found a strength from I know not where. She did sterling work until my mind began to clear and I could take over some of the movements they were trying to get through my thick head.

I walked. I walked some more.

I felt like that fella Christ had told to walk. *'Get up from thy bed and walk'* Soon the wonder of it hit me - I *could* actually walk! The numbness left my body inch by inch - it was over.

Three hours of walking around in a big circle had restored my respiratory system which had been closing down slowly, like the Gates of Heaven - and not a Peter in sight - but, thank God, an Abdul and a Lorna , angels both.

That incident behind us we got back to normality and a few weeks later I met an Englishman named Nigel. Lorna and I were old-timers by now and a lot of new arrivals were pointed in our direction so we could tell them about the best this, the best that, the nearest way to wherever etc.

We got pretty bored with it but one day I was asked by a middle class sounding boy, Nigel, where the best shop to buy gold was. Gold for God's sake!

"Sorry mate, I know absolutely nothing about gold - except you should be careful where you buy it - it can be rubbish."

"Thank you my man, but I think I know a bit of gold well enough when I see it," he said snootily.

'Well go and find it yourself you snobby prick and stop wasting my time," I thought.

I've never liked snobs, or people who believe themselves one or two stages above you - it's the English disease - bring on the Dodo's. We eyeballed each other for a minute and then he ambled away.

I saw this Nigel from time to time in the big square - he didn't seem loaded down with this gold of his. He sent two lemon juices over one day - he was wearing a white hat pulled over his eyes and a white jacket with the collar turned up. I don't know who he thought he was but Lorna said, "Fucking prick," under her breath as she raised the glass in his direction. It took a lot to get Lorna swearing as a rule but he obviously had it.

"Stay away from him Gypsy, he's trouble," she said.

"He ain't nothing my darling, he's just a flyspeck on the window pane of time," I said, laughing at the imagery my mind had just made up. I liked it - but like it or not I should have paid more heed to Lorna's premonition - she had it right.

We had been in Tangier for nearly nine weeks but now the money - and the Kif - were running out. I wasn't smoking as much of the second kilo as fast as I had the first; the novelty was wearing off a tad. Nine weeks of being stoned day and night wore the high a bit thin.

I was thinking of ways to get back to Algerciras so that we could go to the British Consul and get repatriated back to England. We hadn't enough money left to buy tickets home. The thought of hitch-hiking all that way was unbearable. OK - if we had to then we had to, but repatriation seemed like a much better idea - some cock and bull story about losing our money over the side of the boat, but luckily our passports were in Lorna's bag for instance - etc…etc… I was in no doubt it could be pulled off - but we had to get to Spain first.

Was there anything I could sell to raise money for the tickets? Sadly, no.

It was at this time that Nigel walked up to us, as flash as a little fighting cock.

"What about that my man?" he said, looking at Lorna and pushing a huge gold ring into my face.

"Looks like the business," I said.

"Good, isn't it? I've spent weeks looking for the right piece of gold and the right shop to buy it in."

"Well good for you. Who showed you the shop?" I asked casually.

"Abase the Bedouin."

'For fuck's sake,' I thought, *'just the biggest thief in Tangiers.'*

"I had to go to the Arab quarter for the best prices. Look at it my man, wonderful isn't it? It was only £25," he said as loud as he could looking at Lorna.

"Did you get a receipt?" I asked, feeling the tentacles of Fate pulling me towards his story.

"Do you take me for an idiot?" he said, rearing back on his legs as though about to strike. Lorna moved to give me room to swing a punch if need be.

"Abase the Bedouin assured me the receipt is as good as money in the bank," Nigel said looking down his nose at me. "You see the mark there - etched into the gold?" he rambled on in his posh voice. "That says it all."

"Have you got the receipt with you?" I asked.

"Of course I have. Do you think I would leave a valuable document like that lying around in my hotel room?"

"Can I see it?" I asked.

"Yes, but can you read Arabic?"

"No - but my mate here can," I said turning towards Abdul who was sitting in the shade behind us.

Nigel handed over the impressive receipt slowly. Sure enough there was some bold Arabic writing upon it.

"Can you tell us what that says please Abdul?" I said, handing it to him over my shoulder.

"I know what it says," Nigel stammered, "it says that this ring is 24 carat gold."

Abdul looked at Nigel with disgust in his twinkling eyes, "I am sorry my young friend Gypsy, but this says in Arabic, *'Go and get the keys from Kuwait,'* he said.

"Thank you Abdul for your time and translation," I said politely as I passed the receipt back to a white faced and crestfallen Nigel.

He began to shake. "But this cannot be true," he stuttered, "I don't believe you - you're liars!"

I heard Abdul stir behind me.

"If you know what's best for you mate and don't want one of the sharpest blades in Morocco shoved in yer guts I would turn slowly and apologize to Abdul for your insults. - Quickly you fool - do it now!"

Nigel heard the urgency in my voice and turned to Abdul and apologized profusely shaking from head to foot, all his cool melted like rancid butter.

"This is out of my range old boy - don't know what to do here - it's not a situation I know anything about," he said to me, sweat pouring from his brow. All this babble was pouring out of his mouth because he had indeed seen a blade of blue steel in hands well capable of murder.

Take my advice here," I said sternly, "don't insult an Arab in his own country - unless you're prepared to go all the way."

Deflated beyond anything he had experienced in his coddled life he turned and asked me for my help.

Bloody fool that I was I saw an opportunity to get Lorna and I tickets back to Spain. Nigel wanted my help to get his money back for the ring.

"Do you remember the shop?"

"Yes - I know exactly where it is."

"Right, I want four pounds for any risk involved in getting the money back," I said, " - whether we get it back or not - understand?"

"Yes, understood and agreed upon," Nigel answered.

"What are you doing Gypsy my love? What are you agreeing to?" Lorna said in disbelief.

"You know how dangerous it is in the Arab quarter. What you're proposing is madness," she said, turning to Abdul for support - but he had already left.

"We'll go at the afternoon prayers Lorna - that way there will be no one on the streets."

"Then I'm coming with you - and I don't want no arguments as my mind's made up." she said pluckily

"Alright Lorna, but at the first hint of trouble you're to get away and run for the police, is that understood? Not that there'll be any trouble of course," I hastened to add.

"Alright Gyp, you have my word - and it's better than his word by a mile," she whispered glancing at Nigel.

We sat and smoked some small bowls of kif waiting for the afternoon to come. I was feeling a little sleepy as we made our un-merry way to the jewellers, but I knew I had to be on my toes for whatever may happen.. I could hear alarm bells in my head and did my best to ignore my balls as they were pulled up by instinct into my scrotal sack - a part of the 'fight or flight' process I learned later. Slowly we went forward to our dumb destiny as the sun seemed to go into self exile and find a stone to hide under.

Inside the jewellers shop all was clean and quiet as a cathedral. An old man was behind the counter dressed in the usual Arab way with a long robe and a fez hat. He recognized Nigel as soon as we approached him and there was alarm in his eyes for a fleeting second.

"Hello my good man, do you remember me?" said Nigel politely. "I came in yesterday with Abase the Bedouin to buy this ring."

The old Arab nodded his head wisely while looking me up and down with disdain.

"Well old chap, I've changed my mind and would like my money back."

Silence from the Arab and a touchable stillness, like before a downpour in the East.

"You want more rings? Want more rings? I have many," our jeweller said looking up at the low ceiling.

"Your turn Gypsy," Nigel squirmed.

I leaned forward and said, not too forcefully I thought, "Money back, money back, not good ring." Here I held up the receipt for him to see. His eyes widened and looked heavenward again.

"No refund, never give refund, can't give refund," he said determinedly, looking at Lorna hoping to engender some sympathy or support. She looked stonily back.

"Must have refund - ring no good." I threw the ring on the floor where it bounced like it was made of rubber. That was the catalyst for mayhem.

He gave a loud shout in Arabic and there was a shuffling sound in the ceiling. A strong wiry Arab of about 30 dropped as neat as you like on to the marble tiles in front of me like a rabbit pulled out of a hat. All very nice you might think, but this rabbit had a knife with a blade over eight inches long and murder in its eyes as he began to circle me, knife out at shoulder height.

The old man screamed something at him and made plunging gestures. No need for an iota of Arabic to know what he meant. There was a noise behind me and I thought more Arabs were coming, but I was wrong - it was Nigel skidding right out the front door and running away down that deserted street as fast as his long, well muscled legs would carry him.

'Thanks for the help mate,' I thought, as Lorna wisely stood stock still, waiting for what I knew not - but in her eyes I saw a determination to stay and help me no matter what might happen. Her bravery was there shining for me as the first swipe of the blade nearly gauged my eye right out of its socket. This motherfucker meant business for sure! The next swipe was at cheek height and I realized he wanted to cut me to humiliate me before he went for more permanent damage. *'Bastard',* I thought, as I circled the room. I had maneuvered him away from the door which was still open from the fleeing of Nigel.

"Quick!" I called to Lorna. "Out and run for a policeman!"

Lorna did just that and the door ricocheted half shut as she caught it on her way out. The next wave of the knife nearly took the end of my nose off, but as I turned my head away from the stroke I saw a Jalabah hanging on a peg on the door. I grabbed it up and wrapped it around my left arm in as smooth and practiced a move as you could have wanted to see- just as well too as I was able to deflect the next plunge of the blade with the thick wool of the garment. It sliced a groove as neat as you like and I felt the stroke like a punch.

I was now looking around the shop in desperation for something to hit the murderous Arab with. He plunged again and I deflected his arm like a matador onto the wooden counter. Shit, I couldn't take much more of this! Luckily in the time it took him to free his knife from the hard wood of the counter I was out the door. To run would have been foolish, for he would have struck me in the back with the knife. Besides, it was too late to flee - our fight had become a public spectacle The crowd outside in the high walled street made a circle boxing me in.

Out rushed the young assassin knife in hand.

He stopped a grin running from ear to ear - now he had me. He came at me slowly, giving me a little time to search for a weapon for my protection though believe me my eyes were also focused on the tip of his knife. He was getting cocky, wanting to make a show of bravado for the crowd, when someone threw me a cudgel. Talk about throwing a drowning man a piece of wood! You cannot begin to know what that cudgel meant to me you can have no idea what its twisted, grinning roughly carved face represented. I was free, light-hearted - like a man going to his wedding party.

'Right, you cowardly piece of dogshit,' I thought, eyeing the man through new peepers, *'you can have some of your own bloody medicine back'.*

"Fuck you!" I screamed at the top of my lungs and attacked him.

My arm was up before me with the Jalabah attached like a shield.

Whack! I stuck him on the shoulder of his knife arm with a heavy blow. Cheers rose up behind and around me, reminding me of when I boxed a few times as a boy in the gym. Then, in the same breath, the cheer of the audience was disappearing, melting like the man with the knife was fleeing. Surely he was not such a miserable cowardly creep? He still had the upper hand - he had the knife.

"Gyp my love! Gypsy are you alright?" Lorna's voice called to me. I turned to see two uniformed policemen strolling up the windy street as if there was no hurry in the world - and my wonderful Lorna was with them, tears rolling down her face. She flew into my arms. I was alive, the joy was unbearable....until one of the policemen placed me under arrest. Me! The innocent one! I tried to explain, but they would have none of it.

"Give passport - you not need now," the tallest policeman said, his hand outstretched.

"You not need for long time," the other cop said loudly.

Shit - here I was, expecting a hero's welcome being taken to one of the lousiest prisons in Morocco.

"But you don't understand," I tried to explain again, "I am innocent."

The policemen laughed heartily. "Since Allah departed this planet there are no innocents left in the world."

Be that as it may, I felt innocent.

"Passport! Passport!" the tall cop shouted into my face to let me know he meant business.

"Don't have on me," I said. "Lorna will get it - bring to Police Station now," I went on, pointing in her direction.

"Get now," was his command to Lorna. "Bring police station - now!"

'Shit,' I thought 'out of the frying pan and into the fire'.

Once inside the police station they treated me quite nicely - after the show of arresting me had been seen by the public and the police were seen to be doing their duty.

I had been sitting for three hours before I was brought forward to be interviewed by the Chief in his dark and dismal room.

He was thick set and swarthy and very tall for a Moroccan. His dark eyes held hidden depths of cruelty, spiralling their way into his pupils like corkscrews.

"Well?" he said, looking at me as if I was a squashed cockroach beneath his shoe. His English was good - obviously an educated man.

"Well it was like this," I began, "the jeweller sold - "

"I know all about the seller of gold," he interrupted me, "and I know all about the Arabic words on the receipt - the jeweller is very proud of them. Did it not occur to you that although the man was old and a very respectable merchant, he might not be able to write in Arabic? He has been writing the same words for 30 years on his receipts - but his gold is as pure as Allah's heart, my young brave and foolish friend."

He tapped my six months passport. "Are these remarks here true? Are you really only 17 years of age?"

"17 and a few weeks," I said proudly.

"And stupid enough to get yourself murdered before the sun of 18 summers will shine on your portion of dirt," he said in contempt.

He was looking at me as if weighing up all possibilities. I knew that my answer to his next question would make or break me.

"And how long do you mean to stay in Morocco," he asked, staring at me like a spider at a fly.

"Till the day after tomorrow - we have the boat tickets to Spain already booked," I lied.

He weighed the balance of what I had just said as if he were Anubis weighing my heart against a feather.

"Well - I am very pleased to hear it," he said eventually. "If you are one day longer in Tangier I will have you in prison and will take great pleasure in throwing the key away - understand?"

"Understood," I said, "and thank you."

"Go!" he shouted, leaving no mistake as to his meaning.

As I held my passport in my hand and left his office I heard a lightening in his voice from behind the dusty doorway. "oh - and give my regards to Lord Sparkington won't you."

I thought I heard a rumble of stifled laughter, I could have been wrong but there was nothing on earth that would have made me re-enter that room to find out. Lorna, dear soul, was waiting for me hot and bothered in the direct sunshine.

"Ah my love, you're here!" she whispered, as though I had been away at sea for six months.

"Lorna my darling, we got work to do," I said immediately. "We got to get outa here as soon as we can. Come on home - we got to pack."

I told her what had happened at the police station and the Chief's ultimatum.

"You and your blarney Gyp! It's going to get you into as much trouble as it gets you out of! We've got no money, no tickets - and you've told that bloke we'll catch the boat the day after tomorrow!"

"Alright love - I know - but I had to bullshit him or I'm telling you - you wouldn't have seen me for years. Now what's best - you tell me - while we're still runnin' we're still ahead."

"I made you a joint Gypsy for when you was home."

"Thanks love, but I'm gonna quit 'em till we get sorted - give myself some time to think. The thing is I'm stoned enough now to last till next week anyway."

It didn't take us long to get organized to be ready to leave at a moments notice. We were paid up at our pad till the end of the month, so that was cool.

"Right we're finished here my love," I said to Lorna, "let's see if we can get news of that fucker Nigel - he still owes me four pounds, remember?"

"All I remember is his legs running for hell out of it and leaving you to stew in the fire.. He left you up Shit Creek without a paddle , bastard that he is "

"Well I'm gonna find him and get those paddles back - maybe we can paddle to Spain with 'em." I joked although it was no laughing matter .

We walked into the café in the main square and many of the beats came crowding round.

It seemed the news had been spread, by Nigel I think, that I had been stabbed to death in the Arab quarter. Nigel had been seen running for the boat to Spain, suitcase in hand and ticket in his mouth."

"Shit," I said, then told them the story of our adventure in the jewelers. They were all very sorry when I explained that we had to get out of Tangier by the day after tomorrow.

One of the beats, Bix, looked long at Lorna and myself then said, "Leave it to me, I'll get you bread man - I've got an idea. Come on folks," he said to the assembled crowd," we got to find someone."

They scoured the back streets for a chap called Bronx, one of the few Americans there in Tangier. Now Bronx was a great guy but he got stoned every day and would leave his rooms quite often forgetting to bring his money with him. There was no doubt Bronx had money, he was always treating people to things. If he ever needed to borrow money from anyone he always paid it back - he never forgot a debt funny enough.

Now Bix, God bless his cotton socks, had seen Nigel hand over the equivalent of a couple of pounds to Bronx that very morning. Bix's idea was to find Bronx, tell him our story, reclaim the money on my behalf and then bring it to us at the café. The only trouble was no one knew where Bronx lived.

They fanned out, asking anyone they thought might know. Of course the story of my adventure had to be told to each person they met and the upshot of all this enquiry was a spur of the moment whip around for Lorna and myself.

By the time they located Bronx Bix was holding three pounds for us and Bronx chipped in an extra four dollars and the equivalent of the two pounds he owed to Nigel.

With huge triumphant beats on a small Moroccan drum the lads found us still seated in the main square. Bronx wearing his best cowboy hat and neckerchief for the occasion laid the money on the table in front of us with a wave of his hand. When it was explained to us what they had done Lorna and I were flabbergasted. Tears began to flow down Lorna's cheeks onto the metal table, splashing a small token of our happiness and relief.

"Jesus lads, you've saved our lives!" I said, pumping their outstretched hands.

"We couldn't see yer go to that 'orrible prison Gypsy, could we?" Bix said for all. We were saved. That evening I went and purchased the tickets to Algerciras while Lorna gave our room a final clean. We had one more day but it felt as if we had already left Tangier. Everything was so different now. We felt destitute and alone - even though people waved from everywhere as the news spread that we were off.

We went to bed early and stayed in late next morning until we were ready to leave for the harbour. We realized too late that there were a hundred things we should have done and a hundred things to see which we had closed our eyes to.

"Oh well Lorna, we did well enough for now. We'll come back one day and do all the things we didn't do," I said, trying to go out on a happy note.

Lorna gazed up at me with a faraway look in her hazel eyes then she smiled the most radiant of smiles and said,

"We had a ball Gypsy boy - we had a ball and even with the best will in the world, nothing lasts forever."

CHAPTER TEN
<u>BEVERLY REMEMBERS</u>

The boat journey was hassle free and we arrived in time to hunt down the British Embassy building - which was closed. Well, not really closed - it never actually closes - but the man we wanted wouldn't be in until nine the following morning.

"It was repatriation you both wanted, was it not?" we were asked again.

"That's definitely Mr. James. He will be in at 9 a.m. tomorrow. There are some cheap rooms at this address if you require one - or two," the lady in the pink floral dress indicated to Lorna, her eyes raised.

"One will do thanks," Lorna said.

"Ah," the lady sighed, having had all her presumptions verified in one fell swoop. We went to the address, which was half an hours walk away from the Embassy, not knowing if we could afford a room when we got there, but Lorna did the smoothest bit of business you ever saw and got the smallest room in the house for next to nothing.

We asked for an early call and were back at the British Embassy on time next morning. Mr. James was everything I expected. Stiff dark blue suit and white collar, there was even a bowler hat on a stand in the corner of the room. He was very polite and explained that it was every Englishman's - and Englishwoman's - right to be supported if something went wrong abroad.

"Now as I understand it you dropped your wallet overboard on the ferry from Tangier - very unfortunate - and you have only the small change you happened to have in your pockets and purse."

"Yes," I said, "what we have left only amounts to about a pound."

"Hmm - a pound - that's not going to get you far, is it? What we at the Embassy can do is pay your expenses for the train tickets back to Blighty. Mrs. Murray will send for them now - if you agree that is. But we can only pay a maximum of three pounds cash for each persons exspences - will you be able to manage with that?

You can? Marvellous! Then that's settled.

We the British Government will expect a refund of the outlay incurred by the Embassy within two months of your returning to England - is that clear young man - and young lady?" Mr. James said, trying to keep the upper hand in cool.

"That would be wonderful thank you," Lorna and I said together.

"Well that's that then - all above board and ship shape don't you know. Mrs. Murray will sort you out. Goodbye - and have a pleasant journey," he ended, shaking our hands warmly.

"Thank God we're British - where else would we get such service?" I said to

Lorna seriously

We filled in the necessary forms and it was explained that our passports would be taken when we disembarked from the ferry in England.

Mrs. Murray soon had the tickets and the money ready and in half an hour we were walking to the station.

"Blighty here we come," I said.

We boarded the train and leaned against each other in the carriage. We were coming down slowly from the high of the Kif - it made us sleepy - and it made me a bit irritable to tell the truth. We looked well though, suntanned to a burnished brown.

The journey home was uneventful, for which we were grateful.

"We're nearly in Paris Gypsy my love," said Lorna.

"Thank fuck for small mercies," I said, stirring myself from the mental stupor I had vanished into

As we waited at the docks for the ferry back to England I said to Lorna that we should run a little to get our minds back in gear so we did a couple of laps up and down the tarmac, laughing at each others feeble attempts at exercise. But it worked and we felt ready to face the last five or six hours. The kif was almost out of our system and our energy was returning.

The time seemed to drag out forever as we crossed the English Channel until at last a voice on the loudspeaker announced that we would be arriving in ten minutes.

"Thank God," was my response, as we pushed our way down the boat as it ground to a halt. We headed towards the customs.

"Passports please, thank you. Passport young man. Right - come with us please," said a brisk Customs Officer, whisking us away to an office where our passports were confiscated as if we were a pair of dangerous villains.

"Right - let's see your bag - that all you got? Blimey, you two travel light, don't you? What's this here thing? Sleeping bag is it? Empty it out there me lad. Empty your pockets please - put everything in that receptacle there. That's a nifty looking knife me boy - plan on stabbing someone do you? Christ that's sharp! Did you hone it like that? Takes some skill that does - I'm well impressed. Charlie - get Mary out here would yer - I want her to go through the lassie's pockets with a fine tooth comb. So - repatriated were yer?"

"Not against the law, is it?" I said getting a bit narky. "The man in the British Embassy was very nice about it."

"Was he now? Well that's his bloody job, ain't it, but nice or not he was the one to tell us to search you Lad?"

They kept Lorna and I waiting until we had missed the train, then clearly disappointed at not finding anything, the Customs Official told us we could go. We were left with just enough time to catch the last train to London where we sat the night out in Waterloo Station. It felt weird being in a country where we could understand what was said to us. Next morning bright and early, and tired as hell, we started our journey to Manchester. We hitched a lift to a Transport Café and started asking around if any of the long distance drivers were going our way.

A boisterous Brummy, filled to the brim with speed pills to keep him awake, said he would take us to Birmingham. Fantastic!

Two lifts after our Birmingham friend dropped us off we were back in the outskirts of Manchester were we walked the last two miles to Lorna's parent's house - they not having the faintest idea we were coming. Lorna of course was treated like the proverbial Prodigal Daughter returning to the fold. Our news told, they asked about our plans - but we had none.

"Gypsy's going to *The Sovereign* to see what's happening and he'll try to find a room for himself - and maybe me," she said, looking sideways at her Dad.

"Well you keep it a secret if you do live together my lass – 'cause that's no way of carrying on in respectable places. I don't want your mum having them fingers pointed at her."

"Shush Albert - it's modern times we're livin' in. I can give you the fingers of three hands as of youngsters livin' with each other that I know of - and very sensible it is too," Lorna's mum said with some conviction. "Why you and I - "

"Martha!" Albert said sternly as Lorna and her sister looked wide-eyed at each other over the dining table.

Lorna was given the birthday cards and presents she had missed by being away. It was all money from aunts and uncles and her mum said that under the circumstances she would give her money too. Her pretty sister chipped in some cash as well.

"Wow! Lets go on holiday Gypsy," Lorna laughed.

With our new found wealth I discovered a room to rent where we shared a kitchen with the girl in the room across the corridor. She was quite a cutie and Lorna gave her long looks. One night I saw a notice in one of the most exclusive restaurants in Manchester - The Royal. *'Commis Waiter wanted'*. It caught my eye because I thought, for some unknown reason, that the 'Commis' referred to Communists. I was trying to work out why a restaurant like that would only employ our Red Brothers when exiting from a side door a spiff looking Italian came out as though dressed to kill penguins.

"Looking for zat job are zue?" he asked me in totally shattered English.

"Is it difficult to do?" I asked him simply.

"Not in ze leest," he said, "zue just bring zee food from zee kitchens tooze our statchons - from zare we waiterz serve zee patrons weeve zee decorum zay deserve. Come tomorrow at eleven of zee clock wiz zee black trouserz and zee white shirtz and I can getz you workz wiz me, Antonio Belchalotti. Of cause you must ave ze shave young manz."

"Of course, the shave first - see you tomorrow then," I said. Wow! I had the white shirt, all I needed was black trousers and a razor blade. Lorna was pleased when I told her the good news. I borrowed a pair of black trousers from someone in *The Sovereign* and set off next morning to start my new job.

This time there was a Frenchman in charge who wasn't half the fun of Antonio. - but at least he spoke much better English.

"Well," he said, "if Antonio wants you he can have you - but I'm not so sure. The first mistake and you're out, understand young man? Out with your tail between your legs. We don't suffer fools gladly in this business - not at the great Royal Restaurant."

"Why should you?" I remarked kindly.

All went well for two days. Antonio was on the day shift for two weeks, thus so was I. I went into the kitchen at one point, ready to bring the food to the station, when there was an upset from the chief washer-upper nicknamed Mankey. Mankey was a Londoner through and through, he had a gimpy leg from the second world war which he dragged about with him as if it was a prize.

"Mosley you say? Baronet Mosley - that little fucker with his Brown Shirts? What did he order? Cockerleeky soup for starters was it? I'll give the brown-shirted shithead Cockerleeky. Give it to me - come on, give it to me now."

He took the hot soup and poured half its contents down the sink then, right there in the kitchen before us all, he pulled out his dick and topped the soup up with his piss.

"There, now that's fit for a fucking fascist pig, that is." He looked at us youngsters. "Big pals with Hitler he was - and a member of our bloomin' royalty too. Go on then Richard - take it out to him - don't let it get cold."

None of us could understand Mankey's anger - as we had no idea who this Mosley was. We watched from behind the swing doors as Lord Mosley sipped his soup with gusto. He paused for a moment with his spoon held in the air. Then looked into the bowl and nodded to himself with the very air of a Gentleman, seeming to be appraised of the soup's finer culinary delights by an invisible manservant. You might have expected us all to laugh, but none of us did. Somehow it seemed to be far too serious a statement we had all been made privy to.

'That's what you call Pissed Off,' I thought to myself.

One day later I spilled some minestrone from the tureen I was carrying and before I could get it cleaned up a waiter slipped and fell, dropping a Strawberry Flambé for six persons across the length of his body. The restaurant was in tears of laughter as the waiter fled in tears of anguish. I admitted it was my fault and got the sack immediately. Oh well, the guy was asking for his trousers back anyway.

We were living better than we had in our little one room previously. This new room was nice and bright with a view over the garden and was even a few shillings a month cheaper than the other one. It had good furniture too, albeit old.

Lorna and I still spent much of our time in *The Sovereign*. One night we met a young beat with nowhere to kip. He was just passing through. He looked cool enough so we invited him to sleep on the floor of our room - not the wisest of moves as it turned out.

Lorna and I left early the next morning and didn't get back until about three o' clock. Our young friend had departed leaving a note saying thanks. He also left us something else, something Lorna and I never knew existed outside of nightmares - an invisible monster that would have our bodies twisting and turning our fingers like claws scratching till the flesh fell from them like pieces of scalloped meat - but to no relief, no relief at all, no relief anywhere on this wondrous orb of ours. The word was Scabies.

Not such a bad word ultimately if you say it quick - scabies, scabies - but I know that when people see that word they start itching all over their bodies like they were immersed in an ants nest. Scabies is actually very easy to get rid of - if you know you have it - but it took us two weeks before we gave in and went to see a doctor - that is Lorna went to see her family doctor. He had known Lorna since she was a baby and couldn't take what he saw lying down. We in our turn expected him to respect our wishes and not tell her parents, but he was a friend of her father, they played the occasional game of golf together, and he spilled the beans a few days after Lorna's visit. It's true he had thought long and hard about it, but with Lorna only being 17 he felt it was his duty to step in and let her father have our address.

That same evening her father paid us a visit. Distraught was not the word, he was in tears of worry. Although he was relieved to see our room was neat and tidy he wouldn't sit down as the doctor had advised against it. He looked from Lorna to me and back again in despair. I couldn't blame him - we looked a mess. The scabs on my face made me look as if I'd come off worst in a duel with a three foot lobster. We had taken showers and used the white cream the doctor had given us and the beasts inside us were dead, but we knew it would take a month to six weeks before the damage to our skin tissue would heal. The doctor was worried that Lorna might pick up an even more dangerous disease through the open sores - it was a distinct possibility.

Lorna wouldn't hear or returning to her Dad's place without me. Her father, gentleman that he was, said I could come too and sleep on the sofa in the lounge. Well, that was all very well, but I felt to put them out that badly was not a good idea.

"No love, I'll stay on here and you go home, because the doctor's right," I said. "You'll need to be looked after - have regular food and hot drinks and be taken care of good and proper."

"Ah Gypsy my love, don't make me do it - I'll miss you too much!"

"Lorna sweetheart, your dad's right - the sooner you're well the sooner you can be back with me."

"But what about you - who'll look after you Gypsy? You're going to be all alone here!" she cried, tears dropping to the floor.

"You know me love - I'm a survivor. I'll be fine. I'll come and see you all the time till you get sick of the sight of me."

"You miss one day and I'll die Gypsy!"

"Well - with the best will in the world I can't come all that way out to your house every day - but I promise every two days."

" - and stay at the weekends Gypsy - I'm not agreeing less you promise that."

I looked at her father who nodded his agreement. " OK my dove - weekends too."

Poor Lorna cried the whole time we were packing her few things, but I thought I detected a sign of relief there too. It was hard enough on me, let alone a young girl, to go through this fucking itching. I knew she'd have time to recuperate at her mother's place - good down to earth healing.

It was the worst day in my life to see Lorna in the back seat of her father's car being driven away in tears. I was a lucky man in Lorna but Fate is Fate for all that. Maybe she felt something break in her heartstrings that day - knew we had taken different points at the station on our individual tracks - roads converging, roads parting.

After one week of having the room to myself I decided to leave it. There was no way I could afford it and no justification with Lorna gone. I didn't let her know for almost a week. For three nights I slept in an underpass the council was building just 15 minutes walk from Lorna's house. One of the workers, an Irish guy who lived in a caravan nearby, saw me the second morning and said he would look out for a job for me, but kind as he was sharing a hot drink from his flask of sweet tea before the other workers arrived, I didn't feel too comfortable being seen - so the next night I found another place to sleep.

Dossing again wasn't so easy, after having lived so well and comfortably with Lorna. During the day, if her mum was away, Lorna and I usually went straight to bed, after I'd taken a bath. It wasn't just the sex - it was the warmth and companionship that we both needed, all part of sex, yes - but we suited each other so well we were like twin spoons in an empty cutlery box. That weekend I told her I'd given up our room as my scars were healing unbelievably well.

"Just till you're better love - then we can find another room together, I didn't like being in our room on me own sweetheart and it'll only be a few weeks till you and me are together again."

"But where will you sleep Gypsy me darling?"

"Well last night I slept in the bushes by the ditch on the Golf Links by the canal."

"You never did!" Lorna said in surprise. "People say that place is haunted - that ditch was made by German bombs and many souls who lived there lost their lives."

"Ninety nine out a hundred things people say are rubbish me love - although the funny thing is that I woke up this morning with the distinct feeling there were people looking at me and discussing me freely between themselves.

There was no one there when I looked up, but I had the wonderful feeling they were wishing me well. Strange that," I said.

"Maybe there's a change coming for the better," Lorna said prophetically.

That night in *The Sovereign* there was news waiting for me. A friend of Donovan's from St. Albans was looking for me - she would be back in an hour. Lorna had stayed at home instead of coming with me that night as it had turned cold and windy. Not a night for the Golf Links as I reckoned it would rain. I was sitting excitedly, drinking my milky coffee. Who could it be who was looking for me?

It was beautiful Beverly, dressed to kill in a dark velvet mini skirt and matching top that had difficulty holding in her sweet breasts. I had only seen her once before but I knew she had a reputation as an up and coming model.

"I'm only up here for one day and I was wondering if I could kip on yours and Lorna's floor tonight," she explained. "Dono said it would be alright to ask you. I'll be up with the bloody lark Gypo - so I'll be no bother."

"If we had our room it would be cool - but we had to get rid of it. I explained To Beverly. But not to worry," I explained, "I've a place not far from here where I used to sleep sometimes. We could go there - but it's not much to look at, more of a little factory actually."

"As long as there's a bed and it's dry - that'll do." she replied.

"Well let's go and look," I said.

It was a basement where Stephen, the brother of a friend of mine and five assistants made imitation fur rabbits and bears as kids toys to sell to shops. There was a side room with a bed, also a toilet and a huge wash basin.

"I see the bed - but where's the mattress," said a disappointed Beverly.

I disappeared and came back with armfuls of cut-offs from the furry animals, laying them down on the springs to make a comfortable bed.

"Well I never!" Beverly said. "Right, that's my bed - where are you going to sleep?" she said eyeing me with mischief in her eyes.

"I'll put some cut-offs down on the floor, for me" I said.

"I was only kidding you Gypo, we can sleep in the same bed - for the warmth. But I means *sleep* - understand me Gypo? No hanky panky."

We laid out the sleeping bag on the fur and Beverly took off her mini skirt and tight top and laid them flat on the cutting table before entering the sleeping bag with just her pretty skimpy knickers on.

'Bloody Hell! ' I thought, *'If Lorna could see me now she'd have a fit!'*

Feeling it was stupid to wear clothes in the face of Beverly's near nudity I too stripped to my underpants that luckily had come freshly washed from my darling Lorna earlier that evening. Beverly laid her beautiful breasts on my chest while wrapping her arms around me.

"Right Gypo," she said, "this is as good as it gets - I'm very tired and you have your Lorna. In my game it's a total no-no to go with another girl's guy. We would pull each others hair out for starters - and bald models just don't make it in the magazines, so it makes sense," she said sleepily - all the while she was speaking gently in my ear she was running her left hand sexily inside my underpants and over the right cheek of my backside. "Fucking unbelievable arse Gypo.- if mine was like that I'd be famous by now," she said - then fell sound asleep.

It wasn't a con - she was soon snoring sweetly.

It was strange to have another female body next to me, but very pleasant all in all. It took me a little time to fall asleep. I awoke feeling Beverly's lovely body sliding out from beside me.

"What time is it for fuck's sake Bev?" I asked.

"It's five Gypo - I'm just going to freshen up then get the six o'clock back to town."

"What town?"

"The only town silly - London. Got a gig at six tonight at a photo shoot for David Bailey."

"Never 'eard of 'im - what's his number?" I said.

"Takes photos Gypo - fucking good ones too. Thank you Gyp for the loveliest crash in ages. If you ever split up with yer lovely Lorna you let me know, yer hear? Blessings," she said and she was gone - just like that.

She was to change my life was Beverly - change if for Fame even she didn't have the bottle to dream of. I hung around after she'd gone to say thanks to Stephen and make sure it was still cool to stay in his basement once in a while. His van arrived with the workers all excited. They told me they were moving to new premises as Stephen had a contract from two big toy firms who were wanting his products - he was going up in the world. Great news - but that was the doss well and truly finished. The possibilities for crashing down were closing in.

Lorna continued to get better slowly - being a woman her skin took much longer to heal than mine. I waited out the time in a sort of 'No Man's Land'. I had nowhere to go and somewhere to go; a place to stay weekends and nowhere to stay weeks. I believed Lorna's family were trying to entice her back to the fold - they wanted her to stay at home permanently. This made me feel like an outsider - which of course I was. The only way I could prove myself to the household was to get a proper job - settle down and live normally.

I refused to believe this was my lot in life - normality was not my forte. I was fast coming to the conclusion that I had stayed too long in Manchester.

But Lorna's father found me a job where he was the head foreman and I took it. Unfortunately there was some prick who was determined to find out if Lorna and I were sleeping together - and if Lorna's sister and her boyfriend were sleeping together too for that matter. At tea and dinner breaks he continually asked me questions about my private life. *'Frustrated fucker,'* I thought, *'30 odd and probably never had it in his life.'* Finally I got fed up with his constant innuendos and I said to him, "Well what do you think? Would you be having sex with your girlfriend after livin' together for half a year?"

"Ah," he said, "and what about Lorna's sister?"

"For fuck's sake," I said, "use your head - they've been together longer than me and Lorna!"

That was it - off the idiot went to the boss, telling him I was openly talking dirty about his girls and telling anyone who was willing to listen that I was fucking Lorna and that her sister was getting fucked by her boyfriend too. I had no idea there were little shits like this around, let alone dozens in every factory in the world. Lorna was infuriated with me. How could I do that to her poor father after all he had done? I agreed it was stupid of me. I also told her how the idiot had got it out of me and that I was not talking openly of our or her sister's affairs.

"I told my dad it would be something like that my love, knowing you as I do."

"Well we can forget the bloody job now Lorna. Or I'll go in tomorrow and cut the bloke's tongue out with me knife - that way he won't go telling tales the rest of his life, the bastard."

"It's alright Gypsy, I'll tell my dad the truth - he'll know how to treat the pig."

Well, that soured my relationship with the rest of the family.

I was guilty. I should have kept my mouth shut - not that I opened it much. That weekend you could have cut the atmosphere with a knife at the dinner table. I don't like feeling guilty. I thanked them very much for their kind and generous hospitality over the weeks, but under the circumstances I didn't deserve their kindness. That was it. The big speech.

I didn't enter the portals of their house again. Lorna was devastated.

My places left to doss down were becoming microscopic. One night I was wandering around a neighbourhood on the inner ring road of Manchester's central district when I found myself looking into the window of a house that fronted the street. I was attracted by the light and the cosiness of the room. The inhabitants were sitting round a table about to have a party I think. Their smiles warmed my heart - happiness streamed from their faces like a light. They were a normal enough family. Normality wore a very convincing smile that evening and I found myself almost tempted to try it.

On the other side of that pane of glass I must have appeared like a lost spirit looking in, cold, white and bedraggled - shivering within my own world of nonconformity with a bleak future before me and a warmer rosier past tucked up in its pretty painted box of memorabilia.

Shit - was it over? Did it go nowhere from here? I shook my head in sorrow, nowhere to go, no food in my stomach, no dreams for the morrow. I wandered away from that window feeling I had swallowed strychnine my only hope waiting for death to make the pain stop. Christ it was cold - that was it - I just needed somewhere to sleep off this first depression of my life.

Like a sleepwalker I rambled the streets, neither feeling, nor caring, nor seeing. Eventually I looked up to find myself just around the corner from where Beverly and I had stayed the night. The warm memory of Bev put a smile on my face at last. Shit - I would crash there again. Then I remembered it had been quite a few weeks since that night and my mate's brother was long gone from it.

By now my feet had taken me to the entrance. I looked in through the new glass fronted door and could see that the builders had been in transforming the place. I tried the door - it was locked. I wondered if the little window in the toilet had been fixed - it hadn't! The window could still be opened from the outside!

Before I knew it I had scrambled through and into the smell of newly painted walls and windows. God knows what I thought I was doing. I walked into the little room and was amazed to find that the bed was still there. I was so tired that even the prospects of the bare, diamond shaped springs was inviting. Not really meaning to stay, I spread my exhausted body down on them, I didn't even get into my sleeping bag. As I fell asleep I reminded myself to get up good and early before the workmen arrived. I had broken in and could go to prison for that - just like poor Fleet was now in prison for breaking into his own house.

There was a loud smacking sound. It was light and the room was bright cream in colour. Shit - I hadn't woken up in time and the workers were coming into the main room! I had to be quick - if someone was silly enough to try and stop me I would just push them away and run past 'em. My plan set, I dashed out from the little room. Nobody - not a soul in the place. What had woken me then? Well thank Christ for small mercies anyway, now I was up and ready.

I walked across the room with more confidence. I had only to cross the little front garden and I was out Scot free. As I opened the newly painted door and was about to step over the threshold I saw a letter, face down on the paint splattered mat. So *that* was what had woken me! The postman had just delivered this letter - well I was very grateful. I was halfway through the door when, without any introduction, the letter bit me. Well - not exactly - but near enough. It was like an electric shock going straight through my body - from the letter and nowhere else.

'What the fuck!' I said to myself as I bent and picked the letter up. I turned it slowly.

There on the front for all the world to see was *'For Gypsy Dave'* written in red ink as plain as the nose on my face. Who in the name of all the blue jays and peacocks flying down the road had sent me a letter here? I quickly shoved it in my pocket and ran out the door and down to the cheap café at the bottom of the road.

"Watcha mate, you ain't been in 'ere for a long time 'ave yer?" The London owner of the café said.

"Cup of coffee please," I said sitting down near the window and trying to wake up from my spontaneous doss.

I was wondering why my ribs were sore until I remembered I had fallen asleep on the bare bedsprings. This reminded me of my letter.

I pulled it out thinking seriously about the odds of me getting it - they must have been millions and millions to one. On the very morning of the night I had been desperate enough to break into a place to kip - it was unbelievable. I opened it up thinking I knew the writing - I did - it was Donovan's:-

'Gypsy - come on down and help me in the Music Business.
I've found these great Managers who want to handle me.
Straight up mate - they got me on 'Ready Steady Go'
Please Gypsy, come and help me - we're gonna have a ball.

P.S. Beverly gave me yer address.'

CHAPTER ELEVEN
<u>LOOKING DOWN ON DEATH</u>

Beverly had given Donovan my address - but how? Even I had no idea what the road was called - didn't even know the number of the house. I had a mental image of Beverly taking down the number and address in a little pink notebook. *'Them women think totally different from us idiot men,'* I thought. *'A lot more sensible and practical.'*

I gave the contents of the letter some thought - then I gave my circumstances some thought, crossing the 't's' and dotting the 'i's. I was going nowhere fast with only 1/6d in my pocket after the coffee had been paid for - and that only by luck.

Delilah, a half-caste Jamaican and Welsh prostitute, had seen me sitting lost and forlorn by the bus station and come up to me with a big toothy smile on her face and tucked two shillings into my hand.

"What's that for Del?" I asked.

"To tempt yer to be my pimp Gypsy my boy. Big man like you hangin' round me and I'd have no trouble at all."

"Come off it Del, you already asked Joe."

"Yeah, I know - just kiddin' yer. No - it's for the favour you did me that other night - remember?"

Then I did remember. Delilah had come dashing out from an alleyway in front of me with terror, or some relative thereof, written on all over her face. She had looked up as she ran towards me, her expression changing to one of relief as she caught sight of me.

"Here, quick Gyp - get rid of this for me," she said, thrusting a blood covered flick-knife into my hand and running off.

I heard the screams as I passed the alley. Some silly girl had tried hustling into Delilah's patch and would have a scar or two to remind her of her stupidity. It might be the oldest trade in the world but there still weren't that many customers. I had simply walked a few streets onward and then, with a sense of regret - as it was a nice knife - dropped it down a drain hole. Thinking of that incident made me see how crazy my life was becoming. *'I'm bloody well off and that's for sure!'* I said to myself.

Lorna was very upset when I told her my decision. "But look Gypsy, I'm nearly better. Let's go back to St. Albans - you can help Donovan from there till there's some money to be made. Oh please Gypsy, don't leave me - you know how much I miss you and love you! This is all my fault - I left you too long out on them cold streets. Please forgive me my love and don't punish me for it!

Aaaahhhh!" she began to wail - not cry - it was more like the sound you would hear at an Indian's wake. This worried me because I'd never seen Lorna like this.

"Look Lorna my sweet, I have no idea where I'll stay or what I'll do till Dono and I get it together - if we ever get it together. This music business can't be that easy to break into, otherwise there would be hundreds of singers and players. Give me a month - if nothing happens we can go off somewhere nice," I said, trying to placate her.

"Go to your mother's Gypsy," Lorna implored me.

"My mother's? What's she got to do with this?"

"It's near Donovan's house isn't it?"

"Lorna, I can't just walk into my Mums after being away for so long and expect her to put me up."

"Gypsy, you silly thing, your Mum's your Mum. She'll love to look after you, Mums always do, don't you know even that?"

"Well - I'll think about it," I said, entirely unconvinced.

About a week later I phoned Donovan on the number he had scribbled down, obviously at the last minute, on the envelope. He was very excited. He had just done his second week on *Ready Steady Go* on the television.

"Piece of piss Gypo - took to it like a duck to water - I was made for it, sang me song and that was it. They want me back next week as well they say. The record company's falling over itself to get me record in the fucking shops. When can you arrive man - can't do this without yer Gypsy. The singing's one thing - but all these bullshit hustlers, man. I need your clear sight Gypsy, you can see through a con six miles away - you always could, you old bugger. When you coming?"

"Do you have a pad for me to doss?" I asked

"Not yet - but the bread's comin' in man. I'm still at me Mam's till we get some real cash. Come on Gyp, we can share the money 50/50 like we always did. We don't need bread anyway, we know that - but it'll be fun seein' what it's like spending it - just for a gas. Won't yer come Gypo? Come on down man! Yer can stay at your folk's place till we get it together bread wise. I saw yer Mum a couple of weeks back and she was very pleasant - wished me luck when I told her about the music - asked me if I knew where you were. Course I said I didn't, but I said I heard you was cool and healthy and livin' well. She was ever so pleased Gypo. Come on down - you'll make her very happy, you old fucker!"

That's what Lorna had said. "OK mate, I'm gonna start hitchin' down in a couple of days," I said pondering my lot.

Telling Lorna the news was bad.

"Look," I said, "if I am going to stay with my folks I know what that will mean - Mum's always telling me to get a job.....well, maybe I will get a job - if I earn some money I can get the coach to Manchester on Friday afternoon and take it back to Hatfield on Sunday night - sleep on the coach on the way back and go straight to work on Monday morning - how does that sound?"

"Would you do that love? Come all that way for weekends and stay on the sofa like you used to?" Lorna asked.

"I'll try - and that's a promise," I said. "I think it's only a seven hour drive, so that's not so bad love - and luxury all the way. I'm quite looking forward to it," I said, lying through my teeth.

I arrived at my mother's two days later, tired - but just in time for dinner. She couldn't believe Lorna and I had got all the way to Tangiers and quizzed me about it for ages.

"And who is this Lorna then? She must be nice if you've been with her for nearly a year. Do your dad and I have to start saving for wedding bells?" she said with a twinkle in her eye.

"Jesus Mum - marriage? Are you mad! Lorna and I have never discussed marriage for one second," I said.

"That doesn't mean the poor dear soul hasn't been dreaming of it David - and stop swearing please."

"Good God - mothers!" I said in frustration.

"We were sort of expecting to see you David. I saw your friend Donovan just the other week and he told me his news about making it in the record business so I thought, Oh ho - Donovan will want you there if it's true. Made me happy as a sandboy actually."

"Oh yes? And how happy is that?" I asked.

"As happy as a person can get David. I have good feelings about this venture of Donovan and yours - good feelings right through my body."

That was good news - my Mum was rarely wrong with her 'Good Feelings'. "And?" I said, eyebrows raised.

"And you're going to get a job me lad - first thing in the morning."

I laughed at her and put my arms around her neck and gave her a peck on the cheek. "Thank God some things never change Mum, you're as predictable as breathing."

"Well that's good then, isn't it? Because you're as predicable as the English weather," she said sweetly, giving me another helping of her walnut cake with white cream filling.

My father said very little when he came home for dinner - he always left the household matters to my mother.

"Tangiers?" he said. "Aye, let's go there for our holidays next year Nona."

I was up early next morning to go through the local newspaper to find a job.

"Here's one," I said to my shocked mother, who wasn't too sure what to make of this 'new' son of hers. "It's only 10 minutes walk from here - says to report to the Manager's Office."

"Good Luck!" she called out the door as I ran down the road.

The manager was a nice man and he gave me the job even though I said I hadn't had one in ages as I'd been on the road.

He asked me to explain what I meant by that so I tried, but his eyes grew wider and wider as I spoke so I decided to shut up before he changed his mind.

So there I was - working in a bloomin' cardboard box factory.

I was down the far end of this huge machine - and I do mean huge - with Bill who was about 55. We stood either side of some metal rollers. The machine delivered the boxes flat and we had to pick them up and make them neat by hitting each end then swing them onto a pile on a movable trolly that was then towed away when at shoulder height by another worker They were big boxes. Bill was tall and so was I and I began to see why I had got the job. It had nothing to do with my marvelous personality, brains and charm - it was simply because of my height.

"How long you been doing this job Bill?" I asked him, trying to make a bit of conversation.

"17 years, coming up 18 on June the third," he said proudly.

'Jesus!' I thought *'18 years coming to the same factory day after day!'*

"You deserve a bloody medal!" I said, and meant it. "You must know this place like the back of your hand."

"No, not really," Bill said. "I only worked here."

"You mean here? Right here?" I said, incredulous.

"Well - I was on your side for two days, but I didn't like it," he said seriously.

My God! This was not for real! 18 years in the same spot doing the same thing hour after hour.

I was nearly sick all over them shiny metal rollers. Something just turned in my belly.

"Sorry Bill, I got to go to the toilet - come over queer in me stomach," I croaked out.

As quick as you like Bill punched a big round red plastic button with the flat of his hand and the whole machine came to an instant standstill. "That's why I likes it this side," he said, smiling from ear to ear like a fucking demented chimpanzee.

Thank God I had Donovan and the boys to talk to at night in the pub.

Everything was going well with Dono without us needing to do much. I noticed a tad of jealousy in some of the other beats who strummed a tune or two but most of the good players were happy for him. People like Mac Macleod who was a good friend and showed Dono some great actions and techniques on the guitar that helped his playing for sure, but no one could sing the way Donovan could sing. There was a lot of rubbish talked for a while about Donovan copying Bob Dylan, but Donovan's voice was truly what it was - it was no copy. Dylan, ironically, borrowed his voice from Woody Guthrie. Who was the better songwriter is up for grabs. I personally think they were both unique geniuses in their own right - bloody brilliant the pair of them.

But having seen Bob on stage a few times, there was no doubt as to the best entertainer, the best showman, the best performer. There Donovan stands out the winner by a mile. God bless yer Bobby - but most of the time you were lousy on stage. I think I've seen Donovan give one or two bad performances in all the years I was backstage watching him.

He gave many more after 1970, but then again at that time for a little while his heart wasn't really in it. We need our heart in things - and my heart wasn't really into going back and forth to Manchester.

But I did as I promised and got the coach. It arrived in Manchester at 11.45 on Friday evening and after a hurried weekend I left on Sunday night, arriving in Hatfield at 6 a.m. on Monday morning with just enough time to go to my mum's place for a shower before I started in the factory at 8 a.m..

God it was boring. One day during my half hour dinner break I started to walk the length of the machine. I was fascinated because it did so many things. At the bottom of it I stood for a minute admiring this great bit of engineering.

"Hello, can I help you?" came a pleasant sounding voice from behind me.

"Ah no - not really - I was just thinking what an incredible machine this is."

"Are you new here?" he asked me nicely.

"Started a week ago, I'm down the other end - with Bill. I just wanted to see the rest of the machine - it's fascinating."

"Yes it is," he said, "I helped design some of it myself. What's your name?"

"Mills - Gyp Mills - well, David actually - the Gypsy's a nickname."

"Alright Gypsy, you better get going - you're missing out on your dinner hour."

Two days later I was called into the main office and sat wondering what it was they wanted. Everyone was very nice and finally the manager took me into his office and informed me he had been told of my interest in the machine.

"Would you like to start at the end of the week, learning the machine from top to bottom?" he asked.

"Well that would be very interesting indeed, thank you very much," I replied and went back to my job with Bill looking forward to the end of the week.

"What was that all about?" Bill asked me. "Never been in those offices in me bleedin' life, wouldn't want to either - bloomin' snobs they are up there."

"I don't think so Bill, they were very pleasant to me - just offered me a different job actually - learnin' the machine from top to bottom," I said casually.

"Oh 'ave they now, well that's interesting that is. We'll have to see what Taffy the Union man's got to say about that."

Well you could have knocked me down with a feather. I nearly caused a lock-down strike. There was hustling here and hustling there and then I was called into the Union Office.

Taffy, the Union shop steward was a bullshit little sod who seemed to think his actions would free Wales from the English occupation if he just stuck his nose into British industry long and hard enough. He was a stupid, pompous bastard - a man whose sole interest in life was beating back the Management.

"You got no right to that job," he said. "There's places, there's lines, there's priorities me lad, see? Just because the management thinks you got brains - well what the fuck has work to do with brains? It's all brawn me lad and don't think it's not. If they want someone with the brains to learn that machine then they can nick 'em from management - they aren't having any of my boys to turn into snobs and that's the end to it."

The management called me in and apologized profusely. I told them it was no big thing - I was going to leave soon anyway. They didn't understand me and thought it was the disappointment of not getting the new job that made me want to leave.

"You just hang in there young man," they said. "Let a few months go by and we'll slowly teach you how to work the machine, then you'll be ready to take your rightful place in this Great Firm of ours.

I couldn't believe it - they were all bonkers!

In *Goldwatch Blues*, Mick Softly (God bless his cotton socks - and his van) sings,

> *'I did not want no job upon the board*
> *I just wanted to take a broom and sweep the bloody floor'*

I knew how he felt. At the end of the week I left as I couldn't take everyone being either guilty or overly nice. As a going away present I cracked open the factories sweet machine that took sixpences and if you were cleaver enough with one sixpence you could keep opening the drawer and empty each compartment of its goodies. I took armfuls of sweets to the men I knew had children.

That weekend, with my wages stowed away in my jeans, I was back in Manchester. Lorna was so happy I couldn't tell her I had no job to go back to and that next week it would be impossible to get the money for the coach fare. *'Ah well, next week is next week and there's many a slip between cup and lip,'* I thought. On Sunday night I was off again.

Donovan was waiting for some big pennies coming from the *Ready Steady Go* gigs. I went down with him, now I had no work, and we were together when he did his last *RSG* show. It was fascinating to see behind the scenes of the programme. *RSG* was aimed at a young pop audience but there were some really intelligent people behind it all laying down the mechanics and the visuals and sound.

I watched proudly as Don strutted his stuff in an innocent and honest way, putting forward our ideas of freedom and the beatnik life. He was refreshing, stimulating and fun. We were Knights of the Road still on the road sharing our dreams of creativity and freedom with the nation's youth, the feeling of truthful living trailing down the road of self discovery.

Cathy McGowan, one of the main *RSG* presenters, was a sweet, determined girl. She knew how she wanted things and she knew how to get them that way. She was sexier in the flesh than on the goggle box and she got on well with Don's *persona* and liked his cheekiness too. *'You'd take me in wouldn't yer love?'* Donovan sang to the young girls in the audience with a wink and a twinkle in his eye. Would they ever take him in - take him in and eat him all up.

It was fun and from the very beginning it was 'All Happening Man'. And did those girls ever come on to us. I was beginning to see that if I was to get totally involved in Donovan's career there would be little room left for my Lorna.

It took some hard thinking. I knew Donovan needed me and I knew Lorna needed me too. *'Let it ride,'* I thought, *'things will work out in their own good time.'*

The next Friday I phoned Lorna telling her I wouldn't be down as I was knackered. I had not spent a weekend in St. Albans or Welwyn Garden City and I hoped she wouldn't mind if I missed a week with her. She was cool - or at least pretended to be cool about it - said she understood anyway.

That Friday night in *The Cherry Tree* I met a girl called Tammi who was sipping on a Babycham. She was young and beautiful sexy as hell with the air of a swinging beatnik chick. Was she 18, even though being served a drink from the bar, I didn't think so - but no one in our crowd was 18. Tammi had thick, silky light auburn hair that spilled luxuriantly down to a very shapely backside. This wonder of nature supported itself on two magnificent legs and her breasts were like rosy apples that made you just want to put your lips on them in praise of their perfection. She didn't have a lot to say, but the way she looked at me across the Babycham made words superfluous. She was a cross between an angel and a sexy fairy and she fascinated me - and it seemed I fascinated her too.

I took her outside for a joint along with Donovan and Peter, who had just raced up on his big motorbike. Queeny and Beaky came too.

"This one got a fiancé as well Gypo?" Beaky said, nodding at Tammi and laughing her head off.

"Come off it Beaky, I hardly know this lovely lady."

"You and yer bullshit Gypo. Why you silly girls fall for Gypsy's charm I don't know," Beaky said glancing at Tammi. "He's married you know."

"Never been married in my life," I said, giving a wink in Tammi's direction. "Why, I'm still a virgin as it happens," I joked.

"So am I," Tammi said sweetly and we all laughed.

'This girl's cool,' I thought to myself.

"What you doing tomorrow?" Tammi asked me later that night when there weren't so many people about.

"Haven't thought about it to tell you the truth," I said, amazed at her courage.

"Well I've got nothing to do at all - and it's Saturday. I hate that - don't you?

It's like being all dressed up and having nowhere to go. If you'd like Gypsy you can come round to my parents place in the afternoon," she remarked casually.

'Wow!' I thought. *'Is this a put on or what?'*

"Where you living?" I asked.

"Here," she said handing me a piece of paper. "You're not really married, are you Gypsy?" she purred.

"No, I'm not - but I do have a regular girlfriend - and I'm no virgin either."

"Oh but I am - and that's the trouble" she said. "I hate it Gypsy, hate it with a vengeance - and I was hoping you could do something about that," she ended enchantingly.

I looked around thinking I was on *Candid Camera* but there was no sign of a camera anywhere.

"OK Tammi - if you're *really* sure, then it will be my undying pleasure," I grinned, trying to be as cool as the Himalayas.

"I'll see you about one o' clock would that be good for you." I asked still not believing my luck.

"That will be wonderful," she said and kissed me sweetly on the lips before leaving. I sat dazed for a few minutes, then this great big bleedin' silly grin creased my face, like I was an idiot. Then I started to feel a little guilty thinking of Lorna. The hashish was beginning to get the upper hand in the contest with the alcohol to see which would take possession of my soul for the rest of the night.

Jazz strains were floating past and I saw Donovan dancing a jazz stomp with Melanie through the French windows of the dance hall. *'Jesus!'* I thought. ' *No one in their right mind could resist Tammi's offer. Bloody hell - was I dreaming or what?'* Well, I would find out tomorrow at one o'clock .

I wasn't inside the door of Tammi's folk's house before she started to undress me in a playful mock sexual way.

"Slow down Tammi sweetheart - let's enjoy the experience shall we," I said, needing to take over a little bit. "You've got the most unbelievably beautiful body it would be a shame not to appreciate it", I said in delight . That was not just bullshit as I had never seen such a well formed and perfectly proportioned body before."

"If that's true then why am I still a virgin," she asked me wide-eyed. "All my friends aren't. They all have boyfriends - except me. There must be something wrong with me. What is it Gypsy, please tell me."

"I'll let you into a little Male secret lassie - it's nothing wrong with you - believe me. It's something wrong with us men. We see the most beautiful girl and we thinks," *'Can I handle 'er? Can I keep the opposition away from 'er? Do I 'ave what it takes to keep this wonderful girl interested in me?'* It's too much for many a bloke love - just too much effort - too fucking lazy to give a toss. They would rather go for the ugly one, or the plain one - one not strutting her stuff with beauty - a girl they feel there wont be too many men to battle with over the spoils, so to speak. That way they can go to the fucking football on a Saturday afternoons and know that the little lady back home hasn't got any suitors at the bleedin' back door. Not all men are like that of course - but enough to have given you a hard time. You don't know it Tammi - but you are one of the most extraordinarily beautiful women in the world - which means you're going to have trouble all your life with men. Come here and let me kiss it better for you," I said, smiling my most reassuring smile."

You have no idea how incredibly amazing it felt to caress that full on voluptuously womanly body with my own. But there was a price to pay for that and similar joys not so far down that newly opened road. The following Thursday Sammy, his girlfriend Lynn, Tammi and I were waiting for Donovan to arrive. The pubs weren't open yet so we met outside the Wimpy Bar near Welwyn Garden City train station. Donovan got off the train with a grin as far as London was away, he had his Cornish fisherman's hat on, which I noticed was a bit out of shape.

"What do you think I got under me hat Gypsy me old fart?"

"Well - you got some hash for sure."

"Yep, that's right - what else?"

"Dunno - you tell me."

"I'll do better than that mate - I'll show yer."

Here Dono lifted his hat slowly to reveal an ounce of the finest marijuana I had seen in a long time sitting on the biggest wad of money I had ever seen in my entire life.

"Shitting hell! You got your money at last!" I said.

"Five 'undred quid Gypsy - five 'undred pounds. Fucking miracle, ain't it? Let's go up on the department store roof to celebrate. You can roll us one of yer dirty great joints Gypo and you can put in as much as you like."

We did exactly that. We got in the little secretive lift that took us the six flights to the roof. Here we had a panoramic view of the shops below us. On the right was an expanse of concrete that led to a low wall about three and a half feet high. This was our preferred place to blow our spliffs. I rolled up a beauty and put into it what a normal human being would smoke over two or three days.

Dono, Sammy and Lynn were into deep conversation about the myriad tangles of Life.

"What are they talking about Gypsy," Tammi asked in amazement.

"Ah, terribly important stuff," I joked. I took a deep toke on the joint and passed it to Lynn. Tammi suddenly looked so light and weightless in her pretty dress. I wondered if she would float.

I picked her up and turned her round in a circle, my soul filled with her beauty. She laughed - she was no weight at all. In my stoned imagination I saw her float up into the sky like a kite and I went nearer the edge of the wall to get the imagery more real in my mind. Then, like a bloody fool, I lifted her over the wall and suspended her over that six storey height.

It was cool - I was in charge - she weighed nothing.

Tammi wasn't in the least scared. Everything was fine - until I rested my stomach on the wall - and my feet began to leave the concrete floor. I realised I was acting as a balance, my bodyweight from my stomach to my legs versus my bodyweight from my chest to Tammi in my arms. We balanced perfectly - for a moment – then Tammi began to suspect something wasn't quite right and started to struggle in the crook of my arms. I commanded her to keep still but even as I spoke we slipped a fraction lower. *'You God forsaken idiot!'* I thought in my mind. *'This is all your fault - putting poor Tammi's life at risk over a bit of larking around.'*

If we fell - and the likelihood was that we would - then the only thing I could do was to try to shield Tammi's body with mine and try to cushion the blow for her before we hit the bottom. That way there was a slight possibility she at least might survive. There was one chance left however. If I were to call out I knew my muscles would react again and it would give only a few seconds for someone to react. I knew I would start going over the wall the second I shouted out. Who would it be - Sammy or Dono? I knew Donovan could often be slow and laid back when stoned, Sammy on the other hand had quick reactions even when out of his mind on dope. I staked our lives on his reactions and called out his name.

Immediately I felt the wall sliding past my belly. Shit, this was really it - the end. Then I felt a pair of hands grabbing my legs - Sammy had caught me. Dono had lifted Tammi round the waist and with Lynn's help was dragging her over the parapet. We were alive!

I gave thanks to Jesus, Sammy, Dono and Lynn - and I realized I wasn't such a bad bastard after all as my courage had been tested royally and not been found wanting. I believe to this day that my thoughts of saving Tammi's life before my own were powerful enough to save both our lives.

Dono gave me the money to go to Manchester that Friday, with a little extra to buy Lorna a present from him.

It all went well but something was coming in-between our souls. No - it wasn't Tammi - that relationship had nothing of the depth that Lorna and I had.

I gave Lorna the good news that Don was looking for a pad for us to live in.

"And do you want me to come and stay with you then Gypsy my love?" Lorna asked softly.

"Course I do, you silly thing. Just give us a few weeks to get settled in first," I said, "then I'll call for yer to come down my sweetheart."

She smiled a lost faraway smile that reminded me of when we had left Tangier. What was it she had said right at the end?

"We can't expect it to go on forever now, can we? No matter how much we want it to."

I felt a shudder in my soul and shivers in my spine, as if I were a violin being played by a mysterious horsehair bow. That put a bit of a damper on my stay that weekend.

Arriving back in Hatfield on Monday morning I was still strangely depressed. This was quickly dispelled however when Donovan turned up at midday with the good news that we had a pad. He was going to pay the costs of renting an enormous house near Putney, plus electricity, rates etc -and all for a friend who could no longer afford to live there. Of course the friend was staying on free of costs with his arrears paid. Don was happy to help out a friend and get something in exchange. Next day we were up there living in The Smoke - that was the affectionate nickname for London in those days. Me Mum had tears in her eyes when I left, taking the few things I possessed with me.

"Come off it Mum, there's no need for tears - it's a happy time. When we're organized I'll invite you up for cream tea," I laughed.

"It's not that David - I know that everything is going to change for you now - I'm just crying because you're going to be alright - it's such a relief it is."

I gave her one more hug, then turned my back on her watery eyes, and was gone.

CHAPTER TWELVE
COMMERCIAL SUCCESS

The day had passed when Donovan had made his first demo recordings in a basement studio in Denmark Street. They had heard him, they had loved him. His managers, Geoff Stephens and Peter Eden, worked like Trojans and got him a recording contract with Pye. After his performances on *Ready Steady Go* he recorded his first single, *Catch The Wind*. Donovan was really happening - and all before I arrived from Manchester. At some point in all this craziness he had stopped to pen a letter to me.

He was disappointed in his friends. He had told them what was happening but all they did was take the piss.

"Gonna be a fucking star are you Donovan? You wish mate - you wish." came the snubs and derision.

He knew his first travelling pal would understand and support him. Fuck, it had been with me he had first gone out in those little streets to sing and play. He knew I had dug it then and would dig it now - and he was right too.

Within a few short weeks we were well into it. Don was recording and playing gigs at theatres and seaside piers, he was also doing more television. Jesus - he was even being booked for the States! Donovan became a household name as his record rose up the charts - not only in England but all over Europe. I wrote to Lorna shortly before all this went down telling her we would have to part. I had been so busy with Dono I hadn't been to Manchester for many weeks. As much as I loved Lorna, the scene I was getting into had no place for a woman by my side. It seemed Dono and I would be on the road most of the time doing gigs all over the country - no place for a girl like Lorna there.

She sent a friend of mine, Sean, down to talk to me to see if it was definitely over. He told me he was in fact in love with Lorna himself and wanted to marry her, but not until she and I had really split up for good would he attempt to woo her. With regret and sorrow, thinking it best to end our relationship well, I gave my blessing for their upcoming marriage.

Now I really threw myself into work with Donovan. We were moving flats a lot as we moved on - and the newly formed Drugs Squad were showing some interest in us. Twice they came to bust us - without warrants of course - and without much idea of how to find drugs.

The second time a policeman came in through an open window and jumped onto a single bed in the half light. Our mate, Dave Tilling, felt a huge weight fall right in the middle of his stomach and was so winded he couldn't even shout a warning to us. Luckily they found nothing - I think they were only using us as practice for busts to come. All this talk of policemen brings me nicely into my own little brush with the forces of law and order.

Pauli, a good friend of ours who had helped us out with our first pad in Putney, was done for some minor drinking offence. During his trial our names came up and he was asked if he knew where we were living. Pauli said he didn't - said he would be glad to help if he could but he had no idea where we were living now. Of course he was taking the piss and trying to make a good impression on the judge.

After the proceedings an out of uniform police inspector asked Pauli to accompany him to the pub around the corner where he tried to enlist him onto his side.

"What about this Gypsy Dave?" he asked.

Pauli thought that if he acted like he wasn't over enamoured of me he might get some information from the cop.

"That bloody Gypo Dave is a right bugger. I hate his guts for what he did to me," he said.

"Oh yes? What did he do to you then?" the inspector asked, all ears.

"Well, he fucked things up between me and Donovan didn't he? That's why they moved out. Left me with a fortune in rent to pay too, the bastard."

"Did he now," said the inspector. "Well you'll be glad to know that he's in trouble deep - we're going to throw the bloody book at him. Did you know a young girl called Naomi?"

"Yes, I met her once or twice with that shit Gyp,"

"Well we might use you as a witness then if you don't mind."

"Be glad to help - but what's he done?" Pauli asked, all innocent.

"Naomi's mother came to the station and made a complaint against him. She holds this Gypsy Dave responsible for her Naomi leaving home so young. You see she found her daughter's dairy - it's all written down in all its gory details there. He's been making out with a minor - giving her drugs to get his evil way. We got him dead to rights - it's a very serious crime. He's going down for at least fifteen years."

"What?" Pauli blurted out.

"Yep, she was two weeks off from being sixteen when he did his evil deed - we got it all written down in her own handwriting - he can't wriggle out of this one."

"Well good riddance to bad rubbish," said Pauli beside himself with grief.

"If we need you for the charge against him will you be available?"

"You fucking bet mate - I've been wanting to get even with that fucker for ages," Pauli said in shock.

The minute he left the pub Pauli came straight home to our new flat. The news hit me like a ton of bricks, as I hadn't seen Tammi in four or five months. Fucking hell!

"Shit Pauli, were you followed man?"

"No way man - it's cool."

"Fuck man - I gotta split right now," I said in a panic. "Jesus - I've not got a penny on me."

"Here, I've got six quid - you can have that and I'll get it later when Donovan arrives," Pauli said.

"You're a winner man! Look - explain to Dono what's happened - I'm going into hiding till I find out where Naomi is. If I can reach her I can maybe persuade her Old Lady to drop the bloody charges against me. I can't stay here, it'll only take the law a couple of hours to find out where I'm living. Fuck - I don't even have a bleedin' sleeping bag again!"

"Can't help you there Gypsy but you can't go on the road again Gypo - you're too soft for that now," Pauli said.

"Want to bet? I'm going to have to rough it for a while - whether I want to or not. No one will find me on the road - you can't find an address you don't have mate."

I went to my room and quickly stowed a few clothes into an easily carried canvas bag. I had no idea what I was packing - I just knew I had to get out of there as quick as my poor stoned legs would carry me.

"See yer Pauli - and thanks mate - I owe yer, owe yer real good. Let Dono know - he'll understand , tell him I'll get in touch as soon as it's safe to do so."

Giving Paul a hug I rushed out the back door totally convinced in my mind's eye that the Fuzz were entering the front door at that very moment. But where to go? Where to go?

Now I was on the run I felt better and cooled down a bit, I had to get in touch with Naomi and the only way I could think of to do that was to phone her friend Judy. I got her number from my little black book and dialed from a phone box.

"She's in Cornwall Gypsy - gone down to see her brother. He's in a village a few miles from St. Ives," she said.

"What do you want Naomi for Gyp? I thought you and Naomi was over months ago? You got them red hot urges again - you randy sod!"

"Not exactly Jude, haven't got time now to go into it but you'll hear the news quickly enough."

"Gyp, listen love - Tony's just told me she'll be on her way back soon."

"All the more reason I have to go now then - take care you two."

"Bye Gypsy, whatever it is sounds bad by the tone of yer voice - Good luck," Judy called from far away on a phone I was already putting down. I had to set off for Cornwall - thumb out and away.

My first lift took me about 80 miles and I got dropped off on the outskirts of a little country village.

It was getting dark and there was no chance of any further lifts in a place like this. I would have to doss down for the night and get onto the motorway first thing in the morning. I had no sleeping bag, just my leather coat and thick jumper. It was beginning to feel cold, even though the wind was light. I walked slowly along the road contemplating my lot. Before me was a field full of horses As I walked past one he shook his mane and pawed the ground in the direction of a few houses I hadn't noticed till then.

"Thanks mate," I said, moving off towards them.

There were five or six houses in a large quadrangle and in front of them was a row of garages that had no doors on and appeared to be empty. They were just made to doss down in as far as I was concerned so I entered one and laid me down in the furthest and darkest corner and covered myself up with my long leather coat.

The concrete floor beneath me felt strange. *'Fuck it,'* I thought, *'it's because you've got soft Gypsy boy - just like Pauli said.'*

I fell asleep quickly, but woke up shivering right down to my bones. Then I heard a voice I recognized coming from one of those rosy lit houses. It was Joan - Joan Baez. She was singing *'There but for fortune go you and I',* on the television. *'Joan my love - if you could only see me now,'* I thought. I felt damp all over but somehow I got back to sleep.

I arose from the floor of the garage at first light and found I was covered in a whitish grey film. It was all over my leather coat, jeans and jumper. The floor I had been trying to sleep on was newly poured concrete! The bloody cement was wet, but strong enough to support my weight without breaking up. No wonder I was so bloody cold during the night!

I quickly changed my clothes, but what was I going to do about my leather coat? Coming out into the yellow glow of that overcast morning I saw the answer in the paddock where the horses were standing - dew - lovely wet morning dew. Sliding between the barbed wire of the fence I dragged my coat backwards and forwards over the soaking grass to clean off the cement dust. It took a while - but it worked. Suddenly there was a squeal of brakes and a van stopped sharply on the road behind me.

"What're you up to young un?" I heard over my shoulder.

On turning, I found myself face to face with the biggest copper I had seen in my entirety, his sergeant's stripes standing out on his thick muscled arms like whipping scars. God did I panic! My blood pressure went through the roof and I was about to make a run for it when a voice inside said, *'Cool it.'* With a gargantuan effort I did cool it.

"Good morning," I said pleasantly, holding my coat out in front of me and turning it over to see if it was clean. I knew it looked an expensive article.

"What you doing lad? We had a call from one of them houses saying there was someone acting strange in their field," the huge policeman said.

"Sorry," I said apologetically, "I didn't think of that. I'm hitching to see my girl in Cornwall - she's a student like me."

"That's alright me lad - but you've still not told me what you're doing in this field?"

"Oh - I'm sorry - in the first light I noticed my leather coat was dirty - must have come from the lorry that dropped me off fifteen minutes ago - so I had this brilliant idea to clean it up in the dew," I said, trying for the life of me to stay cool. "I need to look clean or I'll never get lifts."

"Well - looks fine to me". Said the Sergeant, "I've seen many a scruffier hitchhiker along these roads. Come on - get in and I'll take you to the Station first then drop you off on the right road, because you're a bit off course here for Devon.

Jesus Christ! I couldn't say no - though I was thinking it could be a clever trick and that there was a 'WANTED' poster of me on the Police Station wall.

"You look cold," he said as we set off in the van, "there's a flask of tea there on the dash board - help yourself to a drink. Me missus makes it up for me every morning., She don't know it - but I stopped drinking tea twenty years back - gives me heartburn - she just won't get it into her head, bless her." He pulled up outside the station. "Won't be long son - just you sit tight and enjoy your tea."

'Please God let him be on the level,' I prayed as I sat there, surrounded on all sides by a swarm of police officers - but soon the Sergeant was back.

"Right, let's get going then shall we? It's only about eight miles to the right road for Devon and Cornwall."

And sure enough that's where he took me. As we said our goodbyes I realised I really liked this Police Sergeant - he had been very kind to me. He gave me hope - hope that there were still some decent lawmen about.

On the road again I felt light as a swan on the water. God, I was flying - and not with drugs either. I got a great lift to Devon and was dropped off in a place where you could see the road tunneled out of the natural scenery like a scar - but a beautiful scar in those delightful surroundings.

'There', I thought, *Man can live in harmony with the earth.*' Then I thought, *'Go get fucked Gypo, you twat! 99% of the scenery we see is man made anyway!"*

Thoughts like that would run through my mind as I waited patiently for my next lift. It was a way to entertain myself on the lonely stretches of a deserted road. There were no Walkmans to walk with you as if they were chummy, mechanical friends; no IPods to squash the thinking right out of your brain like you would squash the innards out of a slug that was on yer cabbages. Yes, I know we live in a modern world - but we've always lived in a modern world.

"Well - you want a bloody lift or what?" came a driver's voice

"Sorry," I said, "I was a bit lost there in the past - or was it the future?"

I travelled on in good company through Bodmin Moor, where Sherlock Holmes had unearthed *The Hound of the Baskervilles*, and the next lift took me to the outskirts of St. Ives.

As I ventured nearer I noticed some advertising for a Folk Club stuck up on a few trees by the roadside.

Maybe I would go see what they were producing as singers in this neck of the woods. I noticed there was an Idriss something heading the bill that week but I felt a little bit superior to these folkies, having had such knowledge of the 'In-Scene' at first hand. *'Stop being a big headed fool and go and see what they have on offer!"* I admonished myself.

I arrived in good spirits in the quaint village of St. Ives for the umpteenth time in my life and there was the same goodwill, same charm and same smell that made me feel at home instantly. God how I loved this place! I promised myself a good wholesome meal and after that a fantastic Cornish ice cream.

I was sitting in the restaurant, having eaten well, when a lovely young lady entered.

She was bright and fair with a face that was glowing healthily from the sun and sea air. I couldn't help but notice that she had a lovely figure too. She was dressed arty - but sloppily smart, if you get my meaning.

From where I was sitting I couldn't help but overhear her conversation with the restaurant owner as she handed him some money.

"Last month is it Idriss? You will come back when the season's over won't you? It's been a pleasure having you rent the flat for the winter."

"I'll have to see how things go Mr. Lobb - can't promise anything yet., but I would like that very much if it's possible," she replied in a voice that sounded London-ish to me.

"Oh - I nearly forgot," said Mr. Lobb, "Johnny brought your guitar in, said it's as good as new. He said, not to fret , it was only the fret."

They both laughed and so did I, which made Idriss look in my direction.

"Hello," I said, "sorry, but I couldn't help but overhear your conversation. I had no intention of being rude."

"That's alright, there's no need to apologize," she said as she held out her hand. "I'm Idriss," she said.

"Pleased to meet you Idriss, I'm Gypsy." Then it hit me. "You must be Idriss - the folk singer."

She looked startled. "Don't tell me my fame has travelled all the way to London," she said with a nervous laugh.

"It most probably deserves to Idriss, but I'm afraid some trees on the way here whispered your name into my ear."

Ah - the adverts on the road - that's good, I told Bernie they might work," said Iris, pleased as Punch. "Are you thinking of coming?"

"I am now," I said, looking long into her eyes. "Is Bernie your man?" I asked with intent.

She laughed out loud. "If you could see Bernie you'd know the answer to that question. He's the organizer of our Folk Club - I don't have a man at the moment. I prefer to be on my own right now thank you, it's easier with the kids and the divorce."

"You have children?" I stammered out.

"Yes, two boys - one five and one three."

"But you don't look old enough to have children - and your figure's still fabulous," I said in shock.

"Well, you're certainly straightforward, aren't you?"

"I'm sorry Idriss, it's just that you look so young," I said, feeling a little stupid.

"That's alright Gypsy, I'll take it as a complement," Idriss replied with a smile. Will you come tonight?"

"You try stopping me!" I said beaming up at her. "Is the Folk Club easy to find?"

"It's about a mile from St. Ives - if you're here at 7.30 you can come with us in the car," Idriss replied as she was going out the door.

"Right you are, 7.30 it is then," I said giving her a wave goodbye.

When I came to pay the bill Mr. Lobb looked at me long and hard.

"You're a bit of a charmer aren't you? I've never seen our Iris in such a flurry. You look after her if you get the chance, she's as sweet as they come," he said protectively.

I was lost in her voice when I heard Idriss sing that evening - God she was good! She sang some Joan Baez songs and also some fantastic renditions of a singer I'd never heard of before, Buffy St. Marie. In the second half her eyes sought mine and she sang straight to my soul and I realized this was what the girls were feeling when Donovan sang to them.

Idriss and I sat together as the other acts performed and it was obvious to all that something was beginning to happen between us.

"You seem very interested in folk music Gypsy," she said.

"Yes, I have a famous friend who's a folk singer," I replied casually.

"What's her name?" she asked, looking at me with intent.

"It's a 'he' actually," I said. Then the penny dropped.

"Not Donovan!" she said incredulously. "Bloody hell - you're Gypsy Dave!" I nodded. "How could I be so silly, I've even got a picture of you somewhere in my scrapbook."

It turned out to be a small world indeed as Idriss was from Hertfordshire and had lived near St. Albans with her soon to be, ex-husband .We were dropped off at Idriss's flat by her friend Jenny.

"Have a good time you two - you look like you were made for each other in our opinion," she said to Idriss sweetly.

"Is that the Royal 'our'?" I ventured to ask.

"No," said Idriss, "Jenny's a good friend and that's her way of saying we both agree that you should share my bed tonight - if you'd like to that is."

"You try keeping me out of your bed," I said, knowing that I had found a kindred spirit in Idriss.

It was her last night in St. Ives and we made the most of it. Next morning I helped her pack her belongings and move to a caravan site about a mile out of town. We had talked through the night and I told her the story of how I came to be there. She asked if I'd like to stay with her and the two boys in the caravan as it would be safe there.

"That would be wonderful," I said with relief, "but first I have some urgent business to attend to. I'll come to the caravan about six o'clock tonight if that's cool."

"Don't get caught Gypsy, I don't want to lose you now - after just finding you," she said giving me a kiss.

I left her then and started to make my enquiries. The first thing I discovered was that Tammi and her brother had left at almost the same time as I had arrived. From her cousin Julian, who lived near Mousehole, I got the news that Tammi knew what her mother was doing and was intent on keeping her from going to Court. She had gone home to play act to the mother that she'd stay at home and be a good girl if her mother dropped the charges against me and if that failed then she'd say her diary was all fantasy, created out of her frustration at not having a boyfriend.

It might just work and at least thing were moving in a positive direction.

"I know her mother very well," said Julian. "She not a vindictive person, but she is a Catholic so you never know how hard she'll react to the loss of Tammi's cherry - it depends on how the priest advises her as well. The best thing for you to do is to lay low. I don't even want to know where you're living - just give me the address of someone who knows you and if there's any news I'll let you know through them."

I gave him the address of Idriss's old flat, knowing that Mr. Lobb would find her, and thanked him kindly.

"That's OK - Tammi asked me to help you all I could. She still holds fond memories of you Gypsy. There's only that fucking priest to worry about - I've met him a few times and he certainly is a vindictive bugger. If he presses hard it's possible nothing will shift my aunt from prosecuting."

In spite of Julian's reservations I felt things were looking up - and felt the luckiest sonofabitch this side of Mount Olympus to have found Idriss. The caravan was the best possible hide out and although I was only eighteen I soon got into the way of playing the father figure to Idriss's sons. Iris was twenty five but looked twenty one. I was eighteen but looked twenty six and I saw no reason to tell her my true age. Not many women like to think they're older than their men. We four as a family had a ball in the coming weeks and months in that caravan. Idriss's kids were fantastic - though as a surrogate father I still had a lot to learn.

Time passed smoothly. I knew Dono was OK as I was constantly reading about him in the music press.

I also knew he was trying to pull some strings with Solicitors who had told him I hadn't been charged as yet - though they thought they could make a good case for my defence if I was charged, as they had found out there was no actual dates in the diary of Tammi. That's what I heard through the grapevine.

Of course I also heard that it was 50/50 and touch and go whether the cops were preparing 'Wanted' posters of me and at one point I was seriously considering paying some Breton fishermen to ferry me over to the coast of France. But then two weeks later Dave Tilling arrived in St. Ives and my friend Chunky brought him to the caravan.

"Dave you old bugger!" I cried leaping up to greet him.

"It's been dropped Gypo - the fucking case against you has been dropped - you're a free man," Dave beamed

"Say that again Dave - just for the wonderment in those unbelievable syllables of saintly sanity," I said.

"Get out of it Gyp, you old con man! You're free man, free."

"I sat down before I fell down. The relief was almost unbearable.

Idriss gave me a huge cuddle, squeezing me half to death with tears falling from her wide, innocent eyes...

CHAPTER THIRTEEN
<u>A BOY CALLED DONOVAN</u>

Dave had some other news too. The television company Granada, one of the biggest in Britain, were interested in making an autobiographical documentary about the Bohemian lifestyle of Donovan and by implication myself too.

It was to be called *A Boy Called Donovan*.

As I was talking away excitedly to Dave, Idriss was giving me long sad looks. She knew our relationship would not be sailing off into the still waters of a red and rosy glowing sunset. I had never promised her more than I could give and now she could hear from my voice that I was off. Donovan and I were Blood Brothers of the Open Road and it pumped through our Ramblers' hearts with the promise of travel, adventure and freedom. Idriss bit back her unhappiness and made smiles replace her tragic feelings as Dave and I continued our heated discourse.

She wore this mask for me, so as not to spoil for the merest second the pleasure I was feeling in my new found freedom. That was love indeed.

Dave Tilling and I left the next morning. He had been given the money to get the train back, but I wanted to hitch - for some reason I wanted to go back the way I had arrived.

During the filming of the documentary, Dono and I moved flats again. This time to Maida Vale and the building of his new manager Ashley Kozak and his beautiful wife Anita. Our flat was several floors above them..

We had just moved in the night before when the director wanted to shoot a short sequence there. Apart from a few things that were our own the furniture in the flat had been left by the previous tenants.

We were filmed in the area that was to be my bedroom, but as yet I still hadn't bought a double bed for the room. The single beds you see Donovan and I in on the documentary, were not ours and were picked up the day after filming by the owners. Dono had bought a beautiful French half-tester bed made of brass but not being very practical he was waiting for me to assemble it so that first night we kipped in the single beds hoping the owners wouldn't mind. Dono had no blanket, so he draped a Union Jack flag on his bed. I had completely forgotten that the TV Company wanted to film us.

Early next morning there was a noise at our door. I was sleeping after a tiring day the previous day and wasn't sure what the noise in the hall was. Still half asleep, as it was only eight in the morning I went to answer the door wearing nothing but my Scants, short modern underpants for men which were fast becoming all the rage. I opened the door to find the whole crew standing in the hall - cameras, sound and lighting technicians and Charlie Squire the director.

"You forgot Gypsy, didn't you?" he said. "I thought you might. Never mind old boy, we'll just film you as you are."

I suddenly realized I was standing at the door virtually in my birthday suit. "Shit! No way man! Let me get some clothes on first Charlie," I said laughing.

"Just put a shirt on Gypsy - it would be great to get you doing the normal things you do in the morning .Go back to bed then and we'll film you waking up, get out of bed, go to the kitchen and make some breakfast old man - anything like that," Charlie advised me - and that's exactly what you see in the documentary - Scants and all.

Charlie Squires was a fantastic man and the perfect fella to direct this film on Donovan. Sadly he died a short while after making this film, his family and the world lost the kind of man it can ill afford to lose.

He was a real gentleman and he left his mark on everyone he had contact with in the finest of ways. God bless you Charlie, Dono and I still hold you warm in our hearts.

There's a party scene at the end of the documentary. It's about as genuine a scene as you could wish to get for all participating were friends of long standing.

It was filmed in Artists studios in Bushy, Hertfordshire and was where our good mate Dave Tilling lived. He rented the studios from British Rail who no longer had any use for these huge storage facilities.

You entered the buildings through a parting in the trees. They were made of corrugated tin, painted black, over a wood and steel construction and must have being built in the 1940's. The really fantastic thing for my friends and I was, they were the most haunted space we had ever come across. The ghosts of a mid eighteenth century Estonian Prince and his beautiful mistress, Lulu, both haunted the grounds. He, as legend had it, sent his castle over to England and rebuilt it stone by stone in of all places Bushy.

Of course jealous rage and murder were all part of the tale. There were many psychic occurrences there One I remember well was when Dave brought me a mug of tea. We had eight mugs - each a different colour. I was sitting reading when Dave set a mug down on the arm of my chair - it was the blue mug with two white chips in the rim. I said 'Thanks' without looking up and continued reading. A couple of minutes later as I was about to turn the next page Dave came and gave me another mug of tea - the same blue mug with two chips in the rim. That's when it hit me.

"Dave, you just brought me this tea a couple of minutes ago - same mug and same resting place."

"Not me mate," said Dave, "must be Lulu up to her old tricks again."

Three of the other studios were occupied. In one lived a painter who had made a name for himself in America in the style that's now called 'Splash & Dribble' he was a cocaine junkie. Next door to his studio was a 40 year old lady painter who was by far the craziest person I had ever met outside of a Mental Hospital. In the last of the studios there lived at times a little old lady as thin as the lace she wore. Her clothes were at least 60 years out of date, but immaculate and as if bought from the tailor's that very day. We never knew when she would be there. She owned a house in the village and her unhelpful neighbours complained about her piano playing so she moved the piano to the studio and at the strangest times through the night she played the most exquisite classical music that can be imagined.

Dave Tilling swore he saw the piano playing itself on one still and pregnant night. I had my own personal experiences to do with distortion of time and space. One time when staying at the studio I went into the corridor late at night after hearing what I believed to be the boots of the long deceased Prince walking there on the bare boards. The corridor was dark as there was no electricity installed there, but the moon was shining through the first window nicely. These windows were spaced at intervals on the right hand side of the corridor. Walking to this window and looking out I leaned up against the wall adjacent to the aperture I was looking through. The view was of a tree, a silvery blue light appeared to transfix everything in place like a photograph.

I enjoyed this scene for a few minutes whilst smoking a cigarette until I noticed what appeared to be a small animal rustling up the leaves under a tree. Fearing it might be a rat I leaned forward against the windows surround to get a better view. As my hands reached out for the window sill and frame my fingers hit solid wood. Before my eyes were a blank wall - there was no window there!

Stretching my whole body to the left with my hand and arm out as fare as it would go I had to take a few shuffled steps before my fingers touched the edge of the windows frame I had supposedly been peering through .. Bloody hell, did it send shivers up and down my spine as I realized that for five minutes I had been looking through a wall of solid wood and corrugated metal. Make what you will of these recollections, that is your right.

We were to lose Dave Tilling about ten years after these events. He was an artist and photographer. He took the cover photo for Barry Gibb's first solo album. Dave couldn't swim but he was out on a windswept sea on a friend's yacht taking pictures of rigging and masts. As the storm got worse his friends came up on deck to warn him to come in for shelter - but there was no one there. He had disappeared, fallen overboard they presumed. He was only 29. The good die young they say - it could be true for Dave Tilling was one of the best there ever was. We can still see him smiling as he always did, with his lover - a model called Roey on camera when they took part in the party scene *A Boy Called Donovan*. Dave is the curly haired chap who escorts the two policemen out of his studio door.

There was some debate as to whether or not these two policemen were real or actors. I can tell you now they were real local bobbies who had come to investigate a theft. A car had been taken and driven at high speed and with such reckless abandon as to be found wrapped around a lamp post in the middle of a roundabout not five minutes walk away from the Studios. The driver, who was described as being male, tall, scruffy and long haired, was seen walking - or rather lurching - away from the wreck, obviously very drunk. He was seen walking into the Studios - did we know anything about it? Well there were about 40 tall, drunk, scruffy, long-haired people at the party to choose from. Charlie Squire had arranged for 30 demijohns evenly distributed of white and red wine to be at the party, to get the scene off the ground so to speak. - after all it was a beatnik party. It kicked off at 7 p.m. but Donovan and I were a little late and it was 9 p.m. by the time we arrived. By then the demijohns were all lying empty and the joints were being rolled. Peter, our dear genius of A-levels and ICI fame, the only junkie amongst us, wanted to score. Whilst walking to his rendezvous he decided on the spur of the moment to take a car he saw by the curbside with the keys in the ignition.

In his drunken state he reckoned he'd be back before anyone noticed the car was gone. Unfortunately he didn't take into consideration the fact that he was drunk, hence the silly business of wrapping the car around the lamp post. Luckily he was only dazed and made his way back to the party - as did the local fuzz a few minutes later - but to no avail. Peter too has passed on now - suicide by an overdose of cocaine. He had tried very hard to kick the habit near to his death and had been off the stuff for over a month when a junkie friend paid him a visit Peter's resolve failed him. He thought one fix would not a junky make; nothing would make him take it up again. Why not have one more hit for old time's sake? Having been off it for so long Peter almost died simply by taking his normal dose. He told it to me like this;

"Your heart pumps in anticipation of the enjoyment - then you find the vein that's had a chance to heal a little in the needle's absence. You push on the plunger slowly and wait for the first effects to take place feeling like a million dollars worth of back pay. Then the Express Train hits you. You fall to the floor believing your heart has jumped from your mouth.

Your body has been taken over by a maniac intent on torture of the most cruel and dire kind.

The mind spins, falls, flies, dives, spilling your poor perforated brain on the floor of thought like a road accident in the making. You're not aware of who you are or what's taken hold of your soul - you just know it has to stop.

Please God let it stop before you explode with fear and disintegrate into a feeling of nothingness bereft of all happiness and joy, suffused with sorrow so deep you shake and writhe in anguish - your mind eventually clearing with the thought I want to live! I want to live! I want to live!'

He told me that he lost something very important to him at that point in time - he told me he had lost his mind, literally lost his mind. It had disappeared. It had died leaving him with a body that could only perform its daily duties. He was in anguish grieving for his lost intelligence.

That was the last conversation I had with poor Peter.

A couple of days after my last talk with Peter, Sammy saw him; it was two days before Peter's sad demise in a broom cupboard under a stairwell. I kid you not - Peter had fallen so low as to be living under a large stairwell in expensive flats in an affluent quarter of London. He lived there free of charge if he kept the marble stairways clean. It was the only job he could hold down as his habit got out of hand once again. Sammy met Peter in a café and they went for a walk down Portobello Road. He could see Peter was extremely agitated.

"What's the matter Pete?" he asked

"Nothing Sammy, it's just Death catching up on me, that's all," Peter said with resignation.

"What do you mean by that Pete?" Sammy asked in surprise,

"Well, for instance Sammy I'll be looking in a shop window when suddenly in the reflection in the glass I see a deaths head staring over my shoulder, it's bloodshot eyes in graying sockets staring at me intently."

"For God's sake Peter, you can't mean that!" Sammy said laughing nervously.

"I mean every single syllable of every single word Sammy.

Another time I'll be walking along the street minding my own business when I hear my name called and on looking up I see Old Father Time with his hour glass beckoning me to walk with him; or I see a skeleton lying in my path that claws at me with its crooked fingers of whitened bone. It's happening more and more just lately .Don't look like that Sammy, because I'm pleased it's happening. You see, I know that I'm dead already. I'm just waiting for this madness to stop. This shame that is my life, now that I have lost my soul, I am just waiting for it to be over."

"Peter, listen to me," Sammy said. "You've got to stop this mate before it takes over your mind." He was appalled at what he was hearing from Peter. "What you're saying is madness - a dangerous fantasy made up by a mind that sees Death everywhere."

Sammy was trying to get some sense into poor Peter's head when he heard a car speeding up behind them. It was a shining black Hearse, complete with floral tributes which passed them bye erratically and screeched to a halt halfway around the corner. Here the back doors burst open with a crash spilling out an ornate coffin. It slid down the road and stopped at Peter's feet. Sammy couldn't believe his eyes. Somebody would surely come to retrieve this macabre relic, but....nothing - nobody came. Stranger still people around them on the streets seemed to think nothing of the coffin lying abandoned by the curbside.

On looking up from the coffin Peter asked Sammy with the slightest tremor in his voice, if he believed him now.

"Look," he said triumphantly. "There you are - the Grim Reaper himself."

Sammy looked to where Peter was pointing and there indeed stood a hooded figure in a bedraggled garment with a huge scythe and skeletal hands holding an antique book of gigantic proportions.

"Jesus Christ help us!" cried Sammy grabbing Peter's arm and running with him in the opposite direction.

"It's no good Sammy, you can't outrun your Destiny anymore than you can outrun Time. My time is up and it's a travesty of nature that I'm still alive - soon I will be gone Sammy. All that you see before you is a shadow cast by another shadow."

Two days later Peter was found dead under the stairs having taken a massive overdose of cocaine. He was 27 years young.

Make of this story what you will. It's the truth as told to me by Sammy - the same Sammy who grabbed my legs before I fell to my own death. The world would be richer if we could teach people like Peter to be able to find there own creativity and not there own destruction, what artist these souls would make.

There are too many artists in this modern world with small unremarkable minds and unremarkable talent.

Hype has become the art while art has become insignificant.

It was during the filming for *A Boy Called Donovan* that I bought a beautiful Chinese screen, with its black lacquer and gold leaf work. It rivaled the Mona Lisa's smile for me. The lovely old lady in the antique shop didn't want to sell it when I enquired about it until by chance I mentioned my name in connection with the film we were making.

"Gypsy?" she said. "Gypsy do you remember a Sonya Cottonwood?"

"For sure I do - we were going out with each other for a while about three years ago."

"Well I'm her Grandmother."

"Well I will be blowed", I said amazed

"She used to come and talk to me about you for hours and hours." said the old lady. I was ill for a while after coming back from China and I was convalescing. Sonya cheered me up no end with her tales, so I feel I know you Gypsy, and I will tell you something else, I know Sonya would want me to sell you this beautiful piece. Let's say £200, shall we?"

"How did you know, that's exactly what the TV company are paying me for my part in this documentary" I said. "I will take it, thanks - and please send my love to Sonya. Is she still living in Cornwall?"

"I'm afraid not Gypsy - Sonya has passed on. A very sad hit and run accident on a deserted road - never did catch the blighter."

"My God - how terrible!" I said in shock and disbelief. I can hardly believe it. Sonya was always so full of life."

"Yes, she was Gypsy and I can tell you one thing, if it'll make it any easier for you. You made her very happy for the short time you two were together. And Gypsy - she understood when you left."

"Yes, I know - she was a bright spark Sonya was," I said.

"A spark that's been extinguished Gypsy."

"Well Sonya's Nan, I'll tell you something - I'll remember Sonya now every time I look at the beauty of this wonderful screen."

"Then I'll have made Sonya happy I'm sure, wherever she may be," said her Grandmother emotionally

. "It was very nice to meet you Gypsy, you've brought my Sonya back to me - even if for a short time."

"Sonya was always talking about you too you know - she loved you very much," I said, my voice full of feeling.

The old lady's eyes brimmed full of tears. "Thank you Gypsy, thank you."

I treasured that screen for many, many years before I was forced to sell it when I was broke and the Self Employed Stamp government people were hounding me for some unpaid stamps and threatening to take my house, chattels and all.

The documentary *A Boy Called Donovan* was an unbridled success. It was released, after some delay, in January 1966. There was a little disagreement between the producer and the director as to whether they should leave the party scene in, but eventually it was decided to use it. The headlines in the newspapers next day were all about ,

'Near Orgy Scene in Documentary A Boy Called Donovan'

The 'near orgy' was simply a silly episode in the life of our friend Pauli. Unbeknown to him we had arranged for his estranged wife Diane to be at the party, hoping we could act Cupid and bring them together again. Pauli, God bless him, on setting his peepers on Diane sitting on the couch, rushed across the studio and threw himself on her at the same time thrusting his hand up her skirt as her legs had gone leaping into the air with his amorous attack. It was just boisterous fun - fun that had been captured on film.

The documentary made Donovan's second album, *Fairytale* , a must- buy for anyone who was a fan and viewed the film. A lot of the new album tracks were featured in the documentary.

CHAPTER FOURTEEN
AFLOAT IN MEXICO

Soon we two Knights of the Road were packing our bags again, this time for America. Donovan was to play at Carnegie Hall in February 1966. That was in New York City - it was the gig of a lifetime.

I watched backstage as my old road buddy transfixed the audience with his singing and playing for almost two hours. Shawn Phillips, writer of that wonderful song *The Little Tin Soldier*, played his 12 string guitar and Indian sitar on some of the set too. This was the first time a sitar had been used in a modern folk concert. Dono was fantastic, Shawn too. I felt after this concert that the world had no limits for the talent that was Donovan - for it was growing day by day.

Donovan was never without his guitar in his hands in those days. He would even take it to the loo, where amongst the raspberries would come melodies fragrant with the musical sounds reminiscent of the Caribbean; *'First there is a mountain, then there is no mountain, then there is'* sang Dono from the other side of the bathroom door.

Boy, did we have fun in Hollywood California. We did ten days at a place called *The Trip* on Sunset Strip. We were amongst the hip of the entertainment business - and Americans have a way of letting you know this. *The Trip* and the *Whiskey A Go-Go* were the best clubs in the hip neighbourhood. We had the best of both worlds, playing at *The Trip* and then going out in the early morning hours to the *Whiskey A Go-Go* to dance and play with the ladies. We were living as guests of Monica Peer and her son David. They had a beautiful mansion up in the hills with a fantastic swimming pool whose water was seemingly filled up by a stream and waterfall. Donovan went down like a house on fire at *The Trip* and the girls loved him. Some of them would jump on our limousine and hang on for dear life until we stopped to let them get off. It was my job to pull them off and try to persuade them not to jump on again.

At one point we had a break in the work schedule and decided to go somewhere we would not be known. A friend of ours, Ben Shapiro, who was involved in promoting Indian music suggested we go to Mexico, to a lovely secluded place called Yelapa. The only way to get there was by speedboat via Puerto Vallarta .Ben made the travel arrangements and got us a reservation in the only hotel there. We needed this break, if only to get away from the hundreds of people we met daily in our work.

Yelapa was incredibly beautiful. We were expected in the little hotel that was placed on the seashore and made cleverly from large bamboos. The walls were also of bamboo but split and woven together in lovely intricate patterns.

Beautiful teak wood furniture and floors inside the hotel spoke of local craftsmanship.

As the hotel was not large Donovan and I shared a double room with two single beds in it. This was cool as we had no ladies with us demanding their privacy - now and again we needed a rest, even from the charms of our American girls we wanted nothing more than to just cool it, soak up the natural beauty of our surroundings and relax away from the crowd.

We had about half a kilo of very nice Mexican Grass to smoke when like idiots we realized we had come without any cigarette papers to roll our joints. I got over this problem by making a pipe from a wonderful mother of pearl shell I picked up on the beach. It fitted into the palm of your hand and a large lip curled back onto itself making a receptacle for the Grass. I made the stem by drilling the first three segments of a radio antenna into the base of this lip. The beautiful shell held about half an ounce of Grass plus a little tobacco to make it burn better. It lit easily and smoked extraordinarily well. The mother of pearl glowed in your hand whilst inhaling on it and looked like a rainbow of sunsets.

We swam from the beach into clear clean water every few hours to cool down and relax and went for sweltering, steamy walks into the jungle forest that grew around our hotel like a green island. Once when we were all out swimming we saw a massive manta ray like a huge cloak being spread on the water with blue-black ink. The locals said it was lucky to see a manta ray - I was soon to have a slice of luck of my own to prove their story true.

A few days after arriving I awoke very early, bright-eyed and bushy tailed , on leaving our room I sat and watched the sun's light creep over the trees behind us while I finished off a full pipe of weed then I took it into my head to walk to the hotel's forecourt. To my surprise there was a lot of activity going on. A large table had been set up on the beach with twenty chairs neatly arranged around it. Cutlery, glasses and large buckets of ice were being placed on the table as I asked one of the waitresses who spoke a little English what was going on.

"It's zee Germans, zay are coming for zee breakfast. We mast not be late or zay will be upset with uz Gypsy. Listen - you can hear themz boat now."

I cocked my head and sure enough I could hear a speedboat out to sea. When it landed I helped the ladies out and onto the shore. The men jumped out with much laughter and splashing. Their leader was very nice and asked me if I was a guest at the hotel and how I found it. I said it was fantastic and by now he had called for another place to be set at the table for me. The buckets now had two bottles of tequila in each and all sort of dishes of crab, shrimp, meat and sausage were brought out. The Germans liked their food but they were drinking the tequila as if water. They drank it in shots, like Schnapps, using salt and lemon correctly. Of course when they realized I was getting drunk they encouraged me to drink more. I pulled out my fancy pipe and filled it with Mexican Grass and passed it around to anyone that cared for a puff. More tequila was called for. Everyone was getting a bit loud and noisy when the leader suddenly looked at his watch, called for the bill and then off they all went. They had another port of call for lunch and were running a little late though it was barely 10 o' clock in the morning. Good God, was I out of it or what! I was stoned out of my mind on that mixture. Tequila did something strange to my head every time I drank the bloody stuff in any quantity. It affected me like absinthe, giving me more of a high than an ordinary alcoholic buzz. What was I going to do with myself? It was too glorious a day for doing nothing. I began to head back to our rooms to see what everyone else was up to.

Walking back slowly along the deserted shell strewn beach I decided to go for a swim. I took my clothes off as I walked and waded naked into the crystal clear water. The feeling was so extraordinary the idea of pouring and melting into a cup of coffee came to mind. It was as if I had been accepted into the sea water like a drop of rain would be accepted, like I was a long lost brother returning unto the fold.

So natural was my blending I sank down in the clear water, my eyes open with amazement. I felt so at home the need to breathe was the furthest thing from my mind. I swan underwater for many strokes, the sea bottom opening out and getting deeper with each moment passing in this eerie silent world of blue glassy beauty.

It was wonderful, the colour of the sea becoming more turquoise blue and the white haze of the sand like the bones of the planet. Gently I took a breath of the ocean into my mouth, half believing I could extract oxygen from it in this frame of mind and oneness with the sea. I had to spit the contents out so I came to the surface and spat the sea water like a fountain from my pert lips. The after taste in my mouth was unbelievably good, the salt and remnants of tequila mingling so well in my drunken-stoned state of mind.

I swam deeper out to sea. Here the waves were coming in measured reels of heightened water. I tried my experiment in breathing water again, this time with the waves. They slapped me in the face and made me take too much water into my mouth. I spat it out with force and felt the dental plate containing my false tooth fall out and sink with a plop into the bright waves in front of me. *'Shit!'* I thought and took a long drag of air before diving under the sea.

I could see my plate plainly. It was just in front of my outstretched hands. It started to go in a sideways motion as it fell deeper into those clear diamond depths. I was determined to catch it and so I put all my concentration into that thought. Down we went, me kicking my legs furiously. I nearly had it - my fingers brushed against it. At that precise moment my chest started to contract in and out in spasms. I had felt three distinct pains in my head during my descent. Was this something to do with that? Was I having a mild heart attack maybe?

My mind cleared from the alcohol in this dangerous situation I realized I had used up all the air in my lungs. I flipped up my body and saw the waves on the surface like a glass lid far, far away.

My brain told me I was in real danger of drowning. I forgot my tooth and concentrated on returning to the surface air. My lungs wanted to breathe the water - anything to stop this desperate need for air. I was out of oxygen with a long way to go to that roof of lapping waves and sunshine. I told myself that I mustn't breathe the sea into my lungs even if my lungs were to burst. The last thought I had was to clamp my mouth shut tight as I kicked for the surface. Gritting my teeth together, I passed out - I went into oblivion.

I don't remember a thing until I felt Donovan on top of me pressing my stomach to get the water out. He turned me over and the sea water gushed out of my open mouth like a stream. He had pressed his fingers into my open mouth forcing the tongue downward to make me sick and the gush of water coming out made me breathe again.

Donovan and Anita had been searching the sea coast in the hope of seeing me after some Mexican children had found my clothes being washed up on the beach and had run to our rooms to tell my friends that I had been drowned. While searching Don had seen strange scuffled marks in the sand. Following these impressions he found me face down deep in the undergrowth, trying to breathe through my nose with ever dire results, my breathing becoming shallower and shallower. I had unconsciously swan for shore and kept swimming even when I reached the sand to come up short in the underbrush. Such is the determination of youth.

When we all sat in our room later that morning I was upset because I would have a gap right in the middle of my mouth - and we still had some dates to do. *'What will those lovely girls think of my smile now?'* I thought.

I needn't have worried. The ladies came fast and left not so furious we hope. We tried to make our lovemaking slow and luxurious - not always succeeding in making our loving into something special I'm sure - but we tried and as the saying goes 'It takes two to tango'. And to those lovely ladies we tangoed with I blow a sweet kiss of remembrance down the winds of time and a haloed thank you for your gift - your beautiful bodies wrapped around ours in joy and harmony.

Donovan and I met some incredibly talented musicians on that trip to the States, good down to earth cats.

People like John Sebastian of the Lovin' Spoonful - an absolute treasure of a bloke; kind, intelligent and helpful even though a genius who penned numbers like *Summer In The City* and *Daydream* which fell from his fingers effortlessly. He was to become a lifelong buddy of Don's after he married Cathy Cozy.

In California we met again The Mamas and the Papas and spent many an evening talking, eating, singing, toking and swimming. Someone, Mama Cass maybe, had a pool virtually inside their front room. Needless to say there were a lot of beautiful girls around to go skinny dipping with. It was a way to advertise their wares to those crazy cats from England who had foreskins - wow foreskins! This was something most of those lovely ladies had not encountered before.

In those days in America, maybe still, the policy was to circumcise all male children at birth. If parents objected they were looked upon as being Un-American. Just the sort of thing those McCarthy 'Reds Under The Bed' would get up to. Jesus, those government chaps the CIA and FBI certainly knew how to indoctrinate their rather naïve general populace. America was becoming more fearful of Communism, especially when dealing with Trade Unions. It's a sad truth that we become the very thing we fear, as in fighting the good fight against The Reds more and more freedoms were being denied the American people. Does this ring any bells? It bloody well should! This is exactly what is happening in Britain and America right now - your freedoms are being eroded day by day. Shaved by the razors edge of fear, cut up through the imaginary knife of those dastardly terrorists. For God's sake wake up before you're shackled, tagged and chipped! Big Brother is watching you on every street corner and if George Orwell wrote his book *1984* now he would be in Guantanamo Bay wearing orange dungarees.

We lived with terrorism for years in England, perpetrated by the IRA, but there was no paranoia - we bit on the bullet and carried on regardless in the usual British way. There were no cameras, no erosion of rights, no security officers carrying guns on the streets of mainland Britain. Of course most of the IRA funding came from America courtesy of citizens of Irish descent who thought they were helping the Old Homeland.

There would be a lot of unanswered questions from America in my youth, not least of them who killed President John F. Kennedy and why? We know who killed Lee Harvey Oswald - but not who ordered the killing - nor who ordered the killing of Jack Ruby or Robert Kennedy. Who killed the thousands of young Americans in Vietnam? The Vietcong you will say - but only with the help of the blind American government and the armaments boys. Where were you Bobby with your, *'And I'll stand over your grave till I'm sure that you're dead'* sentiment? Joan Baez, Donovan and many more singers, writers, poets, musicians, playwrights and ordinary men, women and children saw it and they were not too scared to stand up and be counted. They did something about it too - they stopped the bloody war, amazing as it might seem.

I mention these things only to let the youngsters of today know what drove the youth of the mid-sixties to do what they did and to remind you there is still a war going on - and in your name too. Every age has good and bad signs to recognize, to change or encourage. One bad sign though is when the President of a Democratic America says as good as and with threatening force that... If you're not with us (and our policies) then you must be against us (thus we will crush you for your views against us) - and is not hounded out of office for it.

The youth of the last 25 years have been sadly lax in their duty, mainly because the governments of the free world got the hang of stopping protest before it gets going. But the best thing it has learned is to pretend a protest is not a protest, even when tens of thousands turn up. Newspapers and television seem to go along with this sham while another media tycoon is made a lord or gets first bite at a TV company once under public ownership.

Funny that, don't yer think Old Boy?

The future, like the past, might in reality compare to a Swiss cheese with those dirty great holes in it. If true then we've just been inside a hole for a couple of lines and now we return to the solidity that is the past.

CHAPTER FIFTEEN
<u>LOVE'S FIRST PROPOSAL</u>

Donovan was performing to packed audiences around the world who loved everything he did. He certainly gave them their money's worth of entertainment, I can tell you that. He was brilliant on stage, because he really cared, he gave performances from his heart, a rarely seen spectacle on the stages of today's programmed poseurs.

Donovan loved to perform. It was his way of giving back what the audiences gave to him. He felt he touched their souls - and I believe he did. Donovan truly reached out and hugged them creatively, as if they were friends and loved ones. I was there for almost every performance, hearing the same songs day after day. I loved it, no matter how many times I heard them. I loved it for the main reason that Donovan put himself into each performance. He had the knack of putting his mind fresh into each song, as though he was singing it for the very first time.

When he came offstage there I was in the wings, the first person he saw, the truth of his performance shining in my eyes for him to see as plain as the nose on my face. He would smile contentedly when I would say, "Fucking fantastic Dono!", because he understood that of all the people he had touched that night he had also touched his best mate. He knew I wouldn't bullshit him - he knew me too well for that.

"Was it alright Gyp?" he would ask me, a twinkle in his eye.

"Fucking unbelievable you old bastard," I would say - or words to that effect.

One thing Donovan always got me to do before he went onstage was to write down his list of songs in the order I thought they would go down best. He knew I could make a mood flow throughout his performances, putting the songs together like a string of pearls, giving the best lustre to the inner feelings of his creativity. Donovan liked to have that small bit of paper in my scrawling handwriting stuck to his guitar. It took me with him on the stage he told me once and my written characters brought him down to earth with reminiscences of the simpler times we had shared.

There is nobody more valuable to a commercially successful creative person than the friend he has shared time together with before his success. Donovan needed me as a reminder he was doing fine. He was keeping his head amongst all the glory, thrills and spills, money and the madness of mass adulation. My main job, as I saw it, - as well as all the other jobs I performed - was to keep Dono walking down the High Street of normal life. Keep him in touch with everyday reality - because that's where his songs came from, from the everyday events of an interesting life lived to the full.

Donovan was happy with his creative life, but not with his love life. Linda Lawrence had pierced his soft and gentle heart with her splendid barbed arrows of love. Linda was a truly remarkable young lady. Her beauty shone from her like a luminous dream. To be in love with Linda at that time was to be in love with a fleeting fawn in a wonderful morning mist. Donovan believed that only he knew the real Linda. What he could foresee with her was a rare and unknown happiness, unfelt by him up to this point. He wanted Linda more than he wanted Life itself.

We met her at the same party - it was after a TV show. She was remarkable for her innocence in those surroundings - she was not a parody of beauty, she was the real thing. She was what she was - take me or leave me. No one in their right mind would leave her, and yet she had been left - left by someone not quite in his right mind - Brian Jones, lead guitarist with the Rolling Stones. Linda had met Brian, who was a middle class boy living in Windsor, at a gig he had arranged at a rundown place in the sticks. That night they met and fell in love. Linda was 15, Jonesy was 20. By the time Donovan met Linda she and Brian had had a son together whom they named Julian. I believe Julian was about eight or nine months old when Donovan succumbed to the charm and beauty of his mother.

When Linda told Dono she had a child he was shocked - not by any morality issues but simply because she appeared far too young to have a baby. When Linda told him who the father was Don was even more bemused.

Linda was still trying to work things out between Brian and herself at this point. She felt that her child would need his real father - though she wasn't sure that she needed Brian as much as she had at one time. His treatment of her and the baby had spoiled her love for him and she felt he could no longer be trusted. Wishing to destroy another's will to gain the upper hand was one of Brian's habits. Linda had her pride and would not be put in that position. Her parents, Violet and Alex Lawrence and Linda's immediate family were very supportive of her.

Alex and Violet thought they knew Brian well. He had lived with Linda in their house and because they knew of the youngster's love for each other they apportioned no blame to their daughter's pregnancy and had enough misguided trust to believe that Brian would do the right thing - but he was to prove them wrong. Brian was to throw their decency on the floor and trample it underfoot - just as he was to trample on Linda's love.

With freedom comes a certain amount of responsibility - this isn't always understood by the younger generation, as they're too busy making the changes that freedom requires to come to fruition. Donovan had fought very hard to attain his own personal freedoms. Because of this he was more mature than many others in his age bracket - and now he felt he had reached a plateau where he was secure enough in his feelings to declare his love for Linda in the form of a proposal of marriage.

Linda was flattered - and tempted. She was also scared - and scarred. Once bitten twice shy. She declined Donovan's offer and a few weeks later flew off to America with her independence uppermost in her mind.

Dono went into a slump. I saw what was happening to him, though in matters of the heart we rarely talked or poked our noses in each others business. We avoided judging each others love affairs like the plague, knowing as we did that only the people involved in the affair knew what their heart and mind were feeling.

Work was the only answer and I set about encouraging Don to put his broken heart into his creativity.

"Get it in your songs Dono," I said. "It's what creative artists have done for thousands of years. You're not alone mate - all the best lovers have loved and lost."

My chatter would cheer him up for a while. One good thing for the world of music was that during this period Donovan was more creative than any time before or since. Songs poured out of his fingers, each one as different as chalk and cheese,

Dono, at the tender age of 18, was showing signs of genius and each new song he composed he usually played to me first, fresh from the creative mind's processes. I felt privileged to watch and listen. I felt wonder at his skill and touched by the raw creative power pouring from his soul that transmuted his feelings into musical prose. I was as enthralled as any fan. My old road buddy was holding his own with the rest - and let me tell you, the rest were the best.

Our times *were* the times. The early 60's to the early 70's were a musical extravaganza rarely if ever, seen in history. There were so many brilliant bands and individual musicians, all having something to say and saying it with style and panache.

Amongst the pure exuberance of the raw power of their music they sought to achieve change to the status quo. We youngsters refused to accept the 'Old Boy Network'. This was laid down during the Second World War. It was old hat and based on even earlier thinking in the 20's and 30's - aimed at a higher class of human being having control over the lower species of the working class.

In other words, those that had, should have forever, and those that hadn't should have nothing all their days. The Upper Crust controlled all sources of money - and ultimately the Government - through an unselected House of Lords that controlled Bills passed by the House of Commons. These fine fellows could kill any Bill that wasn't to their liking. Any democratic change which they did not consider suitable to their limited agenda of class would therefore be strangled at birth, wrecked at base one. This by a group of people not voted for by any democratic assembly. Their only claim to run the country was the fact that they were Lords - Lords for God's sake!

A hierarchy of wealthy people with land rights stretching back in history to harder and less lawful times. Three quarters of their ancestors would be clapped into prison for the way they obtained their land and titles is today's society - villains the lot. Democratic? I leave that up to your understanding of Democracy.

In the early 60's the younger generation finally cracked it and were in charge.

England's persona was no longer that of an old man resting on his laurels and bravely awaiting an honourable death.

Its new persona was vibrant and young; creative and cool. England was *the* place to be in the 60's and London was its creative heart and mind.

We felt a brotherhood of understanding that reached the very hub of our existence as human beings. Artists were voted into office by the popular vote of their fans. We changed the 'Rich Stay Rich' system, set up in the eleventh century more in the five years we were influential than in the previous thousand years - and peacefully too.

It was the only time in history that changes were made without a war or by violent means. In fact we called for 'Peace' and we stopped a war - this was our crime. Through peaceful and truly democratic means we stopped a brutal war.

The two foremost democratic governments in the world at that time, England and America, were appalled. Their population was demanding their rights as citizens to get their popular ideas democratically passed through elected government and implemented on their behalf.

Wow! Real democracy in the making.

Try it now my friends and they would shoot you down like the dogs they think you are. Democracy is the will of the majority through its people. If the will of the people changes from government policy then the policies must change - not the will be changed by Draconian methods. 'If you are not for us then you are against us - in which case we must change our policies'. That would be a democratic statement that any President of any country should be proud to make. But I'm afraid countries like America that have been bought and sold by big business have not been democratic for many many years - and Britain is catching them up with every month that passes.

CHAPTER SIXTEEN
BRING YER OWN IT'S A BUST

Donovan and I had just returned from a successful trip to America. We had let a casual girlfriend of mine, an American dancer by the name of Joy, use our flat while we were away on tour. I was beginning to like her a lot. American girls at that time had a free way with them, which was very refreshing and very beatnik.

Unbeknown to me Joy sent her brother to meet us at one of our gigs and he reported back to her that I was making out with other girls whilst on the golden shores of the USA. Joy maybe decided to even out the score by going out with Pauli and living with him in our flat till I returned home to England.

They had some mad parties which lasted for days on end. Dear Pauli was going through bad times, as he and his beautiful wife Diana couldn't get it together again. Diana refused to be reconciled and Pauli in his devastated anguish and disappointment took to hard drugs as a way to forget her. Thus it was that there were some hard drug users in our flat while we were absent. Neither Dono nor I ever met any of them - or ever wanted to meet them.

After the documentary *A Boy Called Donovan* the newly formed drugs squad were watching our flat. This was the excuse they needed - registered drug addicts in our flat having wild parties. The fact that we were out of the country obviously meant nothing to the judge who signed the search warrants - though maybe the police forgot to mention that fact to him. When the police were setting us up they had a bit of luck in the guise of long limbed Samy - a girl I had bedded a couple of weeks previously prior to leaving for Donovan's tour. She had been the girlfriend of Patrick, a friend of mine whom I had met in St. Ives. They had split up and Samy stayed with me for a few nights. We hit it off, but at the time I didn't want a permanent live-in girlfriend so I told her she had to split. She was difficult to get out of my bed so I asked another friend, Bonnie, to take her in as I knew Bonnie was looking to share a spare room in her flat. It was a bit silly of me really because I knew Bonnie was madly in love with Donovan and now Samy was convinced she was madly in love with me. They talked each other more and more into it, as the weeks passed - as girls do.

Samy phoned me twenty times a day until I saw her and when I did see her the inevitable would generally happen and we would spend the night together in her shared flat. Bonnie egged Samy on and tried to get me to bring Donovan to see her again, but I knew how Don felt towards Bonnie. He thought she was a great girl and a sweet spirit - but he knew their relationship went no deeper than the paper around a good joint. It would have taken an atom bomb of a girl to prize away the tentacles of love still surrounding Donovan's soul courtesy of Linda's mesmerizing charms.

In the weeks we were away, these two lovely ladies had got it into their heads that we would miss them so much that the minute we returned they would phone us and come round to the flat to see us.

I must say that I for one had not the least intention of seeing Samy again - and Dono had finished with Bonnie so many months before that she was just a fading memory. I was looking forward to spending time with Joy. We had spent several nights together and I was hoping to spend many more.

On arrival at our flat a group of our friends were there to meet us and welcome us back. Joy threw herself into my arms and made much of my return in her American way and I in my way was very pleased to see Joy. She looked stunning, her dancer's figure and long fit legs made the most of by a short skirt and burgundy tights with short over socks that only dancers wore. 'Extremely sexy' was my verdict as I sat and rolled a gigantic twelve paper joint in the company of our old friends.

Joy came and sat on my lap when the joint was making its rounds and I playfully ran my hands up and down her delightful legs. I caught Pauli's eye and winked at him. There was a strange look on his face that I couldn't work out. He was not very open - very unusual for Pauli, as our friendship went back for years. I put it down to the drugs he was taking.

I had been hearing Pauli was getting into hard drugs and I wanted to have a word with him about it to see if Dono and I could help him quit before it got too heavy a hold on him. Peter had been bad enough - we didn't want to lose Pauli too.

In the kitchen as I was making something to eat a good friend called me aside.

"Look Gyp, I don't want to make trouble, but I thought you ought to know that while you were away Joy and Pauli have been making out - he's been living here with Joy since a few days after you left."

"OK mate, that's great - thanks for telling me. I'll sort it out with 'em - see how the scene is with them both."

I didn't want to get too involved with Joy if she had a thing going on with Pauli. I knew Pauli needed someone he could love after his break-up with Diana - maybe Joy was the one. I went back into the living room called on Joy and Pauli to join me for a drink in the pub which was about four minutes walk from the flat.

We all three walked in silence with Joy's arm threaded through my own. When we got there I ordered up three whisky and cokes. The bar was busy and we were cramped in a corner.

"Well Pauli me old mate, we been friends for a long time now and I love yer Man - so I better tell yer that I've already been told that you and Joy 'ere have been seein' each other while I've been away working," I said quietly

. "Now Pauli, I know you must have fallen for Joy in a big way to have a scene behind my back - that's not your style mate, I know that, I want to tell you Pauli, Joy - it's cool with me. I must be honest Joy and tell you that I was beginning to have some strong feelings for you - I thought we might live together for a while and see how we felt, given a little time. But now love, I want to know how you and Pauli feel," I said with respect.

Joy was shocked at this outpouring of mine, but Pauli was cool.

"Thanks Gypsy, you're right man - I'm in love with Joy. Never thought I could be in love with another girl after Diana, but I am man."

Joy looked at Pauli with new seeing eyes.

"So Joy my sweet, how do you feel?" I asked.

"I don't know Gypsy. My brother phoned me from the States and told me you weren't exactly missing me. I was a bit upset and Pauli tried to tell me it was cool - tried to get me to see that when you were away on tour it was near on impossible for Donovan and you not to get involved with other girls. Well Pauli was so cute I gave him a hug and a kiss.....and it just started like that. We didn't *mean* to start an affair. I don't know *what* to think now that you're here again at my side Gypsy - I think I'm in love with you both!"

Joy had just got this out of her pretty lips when there was a shout and a kafuffle behind her and the bar turned into a fighting match. I quickly grabbed Joy, placed her in the crook of the bar and stood in front of her so that no flying beer glasses and chairs could hurt her. The fists were flying and even the women were fighting. It was then I remembered that this particular Bar had a reputation for this sort of thing. Pauli had been pulled down and was lying under someone on the floor.

I took my new dental plate with my front tooth from my mouth as I knew if I was punched in the face this would cut real deep into my palette. About twenty people fighting fit to bust surged forward towards Joy and myself and she screamed in terror behind me. I reached out for the backs of the nearest two people and with a God awful heave pushed them away from us. As I pushed they all fell, one on top of the other in a great heap of bodies like a rugby scrum. It had been coincidence as they must all have been off balance at that precise moment. It was impossible for me to have pushed them all flat. But from where Joy was looking over my shoulders it appeared to her that I was like Superman. The look on her face was amazing. I smiled at her and she saw the gap where my tooth had been.

"Oh! You're hurt Gypsy!" she cried.

I decided there was no better way of ending our affair than at that very moment. Pauli came up and asked if I was alright.

"We're fine Pauli," I said. "I think you should go to my flat and take Joy's things home to your place mate."

I stayed behind and had a few more whiskeys while awaiting Joy's departure from my flat and arrived back as they were coming from the lift. We didn't say anything - just hugged and smiled. Joy and Pauli moved to the States soon after this incident and I never heard from them again. I hope they made it and still share a great love and life together.

Well, back in the flat the joints were rolled and some wine drank - then the phone rang. It was Samy.

"Sorry Samy, but I'm too knackered to see anybody," I said to her. "All I want to do is kip - I'm so spaced out."

"Give me a call in a couple of days will yer?" she said.

"OK, yes - and if I feel a bit better before than I'll call you sooner," I promised her.

It was all lies but I could not face another break-up scene.
I had had enough with Joy for one day. I went to bed alone that night and dreamed of Joy. I woke up longing for her and hoped that Pauli and Joy were really in love and that it was all worthwhile.
Pauli had saved my bacon once and I hoped I had returned the favour by not making a fuss over his relationship with Joy.

Samy made a nuisance of herself by phoning me constantly from 8.30 the next morning. She was trying another tack - saying if I didn't see her she would commit suicide. I didn't believe a word of it - but you never know.

I arranged to meet her at Hype Park Corner away from her flat and mine. I was determined to tell her it was over once and for all. She threw herself into my arms when I got out of the taxi. I kissed her gently and asked her what all this rubbish was about committing suicide. Samy said she knew she could not live without me in her life. I jokingly said she better do herself in right this minute then, because we were over as from now. Blow me if she didn't walk right in front of a bus! It's fortunate that I have quick reactions, because I needed them that day. I dashed into the road and grabbed her by the shoulders, barely making it back to the pavement in time. The side of the double decker bus scraped my jacket and painfully caught my knee. I was furious.

I walked with Samy still held at arms length and hung her on the railings that surrounded the park, threading her up through her tight jumper. She was held fast by the railing and I think she was in a state of shock at what she had almost done to herself - and me.

"Right my lassie," I said in anger, "I don't wish to see you ever again in my entire life - so think about that while you're stuck up there!"

With that I hailed a taxi and was gone. How she got down from the railing God only knows. She didn't phone me again that day but the following afternoon she came to the flat. I was out but Dono was in.

"He's out seeing a client till six," he told her, "but he'll be at this number after that."

He gave her his manager Ashley Kozak's number, knowing we would all be there that evening.

"Thank you Donovan," she said. "Please give Gyp this and say I'm sorry."

She handed him a matchbox with a small lump of hash in it.

"That's sweet of you Samy. I'll let Gyp know, have no fear," Dono said.

I hadn't confided in him about Samy's stupid behaviour the day before. I was to regret that - we were all to regret it.

I arrived at Ashley's flat about six. His wife Anita had made a Greek dish of vegetables and chicken broth known at Brieam. The candles were lit in her cosy kitchen and the plates set. The smell of the meal wafting into our nostrils was like a foretaste of a culinary heaven. Ashley answered his ringing telephone. It was Samy for me.

"Oh for fuck's sake!" I said out loud in a temper. "Tell 'er I've been busted Ash and won't be around for months."

Ashley had a vivid imagination and we could hardly keep up with him most of the time as he took a lot of pills to give himself confidence to do his business for us. On this occasion he got the bit between his teeth and told a great tale of me being busted, locked up and the key being thrown away. No one in their right mind would have believed it for a minute - but Samy swallowed it hook, line and sinker.

"Do you know what police station they're holding him in Ashley?" she asked.

"No." he replied. "We're waiting for him to get in touch with us - he's only allowed a couple of phone calls.

You'd be best just to forget all about Gypsy Samy - as we all must for a while now.

What can we do? Life sucks sometimes."

"I can't do that Ashley - I love him!" she cried, ringing off.

"You old bull shitter Ash," Donovan said and we all laughed.

"If she believes that she needs her head examined," I said.

We went into dinner and had a wonderful meal without giving Samy a thought, as we had strategy to discuss about the next European tour. There's a lot to think about when you're planning 45 gigs in six countries. Our heads were full of this as we smoked a little of Ashley's weed. Then out came the instruments. Ashley on double bass, Dono on guitar and me on bongos and congas as Anita gave us a rendition of a Billie Holiday song. We were having simple fun after a fantastic dinner. When it came time for us to call it a day Ashley asked if we wanted to take some hash with us. I was just about to accept his offer when Dono said that Samy had left us a piece.

"Sorry Gyp, I meant to tell you but I forgot till now. It's a gift to you from her to say sorry for the way she behaved," Donovan explained to me.

"Well at least that's one useful thing she's done today apart from make a damn nuisance of herself," I said.

"You're too hard on her Gypsy," said Anita.

"You're right Anita my sweet," I replied, "but it's a drag when a girl won't take 'No' for an answer. It's not like we were together for a long time or something - it was only a matter of days."

Dono and I went up to our pad by way of the lift, which made such a noise that I always expected it to break down - but it never did. Dono was excited because Doreen was on her way to see him.

Doreen was unbelievably beautiful and I had fancied her for years but Dono had got the first drop on her. It was an unspoken pact between us that we left each others birds alone - a Cardinal Sin rule. Doreen was half French and had a ravenous figure with all the main features perfectly proportioned.

She was like an exotic flower always smelling of the most exquisite perfume.

I envied Dono his night to come and went to my lonely double bed with Joy in my mind's eye, dancing for me naked - as she had on our second night together. God, what a magnificent figure she had, her red gold hair the same colour as her triangle that glowed like a light beckoning onward the feelings of lust. Shit! I was almost tempted to phone Samy - but I refused to use her like that. Maybe I should have though - it might just have saved us a lot of bullshit. But that bullshit was piling up already and it was soon to hit us.

Samy had been phoning up a number of police stations trying to find out where I was being held after my arrest. Eventually someone told her that if it was a drug related offence then she'd need to speak to the Drugs Squad and they were kind enough to put her call through.

"Hello, Drugs Squad - Detective McDuffie speaking, can I help you? Who? Gypsy Dave? Who is this Gypsy Dave - I know that name from somewhere. Ah - friend and Personal Manager of Donovan the folk singer is he? That's where I know his name from then. What did you say he was arrested for? Cannabis was it? Hold on - I'm putting Sergeant Pilcher on the line - he'll know a bit more about it."

"Hello - can I help you with your enquiries young lady? Yes - I believe we do have Gypsy Dave in captivity - though I'm not sure if we're going to charge him yet, that depends on a lot of things. You want to see him do you? Alright then, come on down to the station right now. I'll arrange for you to meet him - just ask for me, Sergeant Pilcher, and I can take you right to him. No need to thank me lassie, it's all part of the job."

They must have laughed their socks off. Poor Samy fell for it and turned up at the Drug Squad headquarters and was questioned under the pretence that she could help get me out of the charges against me.

She began to smell something fishy when they asked her for the layout of our flat and clammed up realizing she had made a blunder of monumental proportions.

"I'm not saying another word until you let me see Gypsy," she said.

"Put this Samy somewhere she won't be able to get out of for a few hours,"

Sergeant Pilcher said. "We're going in tonight lads - we'll get those bastards - bloody Donovan - bloody Gypsy Dave. We'll show 'em who's boss around here and no mistake - they won't know what the bloody hell's hit 'em."

Samy, poor girl, was in tears of distress - realizing she had dropped us in it royally.

"But where is Gypsy then?" she asked.

"He's in his flat - same as all of 'em. They've been under observation for days now," Sergeant Pilcher said. "We know exactly where they are my girl - and they'll be in custody in this station sooner than they know it - we're going to take their flat apart."

Back at our flat there was a ring at the doorbell. I went to answer it and found Doreen standing on the mat. I gave her a hug and called Dono to come and get his lady. He opened his door, all smiles and soft music playing.

"Want to join us for a smoke Gypo?" Donovan asked me.

"No mate, I'm cool - you two have a blast. I'm going to crash early - feel a bit down to tell you the truth. I think I miss Joy.

I was looking forward to our tryst more than I realized," I said honestly to Don.

"Plenty more fish Gypsy," Dono said with a smile on his face.

"You're right there," I said giving him a wink. We both laughed and it made it easier.

"We're smoking the hash that Samy gave you Gyp, is that cool?"

"Cool as a cucumber mate. Finish it off and I'll go score us some tomorrow morning."

"Sure you don't want to join us for a while?" Donovan asked, concern on his face.

"No man, I'm OK - just tired. See yer both in the morning - have a ball," I said. We smiled at each other and gave each other a hug.

"Goodnight Gypsy," came Doreen's sweet, slightly accented, voice over Don's shoulder.

"Night my little love," I replied and walked to my bedroom.

I crashed - my head hit the pillow and I was out

I slept fit for the dead until I was awakened by a ring at the door bell.

"Jesus! Who the fuck is that at this time of the morning? Shit - it must be Samy! Bloody nuisance of a God forsaken woman," I thought to myself.

There was another ring, Well, if it was Samy I knew she wouldn't leave until I answered the bloody door.

I put my pants on to answer the door, I always sleep naked.

We had a small window with a curtain over it in the door to our flat; I drew it sideways and there to my amazement, on the other side of the door stood a very pretty young lady who smiled at me - a very charming smile. I was racking my brains trying to remember if I had met her somewhere but it was too early in the morning for thought. I removed the chain lock and started to open the door.

There was a crashing sound and the door hit my body with a heavy force behind it.

It threw me across the landing where I bounced off the wall, the wind knocked out of my sails. In through the open doorway came man after man. By the time I could breathe I realized they must be policemen.

Shit - another fucking bust!

A tall, fit looking bugger was holding me with my right arm twisted behind my back. I didn't struggle then, but I called out to Donovan to lock his door quick and throw anything that was left of Samy's gift out the bloody window. I was punched in the stomach for my troubles by the cop standing opposite me. Dono heard that I was in trouble and instead of locking his door he opened it wide.

He was stark naked, without really looking at the situation he dived onto the back of the nearest copper and tried to wrestle him to the ground - it was the nice guy who had punched me in the stomach. He flicked Donovan off his back as if he was a flea and Dono fell hard onto the hall floor. I was afraid the police would damage Dono's polio leg which was weak and had very little muscle on it.

I twisted my arm back around from the grip of the copper who was holding me. I was intent on looking after Donovan in this dangerous situation. The force of my movement twisted the policeman's own arm around and he screamed out loudly. I got another blow in the guts from the same source as before and within seconds four bloody coppers were on me as we crashed through my bedroom door. Donovan was screaming obscenities from the hall floor where he was being held down.

"Leave him alone you fucking bastards!" he was hollering.

The copper whose arm I had twisted was shouting that I had dislocated his arm. In the middle of all this mayhem poor Doreen was pulled naked from Don's bed and told forcefully to sit in the middle of the floor. They would not let her put her clothes back on. By now I had one copper bending my left arm, another bending my right and a third pushing me facedown onto the bed with his knee between my shoulders. I could hardly breathe.

"Let him go you fuckers!" Donovan was shouting at the top of his voice. He was being pulled to his feet and could see me being ill-treated through the open bedroom door. I was determined not to show these idiots that they were hurting me, but to tell the truth the pain in my neck and arms was excruciating.

I knew Dono well enough to know he wouldn't leave it at that.

I understood from the situation that he could get seriously hurt if he tried to interfere on my behalf.

"Cool it Dono, I'm OK Man," I shouted, just as Sergeant Pilcher came out into the hall from Don's room and called his men off.

"This, gentlemen, is a warrant to search these premises," he said, strutting about in front of us like a bantam cock. Finally they had shown some proof of who they were - policemen - not the thugs you would have presumed them to be by the way they made their entrance. We stopped struggling and the bastards let us up.

The coppers in Donovan's room had searched Doreen's clothes and allowed her to get dressed at last. The poor girl was sitting in a chair in her under garments shaking from head to toe. The police had behaved in a disgusting manner. They had a warrant and if they had simply knocked on the door and shown the warrant I would gladly have let them in. In fact it would have been a pleasure, as by luck we were clean that morning - not a bit of dope on the premises.

There would only be one or two filters of the joints smoked the previous evening and in those days they didn't send it off to the Lab to test for minute quantities of hashish. But I didn't trust this lot as far as I could throw them.

Donovan was allowed to put some clothes on too and we followed the cops around as they searched the rooms.

I saw Doreen was still shaking uncontrollably as though she'd been immersed in cold water.

"Make a nice hot cup of tea Doreen," I told her. "You've had a shock love and your body is reacting by shaking. A cup of strong, hot sweet tea will help you."

"Come on darling - I'll help you," said Donovan.

A policeman overheard this conversation and I thought out of decency he had followed to help Doreen too. Did he hell - as soon as Donovan reached inside the fridge for the milk this idiot pulled the bottle out of his hands shouting, "Quick men - the LSD is in the milk!" Two coppers rushed in followed by Sergeant Pilcher.

"Don't be so bloody stupid Jonesy," said Pilcher, "nobody puts Acid inside milk! I told you to look for it on blotting paper or in small pills or lumps of sugar."

"Sorry Sergeant, but he was acting suspicious - I thought he was trying to get rid of something down the sink."

Fucking idiots! We didn't even have an aspirin in the flat let alone Lysergic Acid. From this stupidity I walked into more of the same in Don's room. Dono had bought a most intricate Chinese pagoda made of filigreed ivory that was under a glass dome to protect its delicacy and beauty, it was an antique and unique. As I walked in a God forsaken copper was lifting up the glass dome. He looked up and saw the shock on my face and took it to be a sign of guilt.

"So it's in here is it? This is where you keep the stash do you?" he said thinking he was being clever. The bastard grabbed the Ivory pagoda in his great hoary hands and snapped it in two. Not satisfied with this mindless vandalism the fool broke it in two again then realizing his mistake he threw the pieces amongst the delicate ivory trees, garden and bridge that led up to the pagoda's entrance.

Fucking stupid ignorant animal! I wanted to kill him on the spot!

"You fucking idiot! Look what you've done to that antique pagoda! All those months of painstaking artistic work gone into that and you've destroyed it in a second you bloody ape!" I told him.

"Well, you shouldn't keep your dope in it, should you?" he replied like a child. "That'll teach you a lesson that will."

"But we *don't* keep our dope in it you fool - anybody with an ounce of sense could see that!"

"Well - you could have," he retaliated, beginning to see that he could get into trouble over his actions.

"For fuck's sake - what are you doing Richards?" came the appalled voice of Sergeant Pilcher. Over his shoulder I could see a policeman going into my room. Something had passed between them behind Pilcher's back that made the policeman nervous - I could feel that from where I was standing. As quick as I could I went into my room to find the bugger with his hands in my huge pottery ashtray. He turned on hearing me, guilt written a mile wide over his face, but his features relaxed when he saw it was only me. Then triumphantly he pulled a piece of Red Lebanese hashish, about an eighth of an ounce, from the ashtray.

Now I've never denied taking drugs - but I certainly do deny having taken the dope found in my room - and time has vindicated me.

The dope they busted us with was out of our buying possibilities for a start.

Blonde Lebanese was around at the time but Red Lebanese hash was always rare and could not be bought for love or money as a rule.

"What have we here?" the copper said with a smile.

I was furious.

"You know more about that than I do, you arsehole!" I shouted at him.

"Are you accusing the police of planting this here piece of evidence?" he said threateningly.

"Yes - I fucking am!" I said, knowing as I did that not a soul would believe for one moment that our honest British Bobbies would do such a crass thing as plant evidence. Such was the indoctrination at the time that even I could hardly believe it - and I was the poor bastard they were doing it to!

"OK men, we're all wrapped up here. Let's take them to the station and charge 'em shall we? Oh - but before we go we've got another little visit to make - I was almost forgetting in my excitement," Pilcher said sarcastically. "Right, we'll only need four men - and don't mess up this flat too much please. This little bit of shit could cause trouble for us all if we can't find anything."

The 'little bit of shit' Pilcher was referring to was Don's manager, Ashley Kozak. Bloody hell - and there was no way we could warn him of what was about to come down on him.

Ashley and Anita had similar treatment to us, but without the violence. A warrant was shown as Ashley opened the door.

Some hash was found in a box on the kitchen table and LSD was found in a pill box in a vase in one of the cupboards - the letters LSD written in bright colours on the outside so as not to be mistaken for anything else. The Acid belonged to us but Ashley said it was pointless to say anything about that as it was found on his premises. They also found some uppers (speed) but these had been prescribed to Ashley by his doctor. Apart from Anita the police took us all to the Cop Shop to charge us. They were very up. It had been a successful bust in their terms.

In the police van I said to Don that as they had only found dope in my room I could take the rap.

"Sorry Gyp, they say they found the stuff in our flat, doesn't matter which room it was in - but they didn't find the little hit I was saving you for the morning from Samy's present - I swallowed it."

"You should have given it to the cops - at least it would have been better than having it laid on us," I said.

"What they laid on yer looked nice Dope though Gyp - wouldn't mind a toke on that shit right now."

"Yer right about that Dono - we should ask the fucking coppers to give us their supplier for future business," I said, trying to make light of the crap we were in.

In the Police Station they were very polite to us all. Donovan had several requests for autographs from the cops for their sisters or their kids and he signed them good-heartedly.

"It's not their kids fault Gypsy," he said when I looked down my nose at his signing them.

"Yeah - yer right mate - sorry man," I said.

"It just makes me so mad that they took the easy way out and brought their own bloody shit to hit us with. Did you notice the tall, good-looking guy as we came in? He asked the copper who put it in my ashtray if all went well - if the favour he had done Pilcher had paid off. I'll bet my last dollar he gave the dope to Pilcher."

"We could never prove it Gypo," Ashley said sadly. "But I trust your instincts man. Fuckers!" he said with feeling.

It was hours later before we were finally let out, the charges having been made against us and the time for Court taken care of. There was pandemonium as we came out the main door.

It seemed to us that every major newspaper from around the world was there waiting for us with their cameras flashing and microphones stuck under our noses - there were even some television cameras pointing our way.
Shit! We hadn't even thought of all this bullshit rubbish!

"Jesus Gyp, what we gonna do about all this malarkey?" Dono asked shocked by the malay.

"Grin and bear it mate - fuck all else we can do Dono. Let's get out of here as soon as we can - this is all a set up man. How else have all these newspapers got their reporters here so early in the bloomin' morning. Someone's tipped them off hours before we were busted. No wonder the buggers brought their own."

"They'd have looked fucking idiots if they'd found nix," Donovan muttered darkly to me.

"Where's Ash?" asked Doreen

"He's not photogenic enough for the boys here love," I said pissed off. "He's from an older generation - they want to show the young, depraved youth," said Donovan wisely. "Sex, drugs and rock and roll - and you my little love are the glamour."

I was wondering why they brought you along Doreen - well now we know. Smile for the cameras - it's all a hype sweetheart," I said hotly.

"Bloody hell Gypsy," said Donovan getting upset. "If what we're saying is true then what else have they got planned for us?"

"The circus mate, the bloody circus and no mistake," I said.

"OK, let's cut on outa here," Dono said, his face showing a rare distaste for the world.

We three high-tailed it down a side alley and into a taxi and went back to the flat where we tidied up the mess. The flat felt strange, like it had been violated - it felt like it must feel after a break-in or burglary. We were all feeling depressed when the phone rang. Dono answered it.

"Hi Ash - they let you out at last. Gypsy reckons the whole thing's a fucking set up man. What the hell are we gonna do about it Ash? We need to talk and get organized before we're roasted alive."

"I've already got a barrister for our court appearance," Ashley explained. "Stay calm till then - we should get bail then we can plan ahead."

Next day we were at the court and were charged with possession of cannabis. We were released on bail of £50 per person and told to reappear for trial on July 28th. The newspapers were once again in evidence as we left the court and went home to Maida Vale.

"Do you fellas think I could go home? I'm feeling really down about all this," said Doreen quietly. "I better warn my parents about what's going to happen after this new lot of press hits the fan."

"Sorry, you're right Doreen," said Dono. "Hang on five minutes and I'll arrange a Rolls Royce to take you home to Hatfield. That should help underplay your part in all this and give the neighbours something to talk about. I'll phone Don Murfit to make sure the driver makes a good job of bowing and scraping."

"Tell your folks the stuff in the papers is just a bit of PR that got out of hand," I said. "Say it was a publicity stunt that went wrong."

"That's a good idea Gypsy; I think they'll believe that - thanks."

"Give us a couple of days to get this sorted out," Dono said. "We'll be in touch with you as soon as we know what's going on here. I'm really sorry for this cock up Doreen."

"That's alright Don, it's not your fault - just some mess up of a publicity stunt, wasn't it? I would fire the fuckers if I was you," Doreen said with a smile.

There was a ring at the door. "That's Murfit's boys with the Rolls. OK - head up Doreen - you're a star," I said, giving her a peck on the nose.

"Thanks Gyp - you're a star yourself."

Donovan took her to the door and kissed her goodbye.

"See you both soon," she said and with a wave she was gone.

Don and I went down to see Ash and Anita, she gave us both the biggest hug she had in her arsenal and a smile with so much warmth it could have dried clothes in an arctic storm.

"What's the solicitor got to say Ashley?" Donovan asked.

"I got to tell you lads - he said we did it all wrong," Ash replied. "We should have called him down for the statements and said nothing till then."

"But none of us said very much," I said.

"Yes, I told him that - but he said they didn't need much. They can twist the simplest thing into anything they like."

"Jesus! What's wrong with this fucking country if solicitors talk like that?" Donovan asked in amazement.

"It's all the same shit Don." I said, warming to the topic.

"The Special Police Forces are trained to understand the criminal mind, and in the end they finish up thinking and acting like them - only they think they're cleverer because they've got the Law on their side. It all adds up to a pan full of shit. Stay long enough in the nuthouse and you become an inmate," I said laughing.

"Well, one thing's for sure - we're getting enough publicity."

"Don't forget what Oscar Wilde said about publicity," Dono said his eyes alight with smiles.

"I hate to be a drag Dono, but wasn't the poor bastard put away in jail for a long time?" I said.

We became silent, contemplating our possible Fate.

"Fuck you Gyp!" Dono laughed.

"Fuck you twice Gypo," laughed Ashley as we all cracked up.

It felt good to laugh after all the bullshit.

"Shall I go down to the Gate and score us some dope tomorrow?" I asked Don.

"Better leave it for a few days Gypo. I don't think I could relax with a joint after all this.

Let's give it a rest for a few days."

"That's OK by me mate - won't do us any harm."

"Do you think we smoke too much Gypsy?" Donovan asked me in all seriousness.

"Come off it man! Twenty joints a day isn't much in my honest opinion."

At that point we decided to go back upstairs and get some sleep, but no sooner had we settled down when the phone rang.

"Get that fucker will you Gypsy - it's most probably for you," Don called from his room.

"Right you are," I called back. It was Doreen - and she was in a panic.

"It's everywhere Gypsy!" she cried. "It's worse than the first day - every paper has a report - they even tracked me here to my home. The reporters are wanting to talk to me - they're hustling my parents something rotten."

"Keep cool love - we know a good hotel here in town - very discreet they are - I'll get Dono for you."

Don spoke to her and told her we'd arrange to have her booked into the Parkside Hotel for a week..

I handed him the address to pass onto her

"Take a taxi to the hotel and I'll meet you there," he told her.

No sooner had the phone gone down than it rang again. This time it was Chas Chandler, bass player with The Animals, who was a good friend of mine. He was the discoverer and manager of an up and coming musical feller known as Jimi Hendrix.

"The fuckers Gypsy," he said. "If there's anything we can do for you, let us know - do you hear me mate? Anything."

I thanked him warmly and then I phoned the Parkside Hotel, booked a room for Doreen in Donovan's name and told them he would be there in just over an hour. Once again the phone rang immediately I put it back on the receiver.

"Hello George! How you doing mate - yeah it's a fucking drag. Not a nice thing to have to go through, as you can imagine - but we're cool I think. Trying to look on the bright side - if there is a bright side. Stay with you for a few days? That's very good of you George - but we wouldn't want to put you and Patti out at all. Hold on and I'll put you through to Don."

It was George Harrison and he spoke with Don for quite a while. I overheard some of it.

"Jesus George - Ten thousand quid! That's very nice of you mate, but we're OK for bread thanks. Yes - it would be great to come and stay with you - but I think the coppers might put a tail on us for a few days and we don't want to bring them to your place George. I think we'll have to go away for a few days up to the Highlands of Scotland - find a nice island to get some peace and quiet. When it's all cooled down a bit then we'll be glad to come and spend a few days with you and Patti - we'll love it. Thanks George, you're a diamond - give our love to Patti - bye man."

"That fella is the salt of the earth man," said Don when the call was over.

"He's just invited us to stay with him at his place."

"Yeah, he mentioned it to me just now. Incredibly kind cat - got a heart of gold," I said.

"Right you old bugger, what's all this about going off to the Highlands?"

"I just thought about it right now as I was talking to George Gyp.
We got nothing planned - no gigs - so why not get away for say six days. We can leave the lawyer things with Ash and can be back in a few hours if anything urgent comes up. Let's go Gyp - we can take Doreen with us - give her a nice holiday."

"Why not? We need a break anyway," I said. "By the time we come back our day in court will be arranged - then God knows what will happen to us.
We might as well enjoy it while we got it," I said, smiling at the thought of Scotland.

"Dono, remember to cancel the seven day booking I just made for Doreen at the hotel when you see her there mate."

"Shit! Doreen! - I got to get going - see yer later."

"Alright - I'll get the tickets booked. Which island Dono?"

"How about Islay? I hear it's fantastic. We can hire a small plane from Glasgow to get us there - I remember reading about it somewhere," he said.

"Islay it is then. Go on Dono, poor Doreen will be wondering what's happened to yer. It'll take a day to get things organized, so just make it the one night at the hotel mate."

"Right - got it," he said and was off.

The phone rang again.

"Hi Paul - no, he's just gone out. Yer, thanks - fucking nuisance is right. That's very kind of you mate - George was on the phone a few minutes ago. We've decided to go to Scotland until the fuss is over - no, not with George!" I laughed.
"Sorry - yer, it sounded like it - but I meant Dono, Doreen and myself. Yes, she is a looker. Is she in the papers too? Photos? Ah! No - I haven't been out - haven't seen a paper yet. Shit - well we better get Doreen away from all this puritanical bullshit. Thanks Paul for the kind thoughts and offer of help - I know Dono will appreciate it too. Yeah, I'll get him to phone you when he gets in. Thanks mate, our love to Jane - see yer later."

I just had time to phone and organize the tickets for our trip and then the phone was ringing constantly, most of them from friends commiserating with us over our bust. - but some of the Business in 'Music Business' seemed to be of the opinion that we were finished, over, dead on the hoof .
They were very upset as it wasn't good for the industry.

"Stop being so sanctimonious," I said. "What about Ray Charles? Billie Holliday? A lot of those jazz cats were done for heavier shit than us. People still love their music and buy their records."

I was showing more bravado than I actually felt - we had no idea we were going to face this kind of crap. I went down to see how Ashley and Anita were handling it all. There was a lot of noise from behind their door after I knocked. I smiled to myself and called out.

"It's only me Ash - it's Gyp!"

"Thank fuck," I heard Ashley say as the door was opened.

"Hi you too - Cat got your dope?" I joked.

"It's not funny Gypo - we thought it was the police again."

"Well if it was they could hear a mile away where you hid your dope - you better find somewhere new to hide your stash Ash. Hi Anita love, how's it feel living with a criminal this morning?" I said jokingly as I gave her a kiss.

"No different from the criminal I've been going to bed with these past twelve years," she replied.

"Lucky buggers these criminals," I said. "I would rob a bank if it meant I could wake up by your side each morning Anita my darling."

"You wouldn't have to rob a bank Gypsy - I'd take you as poor as a church mouse," said Anita, her laughing eyes spilling out warmth like a ray of sunshine as she grinned at Ashley.

"Will you two stop it," said Ash good-naturedly. "Anyone would think you're in love with each other."

"Ah but we are!" we said in unison, laughing at the perfect timing of our declaration.

"Have we got anything to do over the next six days Ash?" I asked.

"Why? Want to plan the honeymoon?" he joked.

"No - Dono wants to go up to the Highlands of Scotland for a while."

"Well that's a very good idea of Donovan's Gypsy. There's nothing we can't cancel and there's good sense in keeping you two away from the Press."

"We three, we're going to take Doreen with us - that poor girl's been victimized in the newspapers."

As we talked there was another knock on the door and we all three jumped.

"Fuck!" said Ashley.

"It's cool man, I think it's the tickets - I asked for them to be dropped of here." I said. It was indeed Michael with the tickets for our flights.

"Do me a favour Ash - I've been on the phone all morning - would you call and tell Dono that the flight is at 9 a.m. tomorrow? He's at the Parkside Hotel - most probably having breakfast with Doreen."

"Right you are - pass me the phone....and talking of breakfast - could you make us some eggs and bacon Anita sweetheart?"

As Ashley sorted things out on the phone, the smell of bacon wafted its way down the corridor

"Jesus, that bacon smells good Anita," I called to her.

"Best I could find Gyp - come on you two, it's ready to eat now."

CHAPTER SEVENTEEN
WHERE WAS HIS BAGPIPE?

The island of Islay was wonderful - more than wonderful, it was exquisite. We spent a few days lying on the pebble beach in the northern sunshine. We tried swimming, Doreen doing better at it than us. Donovan and I felt the water was a bit cold after the warmer seas of Mexico in which we had last swam with gusto. The hotel on the Main Street was very old fashioned. It was one of the few hotels on the island, although there were lots of bed & breakfast places.

Doreen rather wisely, believed Dono and herself should be a bit discreet with their relationship as it was obvious to any that cared to look that they weren't married. Dono realized the Highland Scots were a very conservative lot, even puritanical in their outlook towards sex out of the confines of marriage. This was understandable, nay even sensible, on a small island where everyone knew each other. So, not wishing to offend the sensibilities of our hosts, Donovan and I hired a large double room with two single beds in it for us and a double room with one large bed for Doreen. This way there was no embarrassment when Donovan and Doreen felt the desire to spend the night in the warmth of each others arms in Doreen's large bed.

I only mention these facts to explain what happened to Donovan and myself one night when we were deep asleep in our hotel room. I awoke to a strange cat-walling sound. It was in the distance but as it drew nearer it seemed like a chant sung on one note. As the vibration became louder and reached the balcony outside our room the French windows burst open as if by a sudden gust of wind.

On sitting up in bed and looking out the French window, now ajar, I could see a dimly lit street, its lamp posts winding their way to a hill in the distance. A large brick building stood proudly on this mound, with a back drop of strong electric lights. Emanating from below this building I saw a peculiar light floating down the roadway towards me. As it drew nearer to the window it became more like a revolving ball of opaque brightness. The curtains were still moving at the window although I could hear no wind outside. The atmosphere became electric in the room as the temperature dropped drastically. In this cold atmosphere the floating ball of light entered the room through the open French window. There was no heat from it that I could feel, in fact it felt like that light was somehow a sort of dark light which is not what you would expect from such a glowing light source. As I looked on transfixed, the light began to elongate. It did not quite manage to turn into a human figure, when as if felled from behind, it collapsed onto the floor. The chanting sound which I had become used to seemed to stop at the same time as the half figure slumped down on the floor at the foot of my bed.

"What the fuck was that Gypsy?" Donovan asked in a shocked voice.

I didn't know Dono was awake, I thought I was watching this phenomenon on my own.

"I have no idea," I said "but if I was to hazard a guess I would say we have just had a visitation from a spiritual energy .What did you see?" I asked him.

"Just a ball of light that floated through that window - plus there was a noise of a bagpipes drone."

I got up from bed and walked outside onto the little balcony. The building I could see in the distance backlit from behind was a church. At its bass, where the light source had formed, were lots of scattered gravestones. It was the local burial ground for the town's dead.

A few days later at breakfast I asked the owner of the hotel if anyone connected to the hotel had died recently.

"Not at all," he said, "….though there was old Bob. Funny enough, now I think on it, he lived for a years in the room you're staying in now. But that was many a year back - he arrived here soon after the war ended. Bit of a mystery was Bob - had no family…not that we knew of anyway. He died about ten days ago. Even his death was a bit of a mystery - found him with a gash to the side of his head near to the churchyard gates. Poor fellow was smelling of whisky like he had a still in his pockets - even that was strange because he rarely drank. People think he slipped on the wet pavement late at night and hit his head on the little wall that runs around the bottom of the railing of the churchyard. Anyway, whatever happened, there he lay come morning."

"What happened to his bagpipes?" I asked

"They were found broken a little ways away from him on the wet road. Wait a minute young man - I never mentioned he played bagpipes. How did you know that Gypsy?" he asked me suspiciously.

"I think we had a visitation from him two nights ago in our room." I replied. "There was an accompanying sound Donovan reckons could only have been made by bagpipes."

"Well I never did!" said our host. "I never believed in those things in my life - visitations from the dead - might have to change my mind now though....unless you're pulling my leg Gypsy ,are you pulling me pisser?" he asked, looking deeply into my eyes.

"What would be the point in that?" I asked.

"No point whatsoever." he answered

"You've just this very minute mentioned Bob. How else could I suspect he played bagpipes unless what I told you is true?"

"I believe you Gypsy - although I'm telling you thousands wouldn't," he laughed nervously. "On another subject, how are you three enjoying our wee island?"

"It's wonderful," we said

"It's even gifted me a song," said Donovan.

"Not just a song - an unbelievably beautiful song," I said.

Rising from the breakfast table I got Don's guitar from its case and handed it to him.

"Here Dono, play it for our friend here - let him be the judge," I said proudly.

Donovan sang his song, *Isle of Islay*, for the first time to the general public so to speak. Around that breakfast table. I watched our captive audience carefully and was happy when I saw tears fill his eyes. The owner of the hotel was mesmerized by the song.

"That's a beautiful act of creation Donovan," he said. "I can hear your Scottish roots in it."

I was very happy because I could see that the previous few days of trouble had not rubbed off on Donovan's creative soul. He was still writing little masterpieces, little gems of crystallized thought captured for all time in melody and rhyme. I was there, and I know Donovan captured in his music and prose exactly how we felt on that quick break from the inalienable landscape of chaos that we still had to face on our return to reality.

> *How high the gulls fly o'er Islay*
> *How sad the farm lad deep in play*
> *Felt like a seed on your land*
> *Felt like a grain on your sand*
> *Felt like a tide left me here*

Beautiful stuff - and that same tide that left us there was soon to take us away again, back to the madness of the music business. We didn't need the hassle of our bust. Donovan was going through enough hassles over his business machinations. His album *Sunshine Superman* was being held up from release in Britain and Europe by litigation. His intuitive creative music was original and ahead of popular styles of rendition - but how long would it stay that way? Dono wanted his music to be heard in the UK and Europe as well as in America - where it was being received with accolades of good press and a huge amount of pleasure from his audience. Pye records were still bringing out his old hits, revamped into another package in Europe and the UK. It was so frustrating - and also blatantly unfair, as Donovan had made monstrous strides along the path of his personal musical creativity. It was like an Art Dealer telling Picasso to remain in his 'Blue Period' for all time.

On returning from Islay we said our goodbyes to Doreen as she returned to Hatfield and Dono phoned George Harrison just to let him know we were back. We still didn't have the inclination to stay in our flat and were only too pleased to accept George's offer when he asked us to stay with himself and Patti.

We returned to our flat to pack a change of clothes, feeling like criminals in our own pad - though it didn't feel like home anymore. To top it all there was a ring at the door and I answered it to find the Press there. This was just what we didn't need. I told the journalist in no uncertain terms to please go away. The phone rang and was again a member of the Press.

"For Christ's sake leave us alone will you!" I said, feeling very jaded.

"For fuck's sake Gypo, let's get outa here." said Donovan with feeling. "It's not long till the trial - why can't they wait? Let's go to George's in style - get Murfit's boys and his Rolls Royce."

George at that time didn't live in a mansion. He and Patti lived in a modest one storey house in Esher. It was a rather nice bungalow set in well maintained gardens - very un-music business like. This was Beatles manager Brian Epstein's idea - he wanted the boys to have as much peace as it was possible to obtain in the frenzy of Beatlemania then sweeping the world. It was an island of normality where someone of George's fame would be left unmolested. It worked for us, Mr and Mrs Harrison's cosy pad.

Dono and I felt very at home. Patti and George had an easy-going, down to earth relationship with each other that immediately put you at ease. We talked a lot, jammed a lot and Dono talked incessantly with George about their similar interests in Eastern spiritual matters. George was the youngest of The Beatles by a few years and was seen as such by the other band members. Although in a sense his ideas were more mature than there's he was still seen as the younger brother of the group. George was a serious thinker. When he met Donovan he recognized in him a meeting of minds - a touching of their souls through esoteric thought patterns as well as through musical creativity. He loved Don as a true brother - this was a thing he and I had in common and it brought us together.

One thing I shall remember to my dying day is the intimacy of Patti, Dono, George and I sitting on the floor listening to George and Donovan riff off each other in spontaneous rhythms of pure joyful melody. Music by two maestros never to be heard again or shared with the world. They say at the moment of death your life passes before your eyes - if so I will cherish those unique musical moments again. Some evenings I played bongos with them and I remember George kindly winked when I did so.

George, you great good-hearted soul - you've passed on now, but not passed without making a proud mark on our human civilization. You'll go down in history as the voice of Reason and Experiment in the West. The voice that made popular Eastern thought and meditation 'hip', revealing the Oneness of our universal human mind in the process. Yes, you made Yogis famous - but more importantly you and Patti, through your commitment to the Mind, opened up the possibility for young and old to delve deeper into their own personalities and consciousness through meditation. Made it cool to open up the psyche and shed the chains of Christian enslavement in thought that rattled away so loudly in most brains as to make it nigh on impossible to 'Think out Of the Box'.

You made it possible for the young to be proud of who they were through new thoughts of unsuppressed creative Oneness. You opened the box at another angle and thousands jumped out to freedom. It is in the very nature of Thought, for Thought is truly a worked and crafted diamond - the Diamond Sutra indeed.

The box that Donovan and I found ourselves in a few weeks after our stay with the very wonderful Mr. and Mrs. Harrison was in Marylebone Court. Here we were charged with the possession of cannabis, an illegal drug. For all the fuss and all our heartache all our monetary loss and all the publicity Donovan, Doreen and myself were fined £250 each - a pittance compared to what we could earn, even considering Donovan paid all the costs. I'll tell you something. - to be on the other end of a thug who was a Sergeant in the Special Task Force of the Drug Squad is not a pretty place to be. As we came out of the Court - where he had put us - he said,

"I have you now, and anytime I want to, I can just click my fingers and stick you in the Nick - just by bringing the evidence with me in me pocket, see? So you two just watch it - hear me?"

This is not what you want to hear when your whole thing, your whole bag, is Freedom. Years after our bust this wonderful pig of a person was caught bringing his own hashish to another famous bust. He got four years in prison himself and the name of Sergeant Norman Pilcher was splashed all over the newspapers. And what about all his other 20 or 30 busts? Why weren't they looked into again and justice done to his victims - some of whom were in prison longer than him I'm sure. Justice? Come off it - they knew he had been fiddling all along. I kept asking myself what the point of it all was. Although in the court we had been castigated and told to be better examples to the young it was obvious they didn't want that or why make us into a circus? Why bring us into the sawdust of the big tent as the headlining lions of cannabis? Who of the younger generation had been aware of cannabis, marijuana, dope, grass, kif, hemp, shit, pot or any other name you cared to call it, before they started systematically busting heroes of the young - hardly a one. In a thousand white souls you could not find more than twenty that knew of dope and no more than one of that thousand using it for their pleasure. Knowledge of cannabis was rare man. We that knew about it were happy to keep it that way - it was our secret - our way to be cool. I lived in a time when I could walk up to a policeman in the streets of any major city and ask him for a light for my joint. I did this on occasion in Manchester, not out of bravado but because I had no matches. If the Policeman should remark on the smell from the smoke one would simply say it was Turkish tobacco.

In those days society's most popular way to get stoned was alcohol. The few people who toked on joints mostly refrained from alcohol because it seemed a second rate high compared to the simpler, less obtrusive high of Dope. Alcohol was too strong, too erratic. It could be pushy on the personality and could twist your psyche into places your ego would normally hate to go. Aggressive, loud-mouthed, uncontrollably sexually aroused and stupid - whereas smoking a little hash made one relaxed, laid back, peaceful, thoughtful and non-violent. It did not perform miracles however - so the stupid remained stupid.

Usually the knowledge of Dope passed on from good friend to good friend, making a natural microscopic network of like minds - a think-tank of cool cats. Donovan and myself and all the other artistic and musical figures of that time about to be held up to the young as examples did not want to advertise drugs to the wider audience of their fans. They were prepared to put forward the ideas gained through the creative process of thought during these mind altering states. This has been achieved by mankind through thousands of years of our history (usually through Religious Thought). It was nothing new. There's precious little new in the world my friends. We as human beings have had a decent innings but we're poor players compared to how long the dinosaurs were here. If our governments and peoples don't soon learn to be more intelligent, more honest, less violent, more tolerant, less dictatorial and stop their bullshit indoctrination and pure untruths , we as a race are not going to be here much longer on this most wonderful of planets. Nature is the supreme intelligence and referee on this planet, not Man. Not us sick, small-minded human beings - if Nature rules you out, then you're bloody well out mate - atomic bombs or not. Nature always has a contingency plan. It runs on a different time scale from us little second makers.

Its seconds are millions of years and it bases its time on an infinite ocean of suns set ticking when our sun was but one grain of sand on an endless seashore of matter. The history of our earth is but one drawing in of one breath compared to the never ending life of Nature. Wake up, this is fact. In which case, what do you think you are in the scheme of things? We humans think we're clever because we discover things of use in Nature. We look upon these discoveries as if we made Nature in the first place. Well, just because we discovered bullshit doesn't mean we made the bull.

Donovan and I were to suffer a lot of bullshit - bullshit to do with business, litigation, contractual concessions, copyright issues and money interests that business believed far outweighed the importance of the creative process. We all know that it's the early bird that catches the worm - and the Music Business was an unscrupulous early riser.

CHAPTER EIGHTEEN
PARADISE FOUND PARADISE LOST

Dono and I were so pissed off with all the business hassles we decided we'd had enough and would opt for the open road again. We decided to head for Greece to try for the sun. Ashley Kozak's wife, Anita - a full blown Greek, wished to go home for a short break too. When Anita had first left Greece it was as the wife of an injured English soldier, de-mobbed and going home to Swindon. She was just under thirteen years old, although her mother had fiddled her birth certificate to say she was sixteen. Anita had, believe it or not, on her own and in an English hospital with barely a spattering of English her first child at the tender age of thirteen years and four months. She had a husband in bed at home, his condition worsening so that he was practically a cripple. She left the hospital one day after delivering her son John into the world as she wanted to be at home to look after her husband and newborn baby on her own. She saw it as her duty, as wife and mother, to do so - it was the Greek way. I can tell you, her husband was the luckiest man alive and must have blessed his lucky stars every day to have been fortunate enough to have found Anita. Anita wasn't just beautiful, she was *unbelievably* beautiful - bright as a roomful of geniuses. What she must have looked like in the full bloom of youth is hard to imagine, she was wonderful in early middle age - that's for sure She travelled by plane to Athens while we took the train.

Anita was as much a stranger in the Greek Capital as we were, but she could speak the language. We asked her to try and find us a place on an island where no tourists went. She asked the shipping clerk who had no hesitation in naming Paros as that very island. Having phoned home to Ashley she came back beaming.

"That's settled," she said.

"What's settled?" I asked

"I'm coming with you both to Paros."

"That's cool!" Donovan and I said in unison.

"You're lucky," said the clerk. "The boat leaves in two hours - it's the only boat that goes to Paros. It's a bit basic, but it does have three cabins."

"How long is the journey?" Dono asked.

"Nineteen hours."

"Shit!" I said.

"Fantastic!" said Donovan imagining himself as the writer and me as a sort of Zorba heading off to a deserted island to contemplate our novels and navels.

The clerk took our money and handed us three rather bare tickets reminiscent of theatre ticket stubs. When we saw the boat I would have cancelled the trip being fearful of us catching ticks. The open air hold was full of sheep, donkeys, chickens, pigs and people perched just like their chickens wherever they could find a toe-hold. We were ushered to the cabins like Royalty by a crewman with a crooked grin on his face. It was obvious the cabins were being used by the crew and had been hurriedly tidied out for us. They were clean, but very poorly conceived. There were two small cabins and one larger one. The bigger cabin we gave to Anita as there was an armchair and a table screwed down in one corner near to the salt sprayed porthole. On the deck of the cabins was a walkway with two waist high railings, I presume to stop one falling headlong into the hold or the sea in bad weather.

From our higher position we could look down into the hold and see animals, birds and people lazing about on their luggage in the sunshine. There were tight circles of people sharing their bread, tomatoes, olives and cheese. Wine carafes were being passed hand to hand by those not sleeping. If our eye should be caught by the peasant men they would automatically raise their raffia covered bottles in salute and beckon us to join them in their revelries. We waved back, but declined their kind offers. Don was intoxicated by this display of basic peasant culture being played out at our feet so to speak - it reminded him of the book and film Zorba the Greek. I could practically see in his eyes the songs coming from our adventures. Away from the music business, we were already getting in touch with our simpler selves. We left port about one in the afternoon and at six were escorted to a small room where a homely meal and wine was offered to us free of charge. We ate with gusto and partook of the wine in moderation before retiring for the night. It had been a long couple of days on the train and we needed a good night's sleep.

We were awakened at six the next morning to have a hearty breakfast. I'll always remember the first omelette I tasted in Greece. The incredible colour made by the deep yellow of the yolks and the perfect taste, caused partly by the olive oil it was fried in.

Our bags were brought out on deck as we approached a horseshoe shaped bay. In the bright morning light I could see a wonderful little village with what looked like a medieval castle dominating the seashore and a large walled monastery in the hills, but I could see no harbour - the simple reason for that being, there was no harbour. We looked over the side of the ship with trepidation as our luggage was lowered by ropes. A rope ladder with thick wooden steps knotted into it was thrown over the side and we were helped by the crew to climb down to a small rowing boat - which appeared to be dozens of feet below us! Fortunately the sea was calm. Don's eyes were alive with fun and Anita was wearing a royal smile as we were rowed ashore.

We landed on a strip of sand near to a beautifully made windmill with cloth sails which seemed cemented to a rock that was two feet higher than the earthen roadway surrounding it. Here stood a wooden handcart with two large spoked wheels painted cherry red. From behind this cart came an old, dusty man of diminutive stature. He was thin and wiry, but obviously tough and strong as he took our baggage and threw each article into the cart as if it was a bag of feathers. He introduced himself as Baba Dmitri and asked Anita where he was to take our belongings.

"To the nearest hotel - a good one please Dmitri," Anita informed him in Greek.

"Ah - but there are no hotels, good or bad, on Paros," said Dmitri.

"The best rooms for rent then Dmitri, if you please."

"But there are no rooms to rent madam."

Well - it certainly looked as if the shipping clerk in Athens had taken us at our word when we asked to be directed to an island where no tourists went! We looked at each other in wonderment.

"Looks like the beaches then Gypo," Donovan laughed.

"Yes - and with no bloody sleeping bag again," I retorted.

During our banter Anita had been hurriedly talking ten to the dozen to Dmitri.

"OK you two, we're in luck - I think," she said turning to us. "Baba Dmitri has an old farmhouse we can rent. It's about a mile from the village and there's a rocky road going up to it. He's going to rent his donkey to us and can find others in the village if we need them. His donkey only has one eye - but he swears it's very steady on its legs up the path."

"Incredible!" said Dono, loving the thought of us riding on a donkey

"We need to get mattresses, plates, cutlery, oil lamps plus a hundred other things to make ourselves comfortable. Do you want to rent it on those conditions?" asked Anita.

"Of course we'll take it Anita my love," I said, smiling at our new landlord.

"It sounds just the job," Don confirmed.

We knew Anita's bargaining prowess from the Portobello Road. Dmitri, poor soul, didn't stand a chance with her. After a few minutes of smiles, frowns, wild gesticulations and raised eyebrows everything was settled.

"Right," said Anita. "It's 50 drachma per week for the farmhouse and 50 per month for Seraphina the donkey. We can have the chicken eggs free and Dmitri will bring up hay four times a week and leave it in Seraphina's stable. That's the deal. He'll show us up there now and he can get two donkeys this minute if we all want to go together."

"You two go and I'll stay and look after the luggage," I said sitting down in the hand cart.

"Let's be off then Anita," said Don, "and well done on the price, that's fantastic." His voice trailed off as they followed Dmitri into the quaint little village. I lie back in the cart and put my head in the shade, falling into a shallow sleep almost immediately. Peace interwove its silken silence of tranquility into the cloth of my being. It was love at first sight with Paros.

It wasn't just its beauty; it was its feeling as much as anything else. You could feel the eons of history, good and bad, that had visited the island's inhabitants. Thousands of years of history. A history I was to marvel at later in my adventures around the town with history shining from its pure white marble columns, steps and carved lintels. Blocks of marble so big a modern crane could not lift them, yet put there by a people with a determination that would not take 'nay' for an answer.

The Greeks from the islands have always liked strangers. Although strangers have brought them plenty of heartache, they also brought them news and new stock and new genes - even if the latter came by way of rape and pillage in their early history. As I lay on that cart I felt some of this history spiral into me like a corkscrew of time.

"Gyp! Gyp! Where the fuck is he?" I heard Donovan call to Anita.

"I'm here you nutters," I called sitting up in the cart.

"Gyp, you won't believe what we lucked into man - it's fucking unbelievably beautiful. The house is stuck on the side of the hill. We see Parikia out of the right eye and another sea coast out of the left eye - it's incredible Gypo - incredible! A great old place made of stones with a beautiful kitchen, a living room and three bedrooms. All this around a courtyard with a low wall interspaced by high pine beams covered by trailing grapes and bright green leaves."

"It's fantastic Gypsy, you're going to love it," Anita said smiling fit to burst. "Dmitri will arrange to take our baggage up and then he'll meet us at six to buy all the things we need for the house," she gushed, obviously excited at the thought of all that shopping.

"That's great," I said. "Sounds incredible. Now let's go find a restaurant - I could eat a donkey.....that's presuming there *is* a restaurant."

"Don't worry Gyp, there's one on the corner of the little alleyway to Dmitri's stables It looks good too - got my favourite; Dolmatoes," Donovan said, salivating in his enthusiasm.

"I'll have roast chicken with roast potatoes soaked in oil, chicken stock and lemons with a nice Greek salad to go with it," said Anita.

"Bloody hell - let's go, you're making me famished. Is it far?" I asked

"Five minutes walk me old mate. God I love this place already," Dono said, echoing my own feelings.

We walked the small alleyways that were not big enough for cars to go down. Smartly dressed and clean peasants walked the streets nodding to us pleasantly. They were in from their farms and dressed to kill wanting the townsfolk to see them in their Sunday best. We noticed that a few had eggs and cheeses in baskets - the fruits of their labours brought into town to sell.

We settled into the microscopic restaurant and automatically a carafe of

Retsina wine and four glasses were put on the table. I wondered why there were four glasses until our host joined us for a glass and informed us this first carafe was on the house. He was very proud of his wine, as is every Greek I know who makes it. I believe they love the seemingly magical process of making wine as much as the wine itself.

Our meals arrived and they were magnificent - all local produce. Nothing had been saved in a fridge for the simple reason there was no electricity on the island. We were brought fresh grapes, small pears and huge purple figs that Anita went crazy over. It turned out she hadn't had these sort of figs since she was a child in her village on the mainland. When we passed comment on the figs to our host he told us that they weren't native to the island - they had been brought over by the Turks when they had occupied the island hundreds of years ago. Paros had been in Turkish hands for 500 years.

"Bloody hell - 500 years? That's a long time," I said.

"It's a blink in the eye of history to us Paros folks Christo," the restaurant owner said - via Anita's translation of course.

That was the first time I heard myself called Christo - but it was a name that was to stick, as the island people could not say 'Gypsy'. Christi was the nearest thing to what they heard me called by my companions and this soon changed to the softer Christo. I didn't feel too comfortable with this name, believing it meant Christ, but Anita told me that in their dialect it had the same meaning as 'Golden'. Well, I may have been a bit tarnished - but I could live with that.

Poor Anita had her work cut out trying to translate everything but luckily Greek humour is like British humour in many ways. After our meal we slowly wandered back to the windmill where we had arranged to meet Dmitri. He was there waiting with two donkeys and with these we rambled the back alleys for mattresses, cups, plates, oil lamps, a gas stove, blankets and a dozen other things.

The Greeks use wooden saddles on their donkeys, attaching them with a thick plaited strap under the large rotund bellies of the animals. With Dmitri's expert knowledge we managed to put all we had bought onto the backs of our two donkeys with room to spare for our groceries and huge wine bottle. The trick was to be found in the balance, as it is in so many things.

Seraphina took the rough and twisty path to the farmhouse in her stride, wisely and carefully. It was beginning to get fairly dark, the half moon shining like an electric light held high in invisible fingers, but the remarkable thing was how near the brilliantly glowing stars were. You literally felt as if you could pluck them out of the evening sky with your outstretched hand. We realized this was due to the fact there were no electric lights burning bright holes in the night sky and no doubt the lack of pollution in the surrounding air of these treasured islands helped this phenomena.

When we arrived at our new Spiti I saw it was all Donovan and Anita had described. The oil lamps were soon filled and lit, giving us a cosy glow in the whitewashed rooms. I set up the gas stove and within minutes we had our first cup of tea in our new home. We had a well but it was a good way down the garden and I for one wasn't going into that overgrown terrain in the dark until I got used to it. We had brought water with us from the beautiful marble encased tap that had been placed in the centre of town in 1717 for the pleasure of the populace - and which still functioned as good as gold.

Sitting at the table in the living room we looked down a slope and up to a mountain aglow with moonlight. The valley of corn below us was heavy with evening sea mist. The silence was indescribable, almost heavy, like a pregnant pause stretching into the star-studded night on the wings of a butterfly. I had never heard such silence. It entered the soul like the peaceful reign of a benign Emperor. It was the silence of Don's ivory pagoda, now lying in ruins inside its glass dome. Maybe it had gifted this peace to us with its appalling destruction.

The strong black tea in our newly acquired pottery mugs was quenching our thirst made by the dust of the fields we had journeyed by. We felt ridiculously content. Then one lonely little cicada arranged an impromptu concert to dispel its blues and soon thousands of others let it be know that it was not alone in the world by rasping along in unison, shattering our silence. Until I became used to this noise it was a little bit of Hell in Paradise for me. Dmitri, who was still with us, told us the insect had been set off by a night bird hunting - probably a brown owl.

"Cicada don't usually make their noise at night - it's a sexual response and they, like Narcissus, need daylight to see how beautiful they are," he told us, laughing at his joke.

He was a mine of useful information and we were glad of Anita's gently spoken translations. Sitting on the low wall around the courtyard we watched in silence the field of stars above us. They seemed to me to be held up by the sullen heat emanating from the parched land, a cloth of star filled gossamer held above us and ballooning outwards towards the ever-growing moon. The earth and stars felt like twins in the sea of sky, near relations to far relations. On such evenings we were to feel the Oneness in our cosmic journey to the never ending heavens. We three travelers longed for the morning so we could see with our own eyes the landscape to which the Open Road had taken us.

On waking my eyes beheld beauty in abundance. I was in a page of a landscape once sketched by Donovan - drawn with his thin pen in a tattered old book of bleached paper which someone had given him years ago to draw his dreams in.
He had many one line sketches there - and quite a talent for drawing them too. But it was the landscape sketch I recalled seeing in his book as I looked out on the hills of Paros. A dream indeed - but who was dreaming who I might ask? I sat down at the kitchen table and wrote this poem, just for the hell of it:-

The sun sets on mountains of marble quarries

My sun sets on mind of mind with darkness of no worries,
Excepting worries and fears for inhuman world of greed and hate,
Knowing old will rot and young in their hands hold Fate
The God of love-good is awoken in my sleeping mind
For love, beauty, peace, is the one true circle with no end to bind,
As upon the dead minds, going so fast that in their seeing they go blind,
But all will come, as come it must, and in the coming my mind must trust

The young, opening the festering wounds with swords of silver that they thrust,
Cutting from the wounds the rot of ignorance, with golden spoons
For them all to feed on the indigestible food of greed,
And spit from their mouths with shrieking, loathing shouts
Until the true foods of love can be consumed.

'Well - not a masterpiece, but then again, I'm not a master,' were my thoughts.

I woke Dono and Anita with a cup of coffee, pleased with my jottings in my Greek exercise book - if only for the fact it gave me the thrill of writing again, something I thought I had stopped doing.

"What are you so happy about you old bugger? We got no joints, 'cos we got no hash, 'cos we're on a deserted island in Greece Gypo - and you're smiling' fit to burst yer sporran!" said Dono.

"Just look outside at that glorious view and if that doesn't turn you on then I don't know what will," I replied.

"Take a great toke of this air into your lungs and I swear you won't need anything else - it'll get you as high as a kite me ol' mate."

Dono laughed at my light heart and Anita gave me a kiss on the end of my nose knowing I had fallen in love with the beauty of Paros and, by association, Greece. This was the land that made humanity as ancient Egypt had made creativity and religion. Ancient Greece had wed the three like a sea-knot, a wedding ring indeed.

The sea, with its brightly coloured fishing boats near the sand, looked like an Australian opal as I looked in that direction down the beautiful valley of corn and bamboo. I was so much in heaven here that me mind was spiralling through my head like a toboggan run through ice fields.

I went to get some eggs from our pompous chickens who strutted like brides at a wedding banquet. There were exactly six eggs nestled in their jewel box of straw, old paper and coloured feathers plucked out in tenderness by the brooding mother hen. Anita served them up and we ate them with the bread we had purchased the evening before.

"Fuck, these cats can bake bread," Dono mumbled.

"It's the yeast of sour dough Don, it's been handed down, mother to daughter, through the generations for eons," Anita said. "My own mother kept hers wrapped up in a damp cloth, adding a little dough now and again to keep it alive. She treated her yeast like you would a privileged animal."

"Well it was alive and it should be treated with respect," I said simply.

"Oh yeah Gypsy? What about cancer? It's as alive as yeast," Dono stated calmly.

"Yeah, yer right mate but cancer is a killer now - but I'm willing to bet there is a balance to that crap too - I'm willing to bet that they find the answer to slowing down the aging process in the bugger."

"What makes you say that Gyp?" Anita asked.

"Well the cancer cell itself will live forever - as long as it is fed there's no way of killing it - short of killing its host. Mankind had tried for years and years of experiment to kill the cell - but no luck yet."

"Wow Gyp! That's a great subject over breakfast," Anita said laughing at our impromptu discussion.

"You're right love, we should enjoy life to the full - we never know when it will be our turn."

"Let's hope we are all spared that sort of death," she said, crossing herself in the way Greeks have whenever death is mentioned near to loved ones. "You're right about enjoying life to the full Gypsy."

"OK - enough of all that," I said in a lighter mood. "Who's going to Parikia?"

Anita wanted to stay and walk in the hills, breathing in her native land. Donovan climbed aboard the donkey and with me walking at his side we meandered our way towards the café in the little square we had discovered the previous day. As we approached the town a local tried to explain something to us, finally pulling Seraphina's reins in frustration. Finally we realized he was telling us where to tether the donkey. There was a kind of 'donkey park' near to the main church - a small forest of coniferous trees, bent not by the wind but by the donkeys standing there in the shade awaiting their riders return. It's a little known fact that you can leave a donkey tied in a football pitch of tasty grass and it will ignore the grass at its feet as it strains and struggles to get a bite of whatever green stuff there is just out of range of its teeth - strange, stubborn creatures that they are.

Dono and I got a few stares, but in a nice way and no one was rude or pointing fingers at us. We were at our ease, laughing a lot as we drank ouzo with lemonade and ate wonderful cream pies from the local bakery made of sweet semolina and flaky pastry. Four Greek girls came hesitantly up to our table. They were in full view of the whole village, so they had to be cautious with their approach. They spoke to us shyly in very good English. How had we found their island? What was the purpose of our visit? Did I have any relations on the island - as I looked very Greek to them? Two of them were studying English at the main University in Athens and asked if they could practice with us so as to improve their skills. The girls all had lovely long dark blue-black hair, liquid night eyes and lips fit to cause the launch of ten thousand ships. They declined our offer of wine, ouzo or beer but they did let us treat them to a can of Coca Cola - them being modern ladies and all!

We spent a very pleasant hour speaking our language to this lovely captive audience. It was nice too that they had not even heard of the folk singer Donovan, we had the feeling of two ordinary lads just having fun - and maybe trying to score. The music business and fame stole some of the innocent freedom from us but here Dono and I were taken at face value - just a couple of blokes like any other guys.

My eyes were beginning to be caught by one of the girls who held my gaze longer than she should have in her island's culture. Dono too was getting a subtle come on from the most beautiful of the girls. The café owner was looking a little askance at our table

'Shit,' I thought, *'we better be careful here or we could get roasted alive on this small island - 'better put a stop to this right now.'*

I stood up and made a show of saying goodbye to the girls by shaking their hands very formally as the owner approached our table. The girls got the message and with many an *'Epheristo parra Poli'* (Thank you very much), they left us to our own company again.

"Shit Gyp, what a bugger!" said Dono. "But you're right of course - we can't be seen stealing their chicks man. The locals would string us up by our feet from their lamp posts."

"That would be difficult Dono - there aren't any lamp posts - but they have good imaginations and they'd certainly find somewhere as a substitute mate."

"Bloomin' hell! Did you see mine looking at me Gypo? She looked so randy I thought she was going to drop me drawers on the spot!"

"She was a beauty man - but I think they've all got used to Athens where they can be outlandish in the anonymity of the city - I think they forgot where they were for a moment. Here, their families would lock them up."

"Bet they still got chastity belts hanging up in their cellars Gypo," Don said, the ouzo getting to him. "So what we going to do about them lovely ladies Gyp?"

"We're going to let them get a hold of us if they want to Don - but all in their good time mate. They know the island. They know their ways their culture better than we do. In five minutes flat they'll know where we live, where we eat, where we sleep and the colour of our underpants - so we'll leave it up to them shall we? Girls will be girls - for all the obstacles put in their path. It's better we let them lead. If they think it's important enough they'll find the best way," I said, smiling from ear to ear.

"You're bloody right Gyp - look what they did to that widow in *Zorba* - stoned the poor cow to death!"

The waiter was called and a few more ouzos were consumed until Don finally said, "We better head for the hills before we can't find them Gyp - these ouzos get to you after a while."

"You're right," I laughed, feeling the presence of the alcohol in my numbing brain. "Let's go - you want to ride Seraphina?"

"You must be joking Gypo! The state I'm in I'd fall off the bloody thing! You can hold your liquor better than me - the donkey's yours my friend - I'll walk."

We paid the bill and walked to the big church where we found Seraphina none the worse. There was a tin bucket beside her where someone had given her water.

"Look at that will yer - what nice people they are man," Donovan said, touched by this act of kindness. "That's made my day that has Gyp - such caring folks. They most probably realized we were a couple of idiots from the city and didn't know how to look after a donkey."

"We've learned something new," I said, "and we'll always bring some water for the donkey in future."

On our way back home we noticed that a Bar had been opened on the beach. It looked basic, rustic almost, with its bamboo roof and walls. It was as if the tide had deposited it on the sparkling sand like a bit of flotsam and jetsam. The three old metal tables were painted in reds and yellows and the chairs were a deep purple. Two bottles stood on the bar, one of ouzo and one of Metaxa. The café-bar was situated close to a little enclave of palm trees with a trickling stream running to the sea. Overall it was more like something you'd see in Jamaica, not Paros.

"That's great Gypsy!" said Don cheerfully. "Come on man - we got to drink a rum here - if they've got one."

The young, laid back owner was lying in a hammock behind the bar. He didn't have a rum but he poured the Metaxa as if his life depended on it. Each time he came to a halt in his measuring he tipped a little more into the glass until he was finally satisfied and handed us the drinks with a wink.

"Cronia polar," he said, which meant 'long life'.

"Cronia polar," we replied. "See - the girls taught us something useful," said Donovan relaxing in his chair on the sand, his glass of brandy reflecting like gold in his hand. "Shall we have a swim after this drink?"

"No way! Remember Mexico and what I went through there mate?" I replied. "Are you sure you're not too drunk to swim?"

"No, it's cool man - I'm not that drunk and besides, the sea will sober me up for the walk home," Don replied.

"I'm a bit worried about Anita to tell you the truth - we've left her on her own a bit too long I think. Until she gets used to it I better go along and give her some of my company."

"You're right Gyp, Ashley would die if anything should happen to his darling Anita. I won't be too long - see you in about an hour," Don said as he headed for the clear warm sea.

I jumped sideways in the donkey's saddle and we made our way up the track as fast as her short legs would allow. Anita was as good as gold and told me I was never to stop what I was doing on her account.

"You're here to relax and enjoy yourself Gypsy. I'm big enough to look after myself you know - and I speak the language like   a nat....."

"I know - like a native," I joked.

She was right of course and it felt good not to have to worry about her.

I lay down on my mattress on the floor and took in the wonder of this marvelous island.

"How was yer walk Anita?" I called out through the noise of her getting the cooking utensils out.

"Fantastic Gypsy. I found a lovely old mansion that's now a sort of nunnery - though there are no nuns up there now."

"Must've known we were coming and rushed 'em off to the other side of the island before we could get our sticky hands on 'em," I joked

"Is Don coming back soon? I'm going to cook some spaghetti for our evening meal."

"He won't be long love - I'm just going to close my eyes for a bit my sweet."

I was awakened thirty minutes later by Don shaking my shoulder.

"Bloody hell - that smells unbelievable Anita," I said breathing in the aroma of her cooking. "How was the swim - was the water warm?" I asked Don.

"Beautiful - and not deep at all. Went up to the waist as clear as a fish bowl. I think I saw an octopus."

"Why didn't you catch it?" said Anita. "They taste very good."

"I'm happy with this wonderful spaghetti - it's a dream."

After we had eaten I noticed Dono was a bit down. "What's the matter mate?" I asked him

"Nothing really Gypo - it's just that one of them girls reminded me of Linda.
I had an idea for a song," he said reaching for his guitar.

Then he played a tune I had never heard - he had written it in his head on the beach.

Here I sit, the retired writer in the sun
The retired writer in the sun .....and I'm blue.....

He played about three verses and kept working on the melody that had been in his head. I could see it was going to be a great song, as it captured his mood exactly. He would slowly polish the timing until the tune represented what he felt. Jesus! Second night not over yet and already Don was finding songs from a soul that could never be truly happy - not after meeting his soul mate Linda Lawrence at any rate.

I knew it was cool as long as he could express himself. In his creativity he had his sorrow and his guitar in hand and from that piece of wood he could make magic. Magic to soothe a savage breast full of pain, longing, heartache and loving. It took a gentle heart to transfer such agony into such beauty. Dono was the man, I knew I could never come near him in the department of Courage for Love. Here, he was as strong a Hero as any Greek Hero in any ancient legend.

Dono took his guitar to his room and continued to work on the song there. He was propped up by the wall, nestled in the corner, his legs flat out on the mattress and his guitar resting on his calves - a faraway look in his eyes as the music poured forth - music the world had never heard before; music that had not existed until that evening's moment of creation.

These moments, if understood are pure magic - they purge the soul of all negative feelings and fill you with love for human wisdoms and follies alike.

The night wore on - Anita missed Ashley and often said so in her sweet way. Those incredible stars came out again, filling the night sky with wonder.

"There's Orion's Belt Gypo," said Dono.

"Where?" Anita asked as we sipped some wine outside on the porch.

"There love - see? That's his sword - that kite type of configuration," Don replied.

"One of them stars isn't a star, it's a galaxy - but I can't remember which one now," I said, putting my halfpenny's worth of information into the pot.

"A galaxy's a hell of a big thing to forget Gypo!" Don laughed

"Of course it's a Greek word," said Anita.

"What is?" I asked her.

"Galaxy - it comes from our work for milk 'Galla. We call our galaxy the Milky Way."

"Amazing that all those suns can seem so small to us from our position on the wheel's edge," Don said. "No wonder early man was impressed by the buggers - you can see how bright they seemed to them."

It was so quiet as we contemplated the stars. In that silence we three breathed in the universe and it was the perfume of the Gods.

The days went by in peace and creativity. I had started to write again, mostly poetry but then a fairy story came into my mind, influenced by the island we were living on, my friendship with Don and a girl I met on Paros.

I called the book *Sandylea* in honour of Metzi, as we had first met on a sandy lea. There was of course, an enchanted island with a character called Donoleitcho who was a nature spirit and sang about the beauty of his island. The book was in the format of an old fairy tale but had some very modern concepts interwoven through the storyline, such as finding the reason for peace and the reason to abolish war - a very 60's concept but in reality even more valid today.

Don was drawing, writing and making music. I was becoming very friendly with old Dmitri, our landlord. Although he was not of large stature, he was reputed to be the strongest man on the island, the reason being as follows.

One day he was taking his donkey up a mountain path to collect some grapes when he met several friends coming down the other way who told him all the grapes had been picked. On hearing this Dmitri tried to lead his donkey back down the path, but the stubborn beast was determined it would only go uphill. Finally, with his friends laughter ringing in his ears, Dmitri lost patience and spread his arms around the belly of the animal, lifting it from the ground and spinning it around in the opposite direction - downward. His friends cheered him and hailed him as a hero and from that day on he was known as the strongest man on the island.

He had a strong character too. He and his friend, the taverna owner Alexandra, were the only two in the main village who refused to take a siesta.

"I will be dead soon and will have all the sleep I need. Why should I waste the time I have left by sleeping the afternoons away?" was Dmitri's explanation.

So a few days each week I would find myself sitting with the two old men in the taverna drinking ouzo with them while everyone else on the island was fast asleep. I, in my youth, would drink many glasses of ouzo while they, in their wisdom, would mix one glass of ouzo and water making it last all afternoon, sipping with great delight. We had not one word to communicate with but somehow with nods, winks, miming and laughter we did speak. It was to our souls, if not to our intellects. Dmitri and I became good friends and had a great respect for each other deep in our hearts, no matter the difference in our ages.

Metzi was not born on Paros but knew it well through friends' invites over many years. One sunny afternoon I had the good fortune to be surprised by the Lass as she jumped on the donkeys back from a high wall as Sarphina and I were aiming for the Spiti.

"Hi, Mitzi isn't it" I said remembering the girl whose eyes had lingered a bit too long on mine in the square.

"Hi, Gypsy isn't it." she mimicked me with laughing eyes on my face .

"Want to come for a swim with me Gypsy. I can show you a place that the dancing seagulls don't even know about. We can be alone for a few hours there if you would like it to be so."

How wonderful was this offer and said with such confidence in her soft accented voice I could not refuse.

"Lead on, Mc Duff ," I joked.

"Pardon me gypsy, I know not what you are talking off." Mitzi said slightly worried.

"Take no notice of me my love, it just means let's go, show me this private place of yours."

"All that in that one short word. I must remember this McDuff, " she said very seriously.

Cute as hell, I thought and twice as desirable. I was flabbergasted to see she had no inhibitions about nudity and took her clothes off to swim in the still waters of the inlet without a moments thought. God, she was beautiful, nude her skin colour like ancient gold! Well - it would have been bad manners not to comply with her wish to have me in the sea beside her so I undressed and joined her in the mercifully warm water where we chatted away non-stop and I found out she would be leaving on a yacht next morning with her relatives to visit other islands - so this would be her last chance to see me.

Metzi lay down on the shell covered beach and didn't bother putting her clothes back on. She patted the sand next to her reclining figure and I sat down looking at her erect nipples. Reaching for her we shared our first kiss. She was extremely passionate by nature as I have discovered many Greek girls are. I was allowed to do anything sexually I wished to do with Mitzi apart from penetration - in her country virginity is the most important thing a girl can give to her husband. I respected her wishes and resisted the urge to go all the way with her and her wonderful body.

She was no sexual innocent, for all her need to keep her virginity intact, and she had several delightful ways of making a man's body respond to her will and she used them to perfection in our lovemaking. This girl would make her future husband a very happy man in the confines of their bed - that was for sure. She was a truly remarkable lassie was Mitzi and I hope life treated her well and she was and is still happy.

After three weeks on Paros our dear friend Anita left us to go back to her mother's place about 100 miles from Athens. She and Ashley were planning on bringing the old lady back to London to see if it was possible for her to live with them there. Of course we had left Ashley behind in England to sort out the business wrangles that were holding up the release of the *Sunshine Superman* album, the cover of which showcased the artistic skills of Mick and Sheena McCall. We had departed from London disappointed with and thinking that the LP would never see the light of day in Britain and Europe. Ashley knew if he was to get Donovan and I back to the business he had to pull off the deal to leave the Pye label as quickly as his wits would allow him to make the deal. He knew Donovan could be tempted back if all went smoothly and his new album was out there - so he pulled his strings. They took the single *Sunshine Superman* from the album and went wholeheartedly into making it a commercial success.

We sat not even thinking about it, feeling more and more we had made the right decision by quitting. I daresay that in Dono's mind the drag of having your music stopped simply through contracts made years earlier was a real horror story - but that was one of the reasons we had left. Our freedom was being threatened in so many ways - by the police after our bust, by the music business, by contracts - and in a big way by fame. We found the freedom we craved on that remarkable island of Paros.

Five weeks later, our money running out but our needs still easy, we met a couple of English tourists who had found our paradise. They were young girls of about 20 - the eldest reminded me very much of Joy, the American dancer - she had a similar long figure and thick red-gold hair - Jenny was her name. She had come to Paros via Milan and Brendizi, where she began to fall out with her boyfriend and by the time they reached Paros their bumpy romance was over. He spent two days on the island then scampered off into oblivion. We all got together - being the only English folks on the hill so to speak. Jenny let me know she was a mother and had a baby boy at home in Cambridge Youths Freedoms sometimes paid a price in flesh - wanted or unwanted.

There are very few young mothers that want to lose the baby growing inside them but sometimes they realize the person they made life with was inadequate to support or love them. In which case it takes a huge amount of courage to admit the truth and go their own separate ways. There were a lot of these ladies in the mid sixties - and Jenny was one of them. She was a middle class lass with a strong family to help her, lucky girl. There were many from the streets that would be on the streets for a long time - Social Services were in their infancy then. But Jenny felt free of it all for a few short weeks and wanted to ball, in a cool way, on the islands.

We found ourselves in the hay along with the chickens one afternoon and during our lovemaking Jenny did something sexually with her hair that I had only had Joy do to me before. Want it or not I was taken right back to our flat in Maida Vale just before the bust and in that moment I realized that I had loved Joy very deeply and I was still 'in grieving' for her in a strange way. I was stunned by this revelation and lost all my ardour and passion for Jenny on the spot. The poor soul had no idea why. I made a joke of it and apologized, getting to my feet and telling her it was nothing to do with her or her desirability - but something inside me.

What on earth had made Jenny do exactly what Joy had done with her hair - Joy's red gold hair too? It had completely thrown me as it was not a common thing to do. I began to understand that there might be a viper's nest of subconscious feelings deep in my heart and mind. Love's lost children conceived but stunted by neglect and uncaring impulses. New births of love never grieved over at their loss and decay. My God, was I to replay my heart like a tape; was I to rewind the many feelings of love I had felt in my heart and soul? Was I to feel again, like a traitor to itself, all the pain my heart had been cataloguing like a spy, somewhere in my brain.

I was amazed to find this unfinished business in the inner workings of my subconscious. Normally I prided myself on being the sort of guy who was fairly worked out. I thought I didn't have any skeletons in the cupboards of my being, bare boned and rattling. I believed I was free of subconscious hidden thoughts that brought you down flat out of the blue. But now in this light I discovered this wasn't the case. I *did* have unfinished business cluttering up the fabric of my mind - unfinished business with love - and more importantly, with respect for love. I discovered that day that I was building an armoured coating against the pain I had caused the very things I did love - you delicious, delightful, glorious, beautiful, thoughtful, wonderful sensual ladies.

A cockerel entered the barn, jumped on the back of the nearest chicken and jumped off again and ate a big succulent ant nearby as if nothing had happened - he gave the hen not one moments thought. If I wasn't careful there but for its foul nature go I. I made a note to give my new inner discovery some serious thought - and in the not too distant future.

These were the last days of our freedom on Paros, although we didn't know it at the time. Fate was ticking its unknown seconds on its unknowable clock face, a smiling moment of now-ness intent on the blissful ignorance of our joint futures. We had been on the island eight weeks without any Dope but the girl Dono had just met had some with her so she gave a small piece to Dono to share with me. That evening, after a tasty meal and a couple of joints, we went to our usual café. It was the only café that boasted a phone - in fact it was the only phone on the island of Paros. It took hours of waiting to get your call routed to you through the mess of the Athens switchboard, thus we had never thought to use it.

We were told by the café proprietor that a call arranged from abroad would arrive for us at 11 o' clock sharp the following morning.

"Would you please be ready to receive it - it is from a Mr. Ashley Kozak," said Nico the proprietor.

Shit, we wondered in our newly stoned minds - what did he want? We were worried something might have happened to Anita - or our families.

Bright and early the next morning we were at the café for omelettes and awaiting the call in trepidation. Nico, the owner of this new-fangled instrument, was very proud to be getting a call on his phone from London and boastfully mentioned it to all and sundry of his Greek customers. Their eyes raised at the very thought of being able to talk to someone in England from their little sun-drenched island of Paros.

'Who could shout that loudly?' they discussed with knowing frowns.

They dismissed it as impossible but awaited the outcome with baited breath. It was unheard of, preposterous - who did Nico think he was kidding? 11 o'clock came slowly as wise looks were passed by the knowing locals.

'London indeed! Ha!Ha!' I saw some money pass hands and end up in Nicos's drawer - they were betting on the likelihood of receiving a call from England. More and more locals were arriving to get involved with the excitement of this phone call. It would be make or break for Nico.

The phone rang twice - everyone stirred - then it stopped. Eyebrows were raised and there were sighs from the unbelievers and sunny smiles from the believers - who were very much in the minority in the crowd. It rang again - three rings this time which stopped just as Nico was about to pick up the receiver he had specially polished for this occasion. The sweat was coating the brows of the unbelievers. More and more locals were being drawn to the excitement, by whose jungle drums we knew not. Nico was doing a roaring trade in drinks and taking a lot of money in bets. 2....3....4....5....6 rings. The telephone was dancing off its cradle as Donovan stood to take the call.

"Hello? Hello? - Ash? Yes - of course it's me, who do you think it is," he laughed. "Do what? You must be fucking joking mate! I can't believe it - hang on, let me tell Gypo..... *Sunshine Superman* is free out there and Number One in America Gyp. Ash wants us back as soon as we can make it back. Bloody hell Gyp! It's out there man and doing well. What we gonna do?" he asked me - excitement shining in his eyes.

I wanted to shout out for joy for Dono and cry an ocean for my own personal freedom - as I knew this was the end of if for good this time.

"Tell him we'll be on the next boat to Athens," I said.

"It's tomorrow morning lads," said Nico.

"Gyp says we'll be on the next boat tomorrow morning Ash," said Dono. "You can arrange things with the same travel agent in Athens and we'll pick up the plane tickets there. Number One in the States - unbelievable! We're on our way Ash - give our love to Anita."

Donovan replaced the receiver in its cradle to the sound of groans from those that had lost their bets. Would you believe it, Donovan hadn't even shouted down the wires - in fact there were some sitting right there in the café who had hardly heard him.

"We have two first class plane tickets waiting for us in Athens to take us to London Gyp," he said

"That's great Dono - but we've barely got the money for the tickets to Athens and we should try to leave on a high note and treat all our friends to ouzos and mezzo before we go," I said.

"Shit Gyp - you're right. We got to celebrate man - I've got a Number One record in the States!"

Of course Nico overheard our conversation and came up with an idea.

"Right lads, you save whatever money you have for the tickets - I'll foot the bill for the drinks and food needed to give you both a good send off."

"And how can we repay you for this amazing act of kindness?" laughed Donovan.

"You can give me the musical box you always come into town to buy batteries for," said Nico.

"You got yourself a deal Nico - but you must treat anyone who comes in tonight to drink and a little food."

"You're on Donovan. I will get my wife to order your tickets to Athens. It's a proper tourist boat now - they have started a new route to include Paros. We're planning to build a dock right outside my café - amazing, eh?" said Nico excitedly.

"Great," we said, but looked at each other knowing Paradise was most probably lost.

"My wife and I are persuading the locals here to let out their best guest rooms to tourists," Nico continued. "She's making a list and putting a sign in my café to catch the eye. The people here are poor - maybe we can help them get a little."

"They may have no money Nico, but they sure have a wonderful lifestyle and plenty of peace in their life. All that will change and you may look back in regret," Dono said sadly.

"I realise that, but do you know how hard it is for folks here to see our young men and women go off to Athens , never to be seen again because we can't find them jobs here? If we don't get a hold of some commercial enterprise we will just slip into the past. We cannot turn Paros into a museum by putting a dome of stopped time over it Gypsy," said Nico, his face showing his emotion. "We have to grow up and face a modern future - for the sake of our children if for no other reason."

"You're right," I replied, "but do it slowly Nico - don't be in such a rush that your old ways are simply cast aside and forgotten."

That evening, with all our business taken care of, we ate and drank with the mellow natives for the last time. It was a sad occasion for me, as I was loath to leave. This was another love I was walking away from, it added to the scores of other loves walked away from. These were beginning to make themselves felt in the enclaves of my unconscious mind like thistles in hay.

Dmitri and Alex - who had closed his taverna early for the first time in 50 years - arrived wearing their best outfits used for weddings and funerals. I felt very honoured. They drank a few ouzos and we exchanged cheery smiles that masked both their own and my sadness. The island people were used to separations. Dmitri mimed that he would see me at the boat the next morning and I in my turn promised myself in my soul to return to this enchanted island in the future and live here. I would too - years hence. I lived on Paros from 1979 for 27 years - 22 of them with the same girl. A half German, half Czech wonderfully gifted artist by the name of Rita Schmiser. My marble sculptures are nestled in many of the very best houses on the island of Paros as I write this book. But let us continue the story of leaving Paradise, not returning to it.

Miraculously Donovan and I were in time for the boat. We left all the things we had bought for the house there - Dmitri could do with them as he wished. Nico came over and we passed him the record player with happiness, as he had been more than generous with his food and drink the previous evening. He kindly translated for me as I promised Dmitri I would return one day to stay.

"Don't leave it too long Gypsy my dear friend - or you will find me dead and forgotten."

"You could never be forgotten Dmitri, not by those that know and love you," I told him seriously.

Then the ship came around the sweep of the natural harbour into the beautiful bay of Parikia, its pennant flying proudly.

God - the changes we had seen in only eight or nine weeks were amazing - what with this monstrously modern boat bringing tourists new ways of thinking and money by the bucket load which would change the ideas of living, seeing and being for the Islanders. My heart broke for them - but then I remembered what Nico had said about their heartache at parting with their children by sending them off to Athens which was the Pied Piper of commercial success and the only way to put food in the belly for tens of thousands of souls.

We were in Athens ourselves nine hours from waving goodbye to our friends as they stood on the sand. The pace of life for Donovan and myself was about to hit the roof.

CHAPTER NINETEEN
THREE BIG PROPOSALS

Both Donovan and I realized we might not experience such peace again in our entire lives. We had found our personal freedom and it had washed our souls clean. We were stronger in spirit to face the future than at any other time - and we were to need it. Anyone that thinks huge success is easily handled has not even put their toe in the drowning waters of stardoms great lakes. We were to plunge in over our heads….and then some.

We arrived in London without a place to stay, having given up our flat on Edgware Road. Ashley had booked us in at a crazy Music Business hotel where a lot of cats were bopping. As far as my room went I could just about have swung a cat in it - if it had a short tail. After the vastness of Paros it felt more like a cell than a room. The double bed was comfortable enough but the walls were so thin I could hear all the lovemaking going on at either side of me and I felt like I was the third member in a *menage a trios*. I should have recorded some of them sounds and put them on the cat's records - they would have made a fortune.

As luck would have it Chas Chandler and Hilton Valentine, bass player and guitar player respectively with The Animals were among the guests staying at the hotel. Chas had some important business to attend to in town as well as the recording with The Animals in the studio. Unfortunately their lead singer, Eric Burdon, had had a stand up row with everyone in the band as was his want and had found his own accommodation two miles away. This was a pity as I got on well with Eric and liked him a lot - but Chas and Hilton were my good buddies.

Chas had invited his Swedish grilfriend, Lotta, to England. He was seriously in love with this beautiful young lady whom he had the good fortune to meet when The Animals were touring Sweden. They lived in perfect harmony of personality and physical attraction. Chas was a huge man and Lotta was small of stature - but very sexy and self-confident despite her size, mainly I believed because she was very very beautiful. They say opposites attract and that's true - I've had occasion to note that fact myself. Lotta had not dared to come to London on her own so had suggested that her best friend Yvonne should accompany her.

Hilton Valentine had flirted a little with Yvonne when they had first met in Sweden many months before and Lotta thought it would be a real music business dream if she should marry Chas and Yvonne should marry Hilton. Yvonne was not so convinced.

I was unbelievably attracted to Yvonne the second I laid eyes on her. She was seated very demurely by the imitation Greek urns scattered about the lounge. The hotel was in Bayswater Road - a bloody long way from Greece, but it provided a

Gyp and Noel Redding of Jimi Hendrix Experience play a bit of snooker

Gyp and Yvonne

Chas Chandler and Lotte

talking point for Yvonne and myself as I spoke to her of some of my adventures on Paros. She admired my sun tan and said that she wondered if I was from England at all.

We talked and talked - her English was very good considering she had never been in the country before. She had a very sexy accent and an old fashioned way of explaining herself. We got on like a house on fire. She looked a little like Jean Shrimpton, a very famous model of the mid 1960's, although this was just coincidence and not purposefully put on. Nothing was purposefully put on with Yvonne - everything she said and did was 100% her. She appeared thoughtful, good-natured, truthful, beautiful and sexy as hell without trying to be any of these things by one iota of life's trickery. Yvonne was what she was - and what she was was plenty satisfying to me and most people she met. A charming, delightful, intelligent beautiful girl. What more could a man want? This man wanted nothing more. I was determined to court her and make her mine - not just for a fling, but for the real thing.

I hadn't felt anything remotely like this since my love affair with Lorna - though this feeling was totally different of course. From day one of meeting Yvonne I was lost to an emotion that was uncontrollable and destined.

Yvonne was an artist and had already found a job through Chas Chandler, painting a mural above the bar of a Music Business Club called *The Bag o' Nails*, owned and run by Rick Gunnel - a sweet natured gangster from the west end of London. She was telling me of her job when who should rush into the lounge, his arms spread wide for a crushing hug, than Chas himself.

"Gypsy you old fucker - you're here mate! Donovan just told me. How incredible man - it's great to see you. Hi Yvonne, I see you two have already met. You be careful of this bugger love - he's notorious."

"Talk about the kettle calling the pan black Chas," I said laughing.

"Not any more Gypsy - I met the girl of my dreams, a lovely lady named Lotta."

"What's 'notorious' - and what does 'bugger' mean please?" Yvonne asked sweetly.

Chas and I laughed fit to burst our sides at the innocent way Yvonne had of asking.

"When we come back from the airport Gyp can explain," Chas said, a large smile creasing his face.

"Thanks very much mate - but I'll leave the 'bugger' to you. So - what airport and why are we going there?" I asked while putting me leather on.

"Come on Gypo, let's get a cab and I'll tell you all about it," he said walking me outside.

"Taxi!" shouted Chas at the top of his lungs.

I think every empty taxi from there to Marble Arch stopped dead in their tracks.

"I want you to meet the greatest guitar player the world has ever known - or ever will know. Believe me Gypo this cat's out there on his own - no one like him in this world. He's miles in front of anyone playing right now," Chas confided in me. "He'll change the playing of every musician on the entire planet on the electric guitar within weeks of me making him famous - you mark my words Gypsy."

I could see that Chas was really excited about this new guitar player.

"Look Gyp - I know you and Donovan are like one, but I'm looking for an honest and clever guy to look after Jimi on the road - would you be interested? You can have a good percentage if you are Gypsy - there's going to be plenty of bread man once Jimi Hendrix hits the flame, believe me - plenty of the green backs are gonna fly. He told me himself he wanted someone like you Gyp to handle him on tours. Someone that could be a real good friend as well as a business cat. He nearly fell outta his tight pants when I told him we were good friends - said he had to meet you. Fucking unbelievable luck that you're here to meet him. Is it luck or Fate Gypsy mate? Want to come aboard at the very beginning?"

"You know Chas I'm only in this gig to help Dono. To tell you the truth I wouldn't be at all interested in this lark if it weren't for Donovan. At the moment he needs me mate and while he does I wouldn't consider any other offer, although I do appreciate it Chas and I know what it means for you to ask me. Thanks a lot man - but no thanks," I said.

"I thought you'd say that - knew it was a long shot, but I had to ask yer man. For fuck's sake Gypo - don't tell Donovan that I tried to steal yer! He would have me guts for garters in a minute," Chas said.

"You're cool mate - I won't ever mention it to him. I'm looking forward to meeting this cat - what's his name again?" I asked.

"Jimi Hendrix - I've been looking out for a band for him - think I've found 'em - think I'll call them 'The Experience' - how does that sound Gypo?"

"Sounds good enough to me Chas - there's some pretty stupid names for groups out there - like The Animals, The Beatles, The Rolling Stones - people like that will never make it for sure - but Jimi Hendrix & the Experience sounds like a winner," I joked.

At the airport a rather tall, thin cat with a floppy hat, high boots and tight curly hair - dark, three-quarter length coat flapping around his body like he was permanently in the wind and carrying his own electric guitar as if it were a wand and he a wizard, met our joint gaze.

"There he is!" called out Chas and waved Jimi over.

When Jimi smiled he looked liked a shy child about to test the waters of trust and almost sure that the upshot would be to drown in dishonesty's dirtiest waters. Your heart went out to him and you wanted to hold his hand across the road - knowing full well he could look after himself better than you could and you would be the one run over. Jimi was cool and I took to him right away. Chas introduced us.

"This is Gypsy Dave, Jimi - Gypo this is Jimi Hendrix." We stepped forward and gave each other a hug, his eyes shone and I could feel his power - it was as if we had known each other a lifetime.

In the taxi back to Bayswater Chas did all the talking. Jimi said very little although he listened intently. He seemed....not exactly shy, more resigned to his lot in life - whatever it might be. You felt that he knew his worth but that he himself felt that the rest of the world would never know it, or care to know it. As I came to know him better I was to realize this had a lot to do with his American upbringing. In America at that time if you were black or half-caste, you were a second rate citizen. Jimi was half-caste, his father being black and his mother of American Indian descent I believe. Through his talent - and Chas Chandler's managerial skills - Jimi Hendrix was to become a First Class citizen of extraordinary appeal, first in Britain and a little later in the USA. Unbeknown to me at that time I was to spend an unusual amount of time in the company of Jimi, Chas and Lotta through my relationship with Yvonne.

Donovan was talking to Yvonne in the lounge as we arrived at the Bayswater Hotel.

"Oy you old sod! I saw 'er first - you keep your eyes off her," I joked with Dono.

"Hey man - I've just spent twenty minutes talking pretty to Yvonne about you mate. Don't let her see you in your true colours otherwise she'll run a mile," Dono laughed.

I sidled up to Yvonne on the sofa as Chas came in saying Jimi would be honoured to meet Don.

"How's the mural coming on Yvonne? Will it be ready for Jimi's show?" Chas asked.

"Yes, I think - but I would like some help at some background colours. I cannot reach from the ladder these places."

"Look no further Yvonne - Gyp here is a great painter," said Chas. "I've seen murals he's painted - one on the wall of his pad - it was fab - and George Harrison has one of his paintings - you will give Yvonne a hand won't you Gyp?"

"George only has one of my paintings because I gave it to him! No way would he have bought the bloody thing," I laughed at Yvonne's expression of awe. "But it would be my pleasure to assist you Yvonne," I said looking into her eyes.

"Thank you Gypsy, I will be very happy if you help. I work through the night at The Bag o' Nails - could you be there tonight to spend the night together?" she asked sweetly.

All us men smiled, our imaginations working overtime.

"That's the nicest invitation I've had in ages," I joked with Yvonne.

"You bloody jammy sod Gypo," Dono whispered to me after returning from Jimi's room "Yvonne's fantastic - God, what a beauty!"

"Well we can't let you bloody singers get all the girls - us artists got to have our share too."

"Fuck Gypo, I think you've had your share years ago - you're living on the surfeit now for sure."

"Sweet, ain't she?" I said grinning.

"Sweet ain't the word Gypo - you could dip her in your tea for life and she'd still come up sticky. I'm thinking of bringing Enid over - what do you think?" Dono asked me seriously

"Sounds great, she was a gas - and you sure as hell seemed to get on fantastic in the sack. You two was never out of that bloody big bed in LA."

"Yeah - we got on well alright," said Dono, "sexiest thing I ever had when she wanted to be. I think I'll bring Enid over as soon as we get a pad. Talking of pads Gyp - Yvonne's Swedish - don't do what you did to the last Swede you brought home." We both laughed at the memory. "Now, let's go to the Indian restaurant and eat." said Dono, hunger shinning in his eyes

Dono was referring to a very interesting time when on tour in Sweden I had met a young Swedish girl who was the epitome of Scandanavian beauty. I decided to take her home with me to London as she was just too good to put down. She was all for it and ran home, packed her bags and left a note for her parents telling them she was leaving and going to live in London. Meanwhile I had arranged the tickets back to England.

I was leaving the tour before going on to Finland, but that was a one night gig at a very good venue. It was a rest too as Dono would be in a first class hotel for three days relaxing before the concert. He assured me it would be cool.

"I'm going to kip for two days anyway Gyp - have 'em bring me all my meals to the room. I need the break and the gig's easy. They have their own security and the hall will send someone to pick me up. It's all organized, go home and enjoy yer present mate - she's wonderful. Use my room - it's got music and it's cosier than yours and more intimate."

"Why not, the young ones like romance - and your bed is outrageously romantic for sure," I laughed.

"Don't break the fucking thing Gypo - please - it's an antique," Dono said seriously.

"Don't worry Dono - so am I by now."

Anita, the young Swedish lass, was fantastic and as energetic a soul as you would wish to meet. She wanted to go see this, see that and see the other as soon as we landed at Heathrow. I needed to get down to work with Ashley so I cut the sightseeing short.

Ash was surprised to see me home but understood as soon as I introduced Swedish Anita to him and his Anita.

"Jesus Gypsy, she's unbelievable!" Ashley's Anita said to me.

"Couldn't put her down love - had to bring her with me," I explained.

"Dave Tilling's using the flat Gypsy - I knew you wouldn't mind," Ashley said.

"No, that's great. Is he here with his Lady Roe?" I asked, hoping he was.

"No, she left this morning for a photo shoot - that's why they came down."

"Right, I'll go up and see him then - come on Anita," I said grabbing her hand.

It was great seeing Dave and we chatted away until I noticed Anita was yawning. I showed her the bathroom and brought her washing bag for her - meaning to start to get ready for bed myself.

"Fuck Gypsy - she's unbelievably beautiful - has she got a sister?" Dave joked.

I was just about to answer him when the phone went

"Hi - how you doing?" I said. It was Allen Klein.

"Hi Gyp, I was hoping to get a hold of you. Got an interesting proposition for you - could change your fucking life for good and all."

"Can it wait Allen? I got a beautiful proposition awaiting me now," I said, high on the thought of Anita.

"Pussy, pussy.....pussy can be got any fucking time Gypsy - as you well know. Shit, I'm talking about something that'll make you fall off yer fucking bronco! Tonight or never Gypsy - I've got the whole of the third floor of the Dorchester booked. Come on up - I'll get them to lay on a fucking banquet you'll remember your whole goddamn life Gypsy."

I looked at Dave and thought what a treat it would be for him who wasn't used to this lifestyle to come to the Dorchester for dinner with a real rich cat who could afford to rent the whole third floor of one of the most expensive hotels in England.

"Alright Allen, I'll be there - but can I bring a good friend along?" I said.

"Bring the Queen of England and her entourage for all I fucking care - as long as we can have our talk."

"Right, we'll be there within the hour - see yer soon," I said.

Putting the phone down I wondered what the hell Allen wanted.

Anita came from the bathroom in a baby-doll pajama affair that made me smile. I wasn't used to ladies who wore things to bed. It was very uncool in our normal set of wild beatnik ladies - still....it looked very cute on her.

"Look Anita my love - I'm very sorry but some very important business has come up and I have to go to the Dorchester Hotel for a meeting - it can't be helped my dear."

I lifted her off her feet and carried her into Don's room and laid her down on the bed. We kissed sexily and then I went to get Dave and told him we were going for dinner at the Dorchester.

"Shit Gyp! I can't go to the Dorchester looking like this - they would throw me out," Dave said.

"Not at all - they'll fawn all over you if you go through the door in yer birthday suit. They'll treat us like royalty," I said laughing.

I gave Anita another kiss and asked if she was cool and knew where everything was. I told her we would be back in a maximum of two hours so she wasn't to worry. As she curled up in the big bed she asked me to be back as soon as I could as she was a little frightened of this big old flat with its antiques and low light. I felt for her - it was her first night from home and her first night in a foreign country. Maybe I shouldn't go - but I had promised Allen and I would have to go. I closed the door tightly as I left the room with Anita tucked up and sleepy. Dave and I left the flat and got a taxi to the hotel.

We were given long looks until we said who was expecting us, then the atmosphere changed and we were escorted with bows and scrapes to the dining room on the third floor as if we were the King of Siam and the King of Burma. The smiling flunkey knocked gently on the door for us and there was a roaring "Come in!" in an American New Jersey accent making even that small example of the English language sound like it came through an orange grater by way of the San Francisco Bridge.

We entered the hotel suite and Allen shook my hand warmly.

"Fantastic to see you again you old fucker. Who's this?" he asked looking at Dave Tilling kindly.

"A photographer, a friend of many years standing Allen - he came a long way to see me tonight. Dave took the photos for Barry Gibb's new album."

"Did you? Well if all goes well tonight I can get you to take the fuckin' pictures of The Beatles."

Dave and I hadn't the faintest idea what he was talking about

"Look at this table Allen - I've never seen so much food in me life," I said astonished.

"Thought I'd get 'em to put up a few fuckin' cold starters Gypsy. I even taught the bloody Chef here how to make the Waldorf salad properly. What do you want to drink?"

"A whisky would be good," I said. Dave nodding in approval.

"Right you fuckin' are. Get us a bottle of Chivas Regal," Allen said to the waiter who was hovering in the background. "OK you two - sit down."

I had only met Allen a couple of times but I remembered him for his American business suits with their off the ankle high cut trousers. He looked like a Mafia boss, which was a good image for the role he had practically invented - the Business Manager.

The waiter arrived back with the whisky in an ice bucket and put it by my shoulder. I whisked it out and said I preferred it at room temperature thank you very much.

"You have it anyway you fuckin' want it Gypsy," Allen said snappily looking long and hard at the waiter. "Drink up and have as much as you want. Never skimp at my table Gypsy. I've had it hard in my time - believe me - just like you Gypo. But you like an idiot wanted it fuckin' hard I believe," he said with a cackle of a laugh.

"Well, want it or not, having had it hard taught me a thing or two," I said, watching the waiter as he filled my glass and Dave's.

"What you want to try first Gypsy are those prawns in avocado - I can highly recommend them."

I took Allen at his word and we began to tuck in, first to the avocados then to fresh oysters, lobsters and Waldorf salad.

"Want wine boys?" asked Allen.

"No thanks Allen - we'll stick with this lovely whisky, if that's alright with you."

"You're right Gypsy - this snobby thing some Englishmen have for wine sure gets up my kilt. A good spirit far outstrips any fuckin' wine I think," Allen said

"I'm with you there mate. Thanks Allen, this meal is fantastic."

"This ain't nuthin' yet - wait till the main course comes. I've ordered us some fuckin' T-bone steaks, some pheasant wrapped around duck wrapped around turkey with cranberry jelly and creamy mashed potatoes and a fuckin' sauce that's outa this world. After that there's some suckling pig - what do you think - will that be enough for us?"

"Bloody hell Allen! Dave here will never leave if you treat him to all that," I said pouring out another stiff whisky for us both. The Chivas Regal was going down very well with all the rich food.

"Well," I said, "unless I'm wrong this isn't Christmas - so what can I do for you Allen?"

"I'll tell you what Gypsy - it could be Christmas every day from now on, but that's up to you....you and four friends of Donovan. But let's eat first and then I'll tell you a story and you can decide to help me or fucking not."

I was becoming very intrigued - and after our meal which had given me a nice rosy calm what with all the food and alcohol we were imbibing. I looked toward the clock on the wall and realized we had been there well over two hours. We felt like aristocrats, Dave gave up on the suckling pig; I could understand now why the Toffs got gout with their ridiculously rich lifestyle. I decided to give the pig a go and my God it tasted fantastic. More whisky followed, Allen drinking Budweiser from a bucket of ice at his side.

"Now Gyp, the best part of any fucking meal is the dessert. What's your favourite 'sweet' - as you Poms say?"

"I've got two favourites," I explained to him. "Crème Brule and Lemon Meringue Pie with lashings of cream on it - like my darling mother made me when I was a kid."

Allen looked at the waiter with raised eyebrows.

"Yes sir, we have both those desserts on the sweet trolley."

Dave opted for bread and butter pudding with blueberries and double whipped cream and Allen ordered apple pie and cream. We had been sitting over this table for three and a half hours and I knew that coffee, brandy and cigars were still to come - plus Allen's story and more talk - and more whisky. I could see us getting bundled into a taxi about 3 a.m.

Poor Anita! Still, what could I do - it was the sort of life I led in those days.

Dave was talking a lot now about his love of photography and his girl, Roey. The second bottle of whisky was on its last legs. Seeing its sorry state Allen ordered another one.

"Come on Gypsy, it's years since I've enjoyed myself so much," he said. "You cats are really down to earth. I like that about you. So many fucking Englishmen are stuck up and high and bloody mighty. I come from the streets Gypsy - I had to fight for everything I got. Didn't do too bad, did I?"

"Not too bad at all I would bloody say," said Dave looking a bit the worse for wear.

The sweets were brought in and served. My life changed that day, for I was convinced that my mother made the best Lemon Meringue Pie in the world. Reluctantly I had to demote her to second place and hail the Pastry Chef at the Dorchester as the new world champion. I can taste it to this day. For the coffee and smokes we moved to the lounge.

"Simon," Allen said turning to the waiter, "is the bar stocked with more Chivas for our friends here?"

"Yes sir, I took the liberty of putting a new bottle by the brandy," came the reply.

"Well done Simon," Allen said slipping him a twenty pound note for the evening's excellent service. "I think we can do without your excellent help now. Well here we fucking are," he continued as the waiter departed. "I'll tell you my fucking life story after you tell me yours Gyp."

"Jesus! - that could take us till next week, so I'll make it a brief synopsis." I said.

Three quarters of an hour later with Dave asleep and occasionally snoring Allen began to tell me about his life and interests.

"My father was a Jewish butcher from Hungary - but there were hard time there so my folks came to America looking for a better life. My mother died before I could remember her and I was farmed out to various people and institutes. By the time I was in college I was known as a bit of genius for my skill with Mathematics. I paid my own way through college by having three jobs on the go at the same time. I was fucking hungry for a while there Gypsy, I can tell you. But that hard time made me realize that you have to be determined in business and have to work hard twenty six hours a day and not let anyone pull the fucking wool over your eyes. If you're going to be kicked in the butt, kick back twice as hard was my motto. I had a bit of luck along with all my fucking effort by getting into the music business with Bobby Darin and Sam Cooke among others."

Allen went on and on about his clients and his interests until eventually he came to the point.

"Well Gyp, here's where you come in. As you can tell, I demand to be the best in my business of management. Not just the fucking best - the 'supremo'. I want to manage the two biggest groups in the history of music - it's my fucking dream - The Rolling Stones and The Beatles. The Stones I got recently - now I want the fucking Beatles. I tried to get them from Eppi but he would have none of it - no matter what I offered him."

"But Allen, I have no business connections with the boys - how can I be of any use?" I said.

"Ah Gypsy, my old carpetbagger, you can help if you want to. I've been told that you and Donovan have been seeing a lot of George and Paul lately and I have it on good authority that they both trust you implicitly and think you're the most honest guy in the fucking business - especially George."

"That's nice to know Allen," I said pouring another stiff Chivas.

"Well, that's the point Gypsy. You see all I want you to do is introduce me to George as a fucking friend of yours and leave the rest to me. I know that within half an hour George would want me to manage him and by association the rest of the boys will fall into my managerially capable hands. What do you think Gypsy? For the opportunity of putting me in touch with the boys I'll give you ten per cent of The Beatles deal with me - that I promise you Gypsy."

"Bloody hell! Ten per cent of The Beatles!" said Dave in a stunned voice. He must have woken up as Allen was outlining his proposition.

"Fucking worth thinking about, ain't it mate," I said seriously to Dave and Allen.

"You think about it for a couple of days," Allen said to me. "Then, when you're sure, you get in touch with George and arrange a meeting for us three to spiel. The Tea House in Liberty's is a good place to discuss business."

"Listen Gypo," Dave blustered, "I ain't 'alf as out of it as you - just say 'yes' - a percentage of The Beatles! Jesus Gyp - a percentage of The Beatles mate - you got to say yes. There's no one deserves it more than you Gypsy - for the way you treated Donovan all these years - and for nohting too - you go for it man."

I was beginning to have strange feelings about Anita in our flat. I tried phoning her but there was no answer. Where was she? The phone was right by the bed in the room she was in., we had just had it put there. Well, I hardly knew her - how was I to tell what she would do? She knew no one in England so she would probably think the phone call wasn't for her - but surely she would think it was from me? It was a bit of a mystery.

We said our goodbyes to Allen and thanked him for the fantastic evening. Giving him a hug I told him I would be in touch as soon as I made contact with

George to talk things over with him. Allen was knocked out and smiled profusely.

In the taxi home I thought seriously about Allen's proposal - Dave had dozed off again. As I thought about it in my mind I had a strange premonition, or a drunken waking prophetic dream, that came in the form of newspaper headlines:

'ALLEN KLEIN TO BE NEW BEATLES MANAGER!'
'THREE SIGN, ONE WON'T - MCCARTNEY NOT CONVINCED'
'MCCARTNEY TO SUE OTHER BEATLES OVER SPLIT'
'NO WAY BACK - THE BEATLES ARE OVER', SAYS LENNON'.
'KLEIN PAID MILLIONS BY BEATLES IN SETTLEMENT'

I was sitting in the cab groaning and moaning. I felt Dave hold onto my arm.

"What's the matter Gypsy? You're hitting your head on the window and shaking like a beat dog."

"They've broke up Dave - The Beatles have broken up," I said in despair. "And I'm responsible man - it's all over the newspapers Dave."

"How do you know Gyp? You ain't seen a bleedin' newspaper! I been with yer all night long man."

I came to my senses and found myself sitting hunched in the back seat of the London cab with the driver looking at me strangely in his internal mirror.

"Fuck Dave - that was far out! I never had such a strong premonition in my life. Klein will get The Beatles for sure Dave - but it'll be the end of them as a group when he does. No way will I be the catalyst for that mate. I won't be the one that broke up the best and most creative pop group that the world has ever seen - or ever will see. - but it's going to happen with or without me mate, sure as eggs is eggs. What a disaster Dave - I'm having nothing to do with it," I said with deep regret.

"It's just yer mind playin' tricks Gypsy. Don't be a fool and give up the best thing that could happen to a human being man. This offer is a chance in a lifetime Gypsy - don't give it up for God's sake!" Dave said with real feeling and sadness, because he knew I couldn't be reasoned with.

"What? And feel responsible all my life for the break up of the boys? No way man! Nothing can be worth that Dave - no money in the world could compensate for that mate."

"Look Gypsy, I know how psychic you can be, we both saw things in the studio, but don't jump to conclusions - if they *do* break up it might be nothing to do with Klein."

"That might be true Dave, but it doesn't happen until he starts to manage them - that I know.

No Dave - sorry man - I just can't do it, let someone else be responsible - I couldn't handle it mate."

"Fuck Gypsy!" ,Dave said full of feeling. "All that bread gone up in smoke man. Gypo - you're a crazy cat!"

"Oh well, it's only money Dave - and you know that's not one of my weaknesses.

Bread I can do without, but friends are friends man - and more important than anything else. George was so kind to Don and myself after our bust. You should have seen him and Patti Dave - they were angels - no way could I piss on their kindness."

"But Gypo, you don't know for sure this will come to pass - it could have been a dream."

"If it was a dream it was a prophetic dream Dave - that I know for sure. The longer Klein stays away from The Beatles, the longer they'll be together."

By now the cab was drawing into the forecourt of out Maida Vale flat.

"I got no bread Gypo, will you catch the cab?" said Dave.

"Sure man. Been a great evening eh?"

"Evening and morning Gypo."

As we opened the main door Ashley came out of his ground floor flat in a panic.

"Where you been Gypsy? Have we had a to-do over your Anita! Why didn't you give her a number where she could reach you? The poor girl was frantic man - screamed the fucking house down. She nearly knocked the wall down of the next door flat - they were really pissed off. Why in the world did you want to lock her in that room Gypsy," asked Ashley distraughtly. "She couldn't take a pee or anything!"

"But I didn't lock her in Ash. What would I want to do that for?"

"You told her you was only going to be a couple of hours Gypsy, it's not like you to be cruel."

"Sorry Ashley - is your Anita still up? Let me come in and explain myself. Where's Swedish Anita now?" I asked in disbelief at what was going on.

"She's at the airport Gyp - she wouldn't take no for an answer - she was terrified. We gave her the money for the ticket and she phoned home to her parents. They'll pick her up when she arrives there tomorrow morning. Why in God's name did you lock her in? She would have been OK if she would have been free to move about the flat."

"But you can't lock that door Ashley - we took the key away," I said innocently. "It got stuck sometimes when the key was in the lock. We took it out and had no trouble since," I said.

"You pulled the door too hard when you left Gypsy. You must have moved something in the lock and it got stuck again," said Dave.. "I was there Ashley - Gypsy never locked nothing."

"Shit - that fuckin' door man!" I said selfishly. "But what made her get so upset?" I asked Ashley.

"She had just read a big article on Arabs abducting beautiful young girls from Sweden. It said that they were brought to England where some were drugged and sent in packing cases to Arabia - evidently some of the girls were lured by guys from the music business."

"Don't tell me any more Ash, I can guess the rest - poor little soul must've been as paranoid as hell."

"Where have you been tonight Gyp?" Ashley asked, which was unusual for him as he never stuck his nose in my private affairs.

"I been with a dozen Arabs negotiating the fucking fee!" I said sarcastically.

"Sorry Ash - I'm just a bit drunk that's all," I said tiredly.

"Just one of those nights never to be forgotten Ashley," Dave said in absolute frustration.

"Yeah - I'm sorry Ash, Anita - sorry for all the trouble you both had - but like Dave said, its been a night never to be forgotten. Dono will catch the plane ticket when he gets back Ash - I don't have enough bread to give you it now , sorry mate."

"That's cool Gypsy love," said Anita feeling my remorse. "We can get it later."

"We're both knackered - we're going to crash.," I moaned. "Fuck it - and me alone in that big fancy bed when I had that most glorious girl warming it for me. Shit and more shit!" I said, totally exhausted by the toll the evening had taken on my unhappy soul.

"I do believe you're more upset at losing that girl than losing 10% of The Beatles!" said Dave as we took the lift to the flat.

"That girl was worth a million Dave, believe me," I answered as we entered the hallway. "Gotta crash Dave - I'm totally knackered," I said as I fell on Don's bed and was instantly asleep.

Sitting in that Indian restaurant ages after this event I realized I hadn't told Don very much about that evening - in fact I had never mentioned Klein's offer, the reason being that Dono was scared I would leave him in those earlier days - leave him for a reason other than money or fame.....maybe my freedom. I didn't want him to fear on my account as he had enough potential worries. He didn't have to worry about me for it was a truth as old as friendship that while Don needed me I would be there 100% for him and his creativity.

Our Indian meals ordered we sat and talked about Chas's new venture - Jimi Hendrix. Chas was going to put on a PR gig at *The Bag O' Nails* for Jimi - get the music press there and some A & R cats from the record companies to see how much interest he could muster. Rick Gunnel was happy to oblige. His club had been closed for a couple of weeks due to refurbishment, which included the mural Yvonne was doing above the new bar.

Wow! I was going to see Yvonne that night to help her with her work! We would have plenty of time to get to know each other. A lovely tingle ran up and down my spine at the mere thought of her. I realized that I had it bad for Yvonne, almost from my first sight of her. It was up to me to make it work if it was going to work for us. I judged that 'softly softly' was the best approach with this lovely Swedish lady. We had the night ahead to start to get to know each other. I was looking forward to seeing Yvonne's mural. I hoped she was reasonably good, as I was a bad liar in anything that was important to me - like art.

Back at the hotel again I crashed out as I would be up all night with the painting and Yvonne. I asked reception to call me at nine so I could have a shower and get down to the lounge on time.

At 9.30 Yvonne was there waiting for me looking lovely and cool. How could she look so clean? Somehow these Swedish ladies had a knack of looking like they'd just come out of an icy pool, all clear and scaped so clean you could lick 'em to death like a lolly.

The taxi waiting, we said our goodbyes to the assembled mass sitting grinning in the lounge as we ventured into Club Land, not hand-in-hand ,but paintbrush-in-hand. Bloody hell, was it that obvious to everyone that something unusual was happening here? It's a truth that the whole world loves True Love and it was written all over the pair of us from day one.

We might as well have had a three foot sign saying *'WE ARE IN LOVE!'* around our bloomin' necks for the whole world to see - it was that destined to be.

Rick was as sweet as hell in his club, happy and upbeat with the changes going down and as pleased as Punch when he realized I was there to help Yvonne with the work. I could see why Yvonne was having trouble reaching some spots on the mural, as the ladder Rick had given her was too short.

On seeing Yvonne's work I thought it not too bad at all and as my eyes became accustomed to the bright colours I began to like it very much. When the lights dimmed the painting came into its own, making you want to come up to that friendly festoon of colours like a moth to a flame. It drew you into its warmth of brightness like an usher to your seats to watch an opera.

"Good, ain't she Gypsy? It works, don't it? 'ave a whisky and coke on the 'ouse mate - 'ave as many as you like."

CHAPTER TWENTY
WAS IT THE LADDER'S FAULT?

To my mind it was definitely the ladder's fault. Or was it Yvonne's tight Jeans making her pert backside appear so downright enchanting as I held the ladder and she stretched to find those parts on the Mural hard to reach? Whatever it was I believe I had never seen such a beautiful sight. I was so near to those unbelievably well shaped bum cheeks whilst holding the ladder I found them inches away from my vision . For the life of me I could not but help notice their perfection. Yvonne chose to ignore my intakes of breath and exclamations of, "Oh my God." She knew of course who my exclamations were for, she grinned to herself sweetly. I tried not to over do it, still every now and again groans of pleasure would come forth from the very core of my being. Yvonne for her part was working hard to finish this mural her concentration plain to see as she created an Art- Piece over the Bar of The Bag o Nails.

My job, to help her put paint on places she could not reach as well as hold the ladder as she stretched outward. Her commands were in the funniest of English idioms, words she needed not being easy to find in the fading memory of college grammar books. Over Coffee Breaks Yvonne mixed her paints whilst telling me about herself and family. Her Grandmother was Russian and her Great Grandparents on that side of the family White Russians who fled to Sweden during the chaos in Russia at the time of the Communist Revolution. Yvonne's Grandfather though was of pure Swedish stock and a lovely calm wise old man. Yvonne's Parents both born in Sweden had a few years of relative happiness until their marriage failed. Inevitably they became divorced and Yvonne being the middle child was farmed out to the very capable hands of her Fathers parents. They looked after her in their well- run home with much heartfelt love and joy. Yvonne's mother regretted her decision immediately but with the best will in the world she could not cope with the burden of three children. As time passed Yvonne's Grandmother did such a Royal job of looking after the young girl that when Yvonne's mother was in a position to take her back the young spirited nearly- teen refused point blank to go so she stayed in the confines of her Grandparent's home, being brought up as well by her two loving Aunts then living at home. Yvonne's personality as a small lass made her sincerely loved. She retained enough of that natural sweetness and charm to follow her into adulthood. The beauty that radiated from Yvonne's personality was a perfect marriage of intelligence natural cool, a wise innocence and a hopeful disposition capped off by an honest exuberance for the art of living .

At a break in our conversation I looked up to find her eyes searching mine in a strange intense questioning kind of way. I was flummoxed, so vibrant was that look. Had she asked me something of importance? If she had I had not heard it asked. I looked deeply into those hazel- yellow eyes, before I realized it I was kissing those fascinatingly beautiful parted lips. It was as if an unseen hand had guided me straight to the doors of Yvonne's heart. I was dumb- struck with my own reckless impertinence. Had I blown it with this impulsive passionate kiss? Luckily I had no more blown it than I had sank the Titanic. This spontaneous kiss struck a vibrant note in our inner feelings for each other rippling through us as if a silver arrow had passed along our souls, like an unspoken promise, a sliver of shared togetherness yet to come.

It was a promise that was to be tested in the days that followed. Tested by none other then our very talented friend, the one and only Jimi Hendrix. Donovan and myself had work to do, a couple of gigs in the Midlands. This kept us away from the hotel for a few days and like a flipping idiot I forgot to take the Hotel's telephone number which meant I could not be in contact with Yvonne. It was to transpire that after our departure from the Hotel Yvonne, poor soul, contracted a painful and swollen sore throat.

The second day Jimi Hendrix was in London, Chas Chandler, his Manager and Lotte, Yvonne's life time friend, arrived along with Jimi at Yvonne's small flat to see if her condition was improving any. Yvonne had sketches and paintings spread around the living room floor hoping for inspiration for the growing mural in the club .She was working that day on black paper giving her designs a better atmosphere for the darkened Bar area where the mural was to be. When Jimi saw Yvonne's paints spread out on the carpet and her blank papers he asked if he could paint a picture. She was delighted and of course gave the go ahead. Jimi sat crossed legged in front of the virgin paper and before his assembled friends in a few minutes of deep concentration produced a magnificent Poster Colour painting. A spontaneous rendition of a Chinese style Carnival Mask done in brilliant greens yellows and orange paint. All there where amazed at Jimi's artistic efforts; no one knew Jimi could paint so well. Jimi, with a sweet smile said,

"Here, this one's for you ,Yvonne," and handed her the still wet painting. Yvonne was delighted with his work and Chas Chandler never one to miss an opportunity pipped-up with the thought that Jimi might also help Yvonne with her mural in the Bag o Nails Club.

Jimi replied in the affirmative, "Why not?"

A day later when Yvonne was feeling a bit better, Jimi did go to the Bag O' Nails in the wee morning hours and gave Yvonne some ideas and a hand in painting the mural suggesting she should use more vibrant colours and massive swirls of pigment like revolving rainbows. If Jimi suggested any other recreation to Yvonne that evening she would never say, but when I asked if Jimi had asked her out, there was a slight twinkle in her pretty eyes so I had a feeling he had. Luckily for me I was back in London to stake my romantic claim long before Jimi had set his sights with any determination on the young and beautiful Yvonne Pettersson. Jimi, but for my quick and spontaneous determination to woo Yvonne seriously could so easily have become my rival in love. Yvonne and Jimi had a natural affection and trust with each other. It showed sweetly in their fondness to each other in the forthcoming years that destiny was determined to have us meet as friends. Yvonne glued Jimi's painting on two bits of doweling rod and with a simple piece of string hung it on the wall of her rented flat. We were to hang it up together in the Hallway of our newly acquired flat on Wimbledon Common a few weeks later where it stayed for years.

A couple of days after this event Donovan and I returned to the hotel where we had reserved our old rooms after our contractual obligations had been performed. Chas Chandler was still around, working in the studio on bass rifts for the new upcoming Animals album tracks.

He was also arranging with Rick Gunnel the owner of the Bag O' Nails for the Premiere Performance of the then unknown Jimi Hendrix for the Musical Press and friends at Ricks newly renovated club. While Dono and I had been away Chas and Lotte had moved into the same double room in the hotel. Chas had generously insisted that Yvonne should also have a room in the Hotel near to her dear friend. He duly paid down two weeks rent for her.

Immediately I arrived back at the hotel I looked for and found Chas and Lotte they were swooning in the lounge. Laughing at their obvious ardor I asked Lotte if she would phone Yvonne and make a date for me that evening so I could help her once again with her mural. Lotte informed me Yvonne was on the last stages of her work and that she now lived at the hotel. When I asked for her room number Lotte refused to give it to me, but she did say with a wink she would let Yvonne know that I was still willing to give her a helping hand in the club.

"Ok Lotte, I'll wait for her here at nine thirty this evening," I said, excitement in my voice. At that meeting Yvonne's eyes shone whilst laying her pretty orbs on mine. We were like twin roses on the same stalk. If this was not Love then it was an incredibly good impersonation I thought. I felt once again blessed to have the certitude that this new love would be a strong love, as strong as my growing understanding for love could make it. Once again we left for the Bag O' Nails in a taxi, this time hand in hand.

When we reached the club I could see at a glance the mural was nearly complete. I could hardly wait for it to be finished. During the five hours or so of work left on the piece Yvonne and I looked more at each other than we did at the mural. Somehow we felt the few days we had spent apart were an empty lose of time. If it were at all humanly possible we had no intention of repeating that pain. At this point in our relationship I believed our course was set to last a lifetime. Dragging our eyes away from each other we looked to find Yvonne's mural finished.

We left the Club in the early hours finding a cafe to break our fast. Over this simple meal we two became one. Our souls entwined and our hearts beat ten to the dozen like ancient jungle drums, a percussive melody that was as old as the mountains uplifted plains. For a man to find a woman to love wholly and sincerely is an exuberant and satisfying fulfillment of his natural instincts.

We took a Taxi back to the Hotel here the day was just beginning for most people but our needs were for a shower and the comfort of a bed in which to find that heady narcotic sleep. Escorting Yvonne to the door of her room I left her to rest cooling my ardor for the time being in the thought of our next meeting. Curiously when faced by her door I experienced a monumental peace filled by an utmost belief in loving times yet to come

I awoke in the early afternoon to an urgent telephone call from Donovan.

"Gyp, wake up man its time you were here Mate we're going to see that flat on Wimbledon Common, remember," Donovan admonished me. "Come on Gyp George is picking us up at any minute as promised, he wants to show us the house of his friend, the Sculptor David Wynne. So get yer arse in gear Gypo cause I just heard Joani Baez is there too having her Portrait Sculpted. George is also arranging for us all to go for a bit to eat at the Rowalpindi an Indian restaurant he knows in Wimbledon Village. Do you want to bring Yvonne along, she's more than welcome, you know that mate."

"No Dono, I will leave her sleeping it was a long night," I said, trying desperately to wake up

"You Jammy Sod ," laughed Dono

"I don't mean it that way at all you old Bugger, I explained to Don. "We didn't even spend the night together as it happens."

"Plenty of time for that soon enough, Gypo" Donovan said happily.

"You've got that right mate" I replied in joy.

"Let me get me clothes on and I will be down in the lounge in two minutes," I answered.

As it happened, George Harrison the thoughtful and youngest Beatle was a little late too. As good as his word, George picked us up in his supped - up Mini and took us to Wimbledon. George drove well being a natural driver and a calm personality. As we progressed on our journey he chatted about his love for David Wynne and his Sculptures. His voice was full of intrigue as George explained to us he was trying to get a large piece of marble he had brought as a present for the sculptor to Wynne's Studio without letting the artist know in advance. For this subterfuge George had enlisted the help of Gilly Wynne, David's beautiful wife.

The Marble weighed about three tons and had unusual veins of colour running through it. George was convinced David would carve a masterpiece in it.

Our Beetle friend pulled into the front yard of the big Victorian house with a skid on the gravel drive and a loud shrill beep on the car horn. Gilly Wynne opened the door wide for us. She was all smiles, a total sunshine of a person was our Gillie Wynne. Her apron untied around her waist and an armful of Rolly, the latest Wynne child no more then three months old in her care, she was the epitome of the perfect Earth mother. Gilly showed us into the big kitchen where a huge Pine Wood Table dominated the bright cozy room. We could hear from what we presumed was the Artists Studio the sweet dulcet tones of Joan Baez singing on what I thought was a Record Player, but we soon realized this rendering was no recording. It was nothing more then her own masterful voice singing away in the echoing space of David' Sculpture Studio. I judged by this that the Portrait sitting must be over for that day. It was not long before Joani and ourselves were reunited. We hugged each other joyfully around that pine board in the kitchen. Sunshine streamed like a beacon through the large French Windows. Here through the clean glass panels we could see a well cared for garden. Growing rampant on the Wynne's grass lawn and dripping with berries was a huge mulberry tree. Under its leafy boughs and prominently displayed was a life-size bronze work of David's. A Reclining Female Nude, her legs spread open in abandonment and relaxed as only lovers can be in their own sphere of treasured intimacy, in a glance this sculpture spoke volumes to our sensibility Soon David Wynne, a larger than life character, entered the kitchen almost picking George up off his chair in a Bear Hug. Grinning fit to burst, emitting an energy like a whirlwind in a summer's heat we all in our turn received a hug from this obviously boisterous and caring artist. Gilly soon had tea and cakes on the table and we proceeded to talk the hind legs from that preverbal donkey as if we were one family. David Wynne was a Fan of Don's, although we had never met. He got out his mouth organ, found somewhere in the cracks and crevices of the kitchen and blew the Intro to Don's tune Catch the Wind. The young Edward, Gilly and David's eldest male child, ran into the room crying and flew straight into Joani's arms looking for solace after falling from the Mulberry tree. Joani made much of him in her American way; it was the most normal homely atmosphere possible. Dono and I would have taken the Flat before even looking at it if our neighbours and Landlord could be this man and his wonderful family. We were soon to meet two other children from Gilly's previous marriage, Niki and Johnny and what great kids they were too. David soon let us view the two floors of the Flat he had for rent. It was not massive by any means but it was homely, having two double bedrooms and a nice sizable bathroom upstairs a small but well fitted kitchen off of a hallway on the ground floor. But the really fantastic feature was the huge living room. This looked out through the small front garden to Wimbledon Common as did the upper bedrooms. All told it was perfect for us, smack- bang on the Commons edge and surrounded by the most beautiful Horse Chestnut trees I had ever seen.

It made for a charming quiet area, secluded yet not far from the hub of the city of London. I looked to Don and he gave me a wink of approval I winked back and said to David we would like to take the flat as soon as possible. David was very pleased that a more artistic set would be renting his premises

"You can have the flat as soon as you like," said our happy sculptor friend. We shook hands on the deal wide grins on our happy faces at the thought of our friendship yet to come.

"Want to come to the Restaurant to seal your deal with Don and Gypsy", George asked David.

"That would have been a delight George but I have to get back to the clay Portrait of Joan before it dries and cracks on the armature", Wynne said with a smile. "There's still a lot of work needed before I can put it under wet cloths for the night so I will have to reluctantly refuse your kind offer, another time George thank you."

Gilly went off and brought us the keys to our new home. It was a satisfying feeling to think we had a place to call our own again. We were happy and upbeat with the up-shot of our day's Flat hunting. We drove of in George's Mini to go get something to eat - ah, food glorious food. George could sure pick 'em - the Rowelpindi was the best Indian restaurant I had ever eaten in; well, technically Rowelpindi is on the border between India and Pakistan. Maybe that's what made the food taste so good.

That day with some advise from George Harrison, I discovered Chicken Malay plus Potato and Cauliflower Bharji, recommended by Don's favorite Beatle as two dishes that went well together. Dear George with his love for all things Indian was right and the afternoon flew by. After the meal we said our fare wells and thanked him with gratitude for showing us our new pad. We took Joan back in a taxi to the Savoy Hotel where she invited us up to her Suit and phoned Bob Dylan to come down to join us for some wine and a chat. Dylan was leaving for the States the next day so he popped his head in. We sat chatting over the wine but Bob could not stay long he was expecting Ginsburg the famous American Poet and our very good friend Deroll Adams the legionary Banjo player, they were to have a drink together. We wished Bob Bon Voyage and asked him to give our regards to Deroll and Allen. Allen Ginsberg we had last seen as his guest in his Brownstone Flat in Greenage Village U.S.of A, where he was determined to get us stoned on D.M.T. It was a fascinating visit, Ginsberg was rolling up and pouring the D.M.T. on the tobacco with great aplomb while a friend of his was making a psychedelic painting in oranges, yellows and reds on the walls and I believe ceiling of his large front room. I must admit I did not take to the D.M.T. but the original Painting we were privileged to watch happening was amazing. We didn't stay much longer with Joan that day; we had a lot to organize now we had a flat to think about. It was a great feeling and Donovan wanted to get on the phone to call Enid Stulberger, a beautiful young American girl he had spent time with in the States. He intended to put a proposition to her, one he hoped she could not refuse that she should come to England and share his life with him in our new found home on Wimbledon Common .

I intended to put a similar proposition to my new love and growing passion, the nubile Yvonne. Donovan and I saw no reason why we four could not live in happy harmony in our new flat on that as yet Un-Wombled Wimbledon Common. It would be an experiment Dono and I had not tried in the annuals of our personal history. We had never shared any of our flats with live-in girlfriends since being a part of the music business. We had of course shared our individual beds with many a willing maiden. A few nights, even a couple of weeks duration was not unheard of but much longer we both found unappealing due in part to a youthful longing for a certain freedom. A freedom to choose from the multitude of beautiful ladies fate had walk into our enchanted lives. Why ever not for pity's sake we were both young and the temptations faced were extreme to say the least. Our sexual appetites appealed just fine to our less mature testosterone driven minds up to this point. Now it appeared Donovan and I were feeling the self same need to commit ourselves to a longer more permanent partnership with the spirited opposite sex. I had been in this rather uplifting state of near-marriage a few times before in my roving life, my mate Donovan on the other hand had not as of yet experienced this matrimonial style of living. For my part I was looking forward to the pleasures of sharing my everyday life with the same girl in a loving and long-lasting relationship. It was becoming apparent to my mind and inner state of being that I was missing this intimacy somewhat. We had been so busy ridding the superficial Surf of Fames exaggerated waves that I was discovering a rather desperate need in me to find a calm sandy and gentle sunny bay of feelings in which to dry out my sodden and battered soul.

It appeared Donovan and I were taking a lot for granted from our respected ladies at that moment in time. We lived in great and stupendous hopes for a blessed future. Hopes that were in-fact mostly fulfilled for me in the days and years to come. That evening I took Yvonne on our first real date .We went to an Arabesque Restaurant where I knew the owner. Abbass was a dear and treasured friend who originated from Iraq. In his youth he had been a political player, a rebel who for his deeds and believes was thrown in prison where he waited for his death sentence to be fulfilled. However before they could put Abbass to death he escaped. From then on he lived in exile in England banned from his beloved Country. His crime was to attempt to overthrow the Government and kill its President.

Needles to say Abbass was a strong and great character who saw me through his caring eyes and warm heart as his younger brother. Possibly he saw in me the rebellious nature that must have been similar to his own personality in his younger years. Don and I had first been brought to this establishment by Georgie Fame the Solo Singer who later at another juncture joined Alan Price of the Animals to record that great album, The Price of Fame. Abbass had a perfectly respectable and cared for English style family tucked away in a large flat near to his Restaurant whom he loved to distraction. His business however made for a different world in which he felt more akin with his Arabic nature. The warm atmosphere of his restaurants interior plus the constant reminders by the food smells of his longed for country made Abbass a different man there then on the streets at the heart of London's dark and dank Victorian atmosphere. He felt younger, bolder, more attuned to his Arab soul and the freedoms associated with his former protected and reasonably coddled lifestyle (before his arrest and imprisonment for treason and attempted murder).

For these reasons his restaurant was set up as a home away from home .Here he spent time with his old friends and companions smoking the occasional hooker pipe with them in peace and harmony while discussing the fate of his beloved country. This restaurant was a rare find for Dono and myself an island of tranquility in a sea of sanity. A total delight to eat in get high in and listen to the ancient melodies of Arabic music. In short I became an honoured member of Abbass's other family in which he seemed indeed like my caring elder brother and as Yvonne was my choice of lady Abbass made her especially at home in his warm establishment treating her like an honored princess. Yvonne was not used to this treatment it gave the evening a magical transformed feeling. Good food, good wine, good music and good company, the homely feeling and above all the belief in the momentous importance of the occasion set partly in motion by my friend, filled the evening with a sparkle. It made it easy for me to put my proposition to Yvonne and easy for her to accept. It set the mood for our first night of love in our hotel on our return from the goodbyes of Abbas. Dear brother that he was he stood on the pavement outside his restaurant waving us off as if our honeymoon had just begun. In a way I guess it had at that.

Don and I were not the only ones to find a Pad that week. On seeing Chas Chandler the following morning he told me he had just closed a deal on a flat in the middle of London in a tall block of exclusive rentals. Chas Lotte and Jimi were to share this modern home for quite a while. Chas having paid a fortnights rent on Yvonne's room there was no hurry for her to move out. This left me plenty of time to paint our new flat. I enjoyed the act of decorating it was something my Father taught me when I helped him sometimes as a way to earn a little extra cash for our family holidays. I was about ten years old when I started with him and loved every minute of this work, so over the years I learned a lot. Getting down to the work in Wimbledon I would send for Yvonne by taxi while I stripped the old wall paper from the large Victorian rooms. I was in two minds as to what colours to paint the large front room. Asking Yvonne's opinion we came up with a wonderful idea of pink ,violet and olive green which although a daring experiment turned out extremely well. I soon moved a double bed into what was to be our bedroom so I could stay the night if need be while I worked on the old place. Here Yvonne and I partook of intriguing tea and dinner breaks whilst wearing the room in, so to speak. Lotte would call Yvonne to join Chas Jimi and herself for an evening's simple entertainment while she knew I was working away on the flat. I was a little weary about this as I knew Jimi was interested in Yvonne. She had told me on a previous evening they had sat talking about paintings while Yvonne sketched and I had been shown a painting Jimi did for her, which rightly or wrongly I believed was an obvious Come-On on Jimi's part.

Days later there was a Happening that could have been a disaster. This series of events made my mind up not to let Yvonne out of my sight ever again. On this occasion at Chas, Lotte and Jimi's new Pad. they had each dropped a tab of Acid on which they were tripping away quite nicely, thank you very much, when Yvonne, unused to taking such drugs, phoned me up. She told me quite calmly that Jimi and her were sitting on the sill of an open window six floors up while Jimi explained to Yvonne that if they wanted too they could fly out the window and swoop about like pigeons on the wing. Thank God Yvonne had the sense to phoned me, she was quite innocent as fare as drugs were concerned and in that frame of mind, captured by the Acid, it is very easy to think it possible to fly. It was Jimi telling her this and Jimi had never lied to her yet ..

Yvonne knew I had taken lots of different drugs in my time thus the phone call. In the background I could hear Jimi saying, "Let's fly baby, let's fly", in an excited and strident sounding voice, very unusual for the normally subdued and gentle sounding Jimi. I knew I had to be very careful with what I said although my heart was beating ten to the dozen.

"Listen to me Sweetheart, forget about flying for now. would you? Please get Chas to sit Jimi down away from the open window. In fact love, a better idea is to let me have Chas on the phone. Put Chas on the phone for me Yvonne, could you do that for me love?'

Thank God Chas came to the phone at the first call from Yvonne

"Hi Chas how you doing mate? Yes I'm great, I'm sorry I couldn't come over tonight but listen Chas. Jimi's a bit… out of it mate. He's suggesting to Yvonne they can fly out of your kitchen window. Yes, for sure they can't fly, but I know Jimi thinks they can. For God's sake take his mind away from the open window; get him involved in something else before there is a disaster. Then do me a stupendous favor - put Yvonne in a cab when she comes down enough from her high and send her to me in a Taxi would yer? Don't thank me Chas, its cool man, sounds like some strong shit that Acid. Get Jimi's head away from the idea of flying and all will be cool I'm sure. Yer, I know you will look after Yvonne for me, that's wonderful Chas. Yep she is an incredible Chick, oh and Chas save us some of that Acid if possible would you, it seems good stuff . O.K. see you soon and thanks Chas, cheers."

I was relieved to hear Chas was so With- It on the phone. Chas was always such a caring person but in the great frame of a body he inhabited, some people thought him pushy and overbearing, which was mostly not true. I knew all would be fine now and judged that in a few hours Yvonne would be safely by my side.
I was to insist she move in with me a couple of days after this worry was well and truly out of the way. Donovan and I often went shopping down the Fulham Road, Portobello Road and parts of Chelsea for Antiques in the early days of furnishing our Pad. We had similar tastes in furniture and liked big Edwardian style dressers and Cupboards made of Pine Wood these we put in the large living room. We both loved art nouveau; Don's sensibilities even spreading to Art Deco which I found a little too mathematical for my tastes, although I could dig some of the earlier stuff that were still influenced by the floral and flowing styles of art nouveau, which mingled so well with my Cancerian Water Character.

Don had a great sense of Mix and Match in general but at times in fashion he went out on a limb unknown to modern styles of dress. For example, a little known fact, it was Donovan who invented Floral Shirts. Not the big prints of the Hawaiian casual shirt so loved by the American GIs; no, a small and delicate floral print on well cut and tailored designs, this sort of shirt had never been seen before. These shirts became so much the Rage in the mid sixties that even businessmen wore them. This came about innocently enough as I remember. We bumped into Mick Jagger on Carnaby Street one afternoon; he was buying stage gear from Lord Johns if I remember correctly. We got talking about shirts and Jagger gave us the name and address of a great tailor of shirts that he used on stage. In due course we went to see this tailor after which we went to Liberty's Department Store to buy material. On the spur of the moment Dono found some really fantastic floral materials, lovely prints exclusive to Liberty's. We brought yards of different cloth as Don was going crazy for shirts at the time. The manager of the department was informed that the famous Donovan was buying their material. Being a bright spark he asked us what we intended to do with the printed cloth we were purchasing from their glorious establishment. The managers eyes lifted skyward on hearing of Donovan's proposed use and he shivered at the very thought of what Don wanted to do with their priceless goods but wisely he asked Don if he would bring in and show him the finished shirts. Having promised to do so, a few weeks later the finished articles were brought into the store. The manager was duly impressed with the result (the shirts turned out better then I had imagined that's for sure) that three weeks later Liberty's had their own floral shirts for sale at unbelievably expensive prices. This style of shirt did so well the manager for his business acumen if for nothing else should have been put on the board of directors. A few months later flowered shirts could be brought in shops on the high street that sold such weird and wonderful wares. Thus they became Hip, sought after the width and breadth of the land, then the World, all from a simple idea of my old Mate Donovan .

CHAPTER TWENTY ONE
BREAKING UP IS HARD TO DO

Enid duly arrived from the then fairly reasonable if War tormented United States. The young lovers fell into a stupor of erotic love and passion rarely felt by either of them in their short lives as lovers. Locking themselves away for days and reappearing ruffled and crumpled from their sagging double bed like well worn sheets, their sex tainted disarray, charming. Yvonne and myself were in a similar state of Being also. Our new flat picked up the atmosphere as friends popping in would smile from ear to ear in response to the unconscious feelings of lust generated by us all. These were the good old days of contentment and calm in our foursome of family. Yvonne and I appeared at about six in the evening just as Dono and Enid were off to bed. In the spacious living room Yvonne and I were creative most evenings, Yvonne Painting while I wrote Poetry and re-wrote my children's book Sandylea started on Paros Greece. The Kitchen took on new meaning for Dono and myself. Instead of the very simple meals of beans eggs and toast and spaghetti snacks that Don and I made between cafes and restaurant visits we were treated to clean and tasty Swedish food or American homemade dinners. With the difference in times of our use of the flat, Yvonne and I would eat breakfast at Don and Enid's evening meal; our evening meal we would sometimes share with Don and Enid as their breakfast. Yvonne usually ended up cleaning all our plates then the kitchen of Enid's cooking exploits. In general young Swedish Girls of that time were a lot tidier then young American ladies of the same elk .It was not a problem at first, nor was the upkeep of the big front room or the shared bathroom, until it became apparent to my mind that Yvonne was doing all the work .

It felt, rightly or wrongly, Enid was relishing the attitude of using Yvonne as General Maid and Cleaner to our establishment. Yvonne was a softer soul in spirit then Enid so naturally I did not like her being treated in this offhand manner. To my mind Enid was trying to rough shod her way through the responsibilities in the flat by putting the upkeep on Yvonne's very pretty shoulders. I didn't like it; it felt as if Enid believed Yvonne below her in the Pecking Order of things. Enid was the girlfriend of the Star and Yvonne was just with the Star's friend and business associate in her mind's eye. A different class of person it would seem. I knew Enid was not used to giving herself Airs, she had a normal down to earth upbringing as her father was a New York Taxi Driver. I tried saying something to Enid and after awhile to Dono but he seemed oblivious to what was going on in a domestic way around our household. We had never had any problems of this sort before in our shared flats. Oh well, let it pass, it will work itself out one way or another, I thought. If only Enid could see how unfair it was on Yvonne. Not that Yvonne seemed to mind greatly. In her family in Sweden she had been trained in household affairs as a matter of course, her Grandmother being of the Old School. It was me getting peeved by the unfairness of the situation and I found it was getting on my nerves. Dono was a lot more cool, but then it was not his girl being put on.

"It's only plates Gypo and who gives a fuck if the place is tidy or untidy, we never worried about that sort of thing before, man" Donovan explained to me one evening. And he was right, we never had some girl or other would take on the job of tidying up for us so we never bothered with the necessities of household matters. Definitely male indoctrinated stuff but then at that time in history men were not expected to care about the machinations on the household front. It came to a head for me when Enid brought Yvonne a load of her and Don's dirty laundry. She demanded Yvonne wash it for her in our newly bought washing machine.

"Fuck off Enid and wash yer own dirty shit, for Christ sake" I shouted at her, protecting Yvonne from this physiological warfare. Dono and myself were off working quite a lot and it appeared the girls got on very well then. I presumed in that case it was a sort of inverted jealousy thing on the part of Enid over Yvonne and the perceived possible threat to Enid's nest egg in the form of Donovan. Not that Enid was so mercenary in this way, it's just that she was used to a harder reality in her dealings of romance. Protecting your own interests being uppermost on the list of the American Program of Love. Apart from these looming problems the flat on Wimbledon Common was wonderful. Don and I were working hard but there was plenty of time for walks on the common and forays into a quaint secondhand book shop selling Edwardian and Victorian books at knock down prices. Wimbledon Village really was a village in those days and off the beaten track. Our Pad was beginning to attract a few musicians to its warm and usually friendly atmosphere. Chas Chandler, Lotte and Jimi often came as well as Graham Bond. Paul and his love Jane Asher, the young and talented film star popped in once or twice. Maddy Prior and Danny Thompson met at our flat during the time they were forming that fantastic group The Pentangle, with Bert Jansch and John Renbourn. Our dear friend and the first musician on the road with us, Mac Macloud turned up whenever he was in England. At this time he was spending a lot of time in Sweden where he was getting a new band together. Graham Nash loved relaxing on our large sofas and chatting to Donovan and myself. Graham Bond was fast becoming a good friend with Donovan too. Dono and he would spend hours discussing strange ideas to do with musical instruments.

One of these being the colour organ which I would have loved to see invented, interested as I would have been in the results. I had read somewhere that colours as well as sound were nothing but vibrations when you came right down to it. We were causing a lot of excitement with the concert Dono was planning to give at the Royal Albert Hall. We wondered with a little trepidation how the Music Press would take to the musical extravagance Donovan was planning for the opening of this Gig of Gigs. Donovan wanted to use Jazz Musicians, Rock and Roll Musicians plus Orchestrated Strings, Harpsichords plus Wind Instruments and a full Orchestra Percussion Section. All this was to be in the care of the very inventive baton of our Arranger and dear friend John Cameron. John would work miracles with Don's songs setting the mood of these songs to perfection. Donovan and he found they had the same interests in a wide musical acceptance. They also felt deeply for one another in a natural warmhearted genuine way. Mickie Most had brought them together with his genius for blending personalities and talent. Mickie was a welcome visitor to our Pad on the Common in those early days of their partnership and I remember him seeming paranoid about Paul McCartney's visits with us. He was afraid Paul might get ideas for their prolific albums from the new style music Dono and he were producing. I knew that Paul, being the nice guy he was and with his phenomenal gift for writing songs himself, would never do anything so crass. Months in the future from the time I am writing about, Paul invited Yvonne and myself to his Pad in St Johns Wood to celebrate the American Holiday of Thanksgiving with his new girlfriend Linda and her beautiful child. It was fun and Linda served us among other food some button mushrooms in a cold salad sauce. The mushrooms were raw I remember and although they tasted very good, it was the first time I realized normal mushrooms could be eaten uncooked. No earth shattering knowledge I must admit but something I remember to this day. Also we could not help but notice how truly fond of Linda's little girl Paul was becoming even then. I don't blame him either, for she was charm itself and as cute as a button with the tip of her nose painted black like a young puppy. Whiskers painted by Linda at just the right angle finished off this deception very adroitly. Linda was at home with her and Paul's table it was easy to observe her obvious love of cooking and food. They made a very natural couple, which I realized was what he and Jane Asher had never been. It seemed to my mind they had always been individuals in a relationship, not a couple as such. Well good luck, I thought, knowing how lucky Paul would be to find a simple but real love in the madness of our lives as we were living it then. I too was finding this simple but real love with my darling Yvonne and just as happy for this fact as Paul McCartney and Linda Eastman were. The lively, intelligent , hugely good looking Beatle Paul was to go on to marry his Linda as indeed I was to go on to marry my Yvonne , for sure at that time in our history we were not to know that and would have laughed at you for suggesting such a thing, two wild and free young men. Such is life and all the more interesting for it.

Before the Concert at the Royal Albert Hall, Dono and I were in the studio a lot for the new songs that eventually became the tracks for the Mellow Yellow Album. As I remember it the song Mellow Yellow was arranged by the affable nice natured and vastly talented John Paul Jones, although the first playing was a bit too strident for Don's taste. Mickie Most liked the Stripper feel though, Donovan however wanted the sound a bit more mellow but could not describe what he meant. One of the Jazz musicians said;

"I know what Don means, he wants the 'Ard 'Ats."

The Hard Hats where duly put on the trumpets and brass and the sound was perfect exactly as Donovan heard it in his mind's eye. Mickie Most had us make a film for the promotion of this single where he literally hired a Stripper to take her clothes off in a field on a very very cold morning. We were also in the field but sitting like spoiled Brats comfortably in Mickie's Gold Plated Rolls Royce, warm and snug with the engine running for the heat that was in it. This short film also included me and Don on horseback where I seem to be at home dashing off at breakneck speed on the horse's withers, whereas the bloody horse had in fact got it into its head to take off like greased lightning with me terrified on its back. Both feet free of the stirrups looking for a safe place to jump off; this insane animal crested a small hill. By some miracle I was still glued on its prancing back and in the dell below a herd of cows panicked by me and this mad horse bolted off as if the very Devil had made an appearance amongst them. I deemed it prudent to remain bouncing on me Gullies rather then be trampled to death by a herd of desperate Milking Cows. Mickie was very happy with this film and laughed himself silly at my groans of pain .It was Aired on Ready Steady Go or one of the Pop Musical Television Shows I was told, although to this day I have not seen it personally.

That winter found us warm and cozy in our shared flat on Wimbledon Common, David Wynne and his beautiful family our direct neighbours and friends in the Victorian house. Donovan took stock and found he had five hit singles, two hit E.Ps, three hit albums and two new singles all lately in the American charts, as well as Europe and England. We were doing very well thank you. Not bad for a couple of penniless bums quite recently from the shores of Cornwall's enchanting coastline.

By mid January Donovan and I were sitting on our Loral's after the Concert at The Royal Albert Hall. It was a sell out and we hoped the happy punters would be glad Donovan was back in the lime-light yet again. One evening Dono returned home with two dogs that were brothers, one a dark blue and black Collie and a black and tan character that had mischief written all over his bemused and endearing puppy face. Donovan and Enid had the Collie and called it Banjo. Yvonne and I had the little black and tan monster calling him Magnus. I was fast becoming a Number One fan of David Wynne's Sculpture, spending a lot of time in his studio. We talked about art, sculpture in particular, I learning unconsciously all I could by watching intently as David worked, showing me how it was done and explaining little details of form and shape, which for some unknown reason I seemed to have the understanding for already. David Wynne it turned out was totally self taught in the realms of his art, although he had been to Cambridge University to study Anatomy. It was during this tuition that he realised his love of form and his understanding of it naturally led him to Ancient Greek Sculpture. His Farther a Sea Captain bankrolled his youngest son, helping David with his first Studio. From some of his connections from Cambridge University he met a very interesting fella by the name of Alistair McAlpine, a younger son too. Alistair McAlpine became David's patron for many years, buying everything that David made and also getting him the house on Wimbledon Common, having his builders refurbish it for David and his young family. Alistair brought sculptures for the bills instead of wanting cash, which was a huge help for David. Oh, if all Serious Sculptors could find such a person to help them, this World would be an Artistic Heaven

We were going off on the road again on a short European tour. Just before we left Donovan received the good news he was to become a father. I hoped that Donovan's obvious joy at the acceptance of this news would make Enid feel more secure. Usually reactions speak louder than words and Donovan's reactions were over the moon. Unfortunately, in Enid's case the strain in all our relationships became more apparent, the more she grew the more the rift between us grew. Some little time later Donovan and I came back from another tour of Scandinavia where we had a chance to talk over our problems of domestic bliss, or domestic blisters, as it was fast becoming. I asked Don if he intended to marry Enid and received the answer as a negative.

"Well Dono if you don't give Enid the security of marriage when she's in the position she's in my old mate, we are never going to have harmony in our home."

Dono saw this plainly but no way could he see himself as a Married Man .

"Ok Gyp. I will get me father to look for another pad for Enid myself and the baby. Our flat in Wimbledon would not be cool anyway for a child, not with the road in front." Dono said in reflection. "Gyp I suppose I knew this was about to happen man, I've been putting it to the back of my mind because I really don't want to face this fact me old mate."

"Well Dono, I don't want it either, but something has to be done. Shall Yvonne and I look for a pad of our own, would that be easier?"

"No way man, you both stay. You and Dave get on so well having the same love of sculpture in your souls; it would be a shame for you to have to leave. No, the old man will find me and Enid a place in the country of Hertfordshire." Dono said beaming. "I see us as a happy family living by a stream in woods in an old cottage surrounded by lush green countryside."

"Can't be so bad," I reflected. "Sounds like a good place to bring up kids and you've got plenty of the readies to buy it with so no-problem there," I said, feeling relaxed and happy for them.

"It will make Enid a lot more content knowing there is just the three of you to worry about "

"You're right Gyp, sometimes I get the impression that Enid's so uptight because she really wants you and Yvonne's approval and feels she isn't getting it"

"I never thought of it like that Dono, but maybe your right. O.k.,. We will make a supreme effort to show Enid that we don't dislike her. Actually we don't dislike her at all and she is going to be the mother of your child mate. Wonderful"

A few days later, Donald Leitch, Donovan's rather unusual father, found the perfect cottage in the location that Don had been dreaming of. A sixteenth century building tastefully restored to a more modern style while keeping the charm of its origins. Enid was delighted with the cottage too, as it had an old feel not found in most American houses. In fact the house was older than America, well older than The United States of America anyway. We tend to forget that the Native Red Indians lived on this land for thousands of years.

One of their heroines was a girl called Buffy St Marie; she wrote an incredible track called Soldier Blue which later was used in a film about the cruel treatment to the native people by the American Government Soldiers .

Buffy, herself from Indian stock wrote the song that Donovan made his own and a hit for himself, The Universal Soldier. This song I had first heard performed by Idriss, my then girlfriend in St.Ives Cornwall when I had been on the run.

But I digress ....

Donovan, before the Albert Hall Concert even, was beginning to conceive some of the songs for what would become the double album A Gift From a Flower to a Garden. He had three or four of these songs penned but needed the influence of his knew-found cottage to realise his concept. Donovan was to become his own producer on this double album when the time of its consummation was to arrive. He did such a good job of it too that Mickie Most was happy enough to have it under his name as contracts demanded it to be. Mickie also received the tidy sum that was the producer's right and put aside for him. A very nice present he must have thought.

It wasn't till I started living alone with Yvonne in the Wimbledon Flat that I needed a wage packet, as I rarely needed money for myself up till that point. I wished for little as a rule, of course my daily living was taken care of and I had money whenever I needed it for whatever purpose. Donovan used to say in the early days in all his interviews with the press that he and I were to share the money earned Fifty –Fifty, which I believed was his wish. It was my wish not to take the money; I had no need of it.

More important to my way of thinking was my experiences throughout life and these were very unusual and I could learn a lot by these experiences and get to see the world, which was great. I knew that if ever I wanted money for anything it would be there for me. In fact I was thinking of buying my mother a cream tea establishment in Devon. I asked Estate Agencies to look around for a place on several occasions but my dear mother thought it too much to except from me. Silly as I believed it to be, I respected her decision, thinking I would buy them a place as a surprise one day

But as it turned out I never had the time to look for a teahouse for them. Shame really, as I felt I owed my mother something nice for all the heart ache I had brought her by leaving home so young. A little recompense for the worry and pain I had brought her for not knowing my fate as a young man, this being the worst of it for her.

The last interview I allowed myself to do in the early days was an interview where the girl interviewing me mixed up what I had told her of my actions as a nine year old with my actions on leaving home at fifteen, making it appear as though I went back home often to torment my parents after leaving. Even these supposed actions of mine if they had happened would have been greeted with joy by my brokenhearted mother. At least she would have known I was alive and well enough to be behaving in such a dastardly fashion.

Let me tell you its very annoying to be miss- quoted or have total drivel written about yourself for all the world to read as if it came from your own mouth. It beholds those with the responsibility to write for newspapers or magazines to report correctly and as accurately as possible things stated in an interview. The interviewee puts themselves in the reporter's power and it should be a natural right to have the truth of what is said be published. I felt a fool for months after reading this false statement in this particular music paper every time I remembered it.

This was the reason I said no to any more music paper interviews. At least it made me see how unbearable it was for Donovan when the reporting of what he said was ridiculously misquoted. I sat in on all interviews Donovan did from then on. Soon the portable tape recorder was to come into its own, making it considerably easier for the reporter to follow the statements made rather then rely on their own scribbled short-hand notes.

There was one exception to this general malaise and that was a chap named Keith Altham. He worked for The Melody Maker as well as other magazines like NME. Keith reported factually even if sometimes tongue in cheek, and he had a wicked sense of humor He became a very good friend of mine and many other people from the music business of that and later times. Keith left reporting and started his own P.R. company. It was very successful and it took him into the lives of many artists with his ever knowing interests in the music game. Altham is one of the true characters of the music business and was as well known as many an artist from the period, his fame, stretching from the very early sixties to the mid nineties. I think the only major group he didn't have anything to do with was the Beatles. It was Keith who suggested to Chas Chandler that Jimi Hendrix should set fire to his guitar on stage, thus making a landmark in modern music. He left Chas to work out the mechanisms of that trick and how it could be used on stage. Jimi managed it with the help of lighter fluid. As the combustion element was so dangerous, Jimi could have so easily burnt his fingers to the bone, especially on that first occasion but he was lucky and got away with just one burn. He soon learned how to make his guitar flame without losing skin, but it was still a bloody dangerous thing to do so he was advised by Chas to give it up. His fame as a master of the electric guitar would soon spread like fire anyway, making his name burn into history like the Firebrand he was on stage. There has been unconfirmed talk lately that Jimi was murdered, some say by Mike Jeffreys, Chas Chandler's business partner of the time who was supposedly into the American Mafia for a million dollars or so. I do know for a fact, because Chas told me with his own lips, the night before Jimi died that Jimi had been on the phone begging Chas to handle him again after a splitting of their ways. Chas I know complied with his request but only on the terms that Jimi was to boot-out all his American hangers on which would include Mike Jeffreys, Chandler's estranged business partner.

Life went on smoothly enough for all of us and I decided to concentrate on my own creativity during the days of no work. After my never to be forgotten experience life modeling for David Wynne's piece called The Tynne God and all our conversations in his studio during these working sessions, I was becoming passionate with my own attempts at sculpting. I realized sculpture was taking over my other creative endeavors in painting, book writing and poetry. David Wynne encouraged me in every way he could in my sculptural efforts convinced as he was that I was a natural sculptor.

CHAPTER TWENTY TWO
HENDRIX'S DEMISE

Going back to my comments on Jimi. Now my friends I am not saying in any way that the information of poor Jimi Hendrix's demise contained in the last chapter is true in any way shape or form. It's just another brick in the wall of ideas that circulate after a well known personality dies unexpectedly. I can tell you that Chas Chandler, God bless his soul, was appalled at the news he received and the way he was informed about Jimi's tragic death. This by way of a newspaper reporter phoning him in the early hours of the morning to seek out his reaction to the untimely death of Chas's protégée. Chas had no idea that Jimi was no more with us until this rude awakening by a reporter. This appalling news for Chas was to be at the end of 1970, September 18 If I remember rightly, just over a month from my son's birth in October.

In this epistle you are reading now we are still in the innocent times of Jan 1967 and Jimi was about to become a superstar in his own right, not die as one.

Many strange experiences were awaiting in the wings for me around this time. For instance before the Albert Hall gig Donovan had me go to Positarni on the southern coast of Italy to pursue a wonderful woman, our dear friend Valley. My mission was to ask her if she could see her way clear to perform a spontaneous dance on the stage of the Albert Hall. She had the choice of any of Donovan's tunes she wished to dance to. Relaying Donovan's message, the dear girl answered in the positive saying she would gladly come. When I asked Valley what she would like as payment for her performance she instantly said " One Nubian goat, would be lovely Gypsy" .

"Rubbish," I said, " You must have at least a pair of the buggers" at which she roared with laughter at the thought of the air flights, the hotel and the dance she was expected to perform at the Royal Albert Hall. I must say I saw the novelty too as Valley and her man Ruddi lived in a fallen down chapel hidden away down a deserted overgrown track invisible to most eyes.

There is a true and wondrous story about our lovely Valley, I heard it strait from Ruddi's lips (and had indeed met the young animal mentioned.) The story had to do with a beautiful young fox cub. Ruddi and Valley were now painters (Valley having been a well known modern dancer in her youth). They loved the secluded spot they had found in Italy. Here they spent many hours a day painting with nothing to distract them from their work. One morning partaking a vigorously healthy walk, Valley found in their path a dying young fox cub. Valley possessing a soft and gentle soul could not look on this tragedy with hard eyes. Picking the softly barking fox up she took it to their home in the chapel where Valley attempted to nurse it back to health. The food or the tender feelings from the soul of Valley worked wonders. The endearing wild creature returned to life, adopting our two friends as its parents. Valley in particular had what would be called an unusual re-pore with this young beast. They gained subconscious understanding of each other way beyond ordinary knowledge between animal and man. As the fox began to grow, it found a natural way of fitting in with them in the small and charming fallen down chapel. At night the growing fox would hunt, roaming around in the different quarters of the moon. One evening Valley, fast asleep, had a dream of their beloved fox. This was a reoccurring dream where she and the fox hunted together, but on this night Valley woke up with an agonizing crick to her neck. The pain would not let her turn her head one excruciating inch. Valley was in such violent distress she could not sleep more that night. The following day the pain stayed with her and she could not move her head from the angle it was stuck at. Ruddi became frightened for Valley's hurt saying they must find a doctor, but Valley would not hear of it. Their little beautiful fox had not returned from its nights wonderings and she did not want the creature to find the church empty on its return.

"Don't worry Ruddi, my neck will get better soon." Valley said .

A few hours passed and Valley's neck was no better. She lay hoping for respite from the pain, her head being filled by the thoughts of the fox, which had still not returned. Thoughts loomed ever larger in her mind until she could think of nothing else but her missing fox cub. Valley realized the more she thought about their fox the more she was convinced their young charge was also in pain.

What could have happened? Valley persuaded Ruddi to pack up work on his painting and come with her to look for their beloved wild animal. The walk was very hard for Valley, no matter what she did she could not move her head to a straight position, she had to amble forward with her eyes and head at a strange angle. They searched and searched in the surrounding area, winding up in all the places the young fox loved to go. Suddenly, the pain in Valley's neck became unbearable and she screamed out

"Ah, he is near Ruddi, " she moaned and stumbled on towards a covered bank her neck in such distress she crooned fit to die. Valley fell forward and let the incline take her. Ruddi followed in despair at her pain. She rolled on and on into a jumbled pile of leaves. "Ah he's nearby I can feel him," she moaned in utter despair. "Look, there, under the bush," Valley deplored her man, her hands trying to hold up a neck that looked to Ruddi as if it had been broken in her fall.

"But you're hurt Valley, let me look at you," Ruddi shouted at her in shock.

"No my love, don't worry about me, look for our dear fox. He's over there Ruddi." Valley said pointing to a hidden spot under the bushes.

Not quite knowing what he was doing, Ruddi did as Valley advised. Crouching down low he cleared the debris in his way and there to his dismay was the fox.

But here is the strangest of things. The poor animal had its head held tight by the neck at a cruel angle by a man- trap, its blunted teeth all but severing the fox's head from its young body. The man-trap was pinned down to the earth by a metal stake on a rusted open- link chain

"Have you found him Ruddi?" Valley called out.

"Yes I have, he's in a trap and barely alive. I will take him out as carefully as I can, but there is no help for him Valley, he's as good as gone." Ruddi stepped on one end of the man-trap and pulled outward until the spring gave way, and the blooded fox slid out of the metal jaws into Ruddi's arms. The instant the fox was free from the vice like grip the pain around Valley's neck disappeared. She ran forward to take the dying fox into her arms. Valley and the dying fox looked eye to eye for a few moments when the young animal gave a small bark, a shudder and a lick to Valley's hand. It then died with a long drawn out sigh. Ruddi and Valley carried their fox friend home to bury it somewhere special to them. The amazing thing was Valley could now walk home quite normally, not one tiny twinge of pain in her neck now that the fox was free.

This, my friends, is a true story. It shows how interconnected we are with the natural world around us. If we can see it and feel it like dear Valley and the fox we could add worlds to our understanding.

Valley's subsequent dance on the polished boards of the Royal Albert Hall while Donovan sang one of his sensitive ballads went down a storm. Valley brought the fresh salt breezes and free flowing spirit of the coast of Italy with her. She brought too the sun filled wonder of her creative life and it was as if a spell of freedom had fallen like a fisherman's net over all that saw her dance. A certain kind of perception opened up for us that night and through the mixture of melody song and dance, doors of another reality were thrown open with such gentle force I remember that night as if yesterday

Always influenced by nature, Don's songs took on a more natural essence. He was painting with words, with rhythm, things he was observing in his daily excursions into the woods and fields around his cottage. Although always a Troubadour at source, it was here that Donovan touched an older spirit in himself. It was around this time on one of our many tours of Scandinavia we were booked to do a gig in the luxurious surroundings of The Royal Opera House in Gothenburg Sweden. It was a mistake by the bookers. The Opera House believed Donovan was a folk singer of the Eighteenth Century tradition. A serious singer of German, French, Italian style ballads sung in a casual operatic way, usually accompanied by a virtuoso piano player. A few days before the sell out concert began, the organisers and owners found out they were to have their wonderful velvet seated and carved guilt hall filled to the brim with screaming demented teenagers. Horror of horrors, what to do? They were under contract so they offered us a mountain of money not to do the gig. Dono and I would not hear of that. We would not disappoint hundreds of fans who rightly would be unhappy. I tried to convince them that Don's fans would treat their place with the respect it deserved. They panicked outrageously, offering us an even bigger mountain of money. We just laughed and carried on preparing for the gig. Something touched Donovan on that night's performance. Was it a long lost talent, possibly from previous lifetimes of musical skill? Was it a talent that had been resting in the very integrity of his being not leaving his eternal soul through many transfigurations? It gave him a musical authority far and away greater than his few short years on this earth could have assumed.

On that beautiful stage in front of hundreds of dumb- struck fans I watched my best mate become a master, a man of profound natural artistic musical expertise. I was so proud of him and felt for him that night as the audience experienced the unearthly sense and knowledge of his ancient genius, lifting them to new highs of creative understanding. Donovan had arrived yet again, he had re- invented himself on a new level and I was to insist that we only performed at concert halls from that moment on, if at all possible.

Life went on and in the peace of our Wimbledon flat, Yvonne and I felt our love grow to such an extent that one night after a love poem had made its strange journey through the portals of my romantic mind I asked Yvonne to marry me. Yvonne was very excited and agreed sweetly to my request

Not wishing to delay this idea we went to the registry office in New Maldon to find out exactly what would be needed if we got married there. We were kindly given all the information, also a date for the ceremony a couple of months in the future; they were pretty much booked up, marriage still being all the rage. Needless to say what with one thing and another Yvonne and I totally forgot about our proposed wedding. Three days before the momentous event Yvonne said very casually,

"Are we not to get married in a few days Gyp?"

"Bloody hell you are right my sweet," I said, realizing it was up to me to pull me finger out and get on with the event. Post haste, I went down to the village and booked a table for twelve at a very posh French restaurant. They were a bit flummoxed at the short notice but agreed to arrange matters nicely for a wedding reception meal. We phoned up Yvonne's Grandparents to invite them only to find they both had symptoms of a really bad flu going the rounds in Sweden. Yvonne was naturally disappointed but did not want any members from her estranged family there, seeing as her Grandmother and Grandfather were the ones she really wanted. The lunch taken care of, I turned my attention to our friend's entertainment. I wanted them to join us somewhere special for the night's celebrations. I had the brilliant idea to phone Abbass to see if it was cool to go there. I prayed the restaurant would be free for us all to partake of his brilliant Arab Fare. When I explained to Abbass Yvonne and myself were getting married and would love to have the evening party at his place, he was ecstatic .

"Leave everything to me Gypsy, all will be done in the correct manner my brother," Abbass affirmed to me over the telephone.

"Sorry it is such short notice Abbass, is nine o'clock O.K? I think there will be about thirty or forty of us," I asked

"Not a problem Gypsy, nine o'clock then," said Abbass, sounding delighted.

"Thanks Abbas you're a diamond."

I hoped against hope our do would be held in the basement, but I knew how private a space that was for him so I did not ask for it. Now that that was taken care of, I felt full of energy as I phoned many friends to invite them to the party; most were able to come it transpired. O.K. what next? Wedding rings of course. There was a brilliant jewelry shop in the village so we rushed there and chose a matching pair of platinum rings. Next part of the program, to get Dono to be me best man and David Wynne was kind enough to step in to give Yvonne away at such short notice. Next thing was the dress for Yvonne. She did not like all the thrills or bibs and bobs of the wedding dresses she saw. Instead Yvonne brought some beautiful yellow coloured material that glowed with the intensity and colour of Sun Flowers. Yvonne managed to get the seamstress (who had just made her an outdoors coat in brown velvet) to make her a mini style dress with this yellow cloth, intending it for the great occasion.

Yvonne looked a million dollars on the day, wearing the brown velvet coat casually open outside the yellow dress. In the sunlight of that morning she looked like a magazine model. She was wearing very little makeup as was her want. Yellow and white flowers pined into her lovely light brown hair and a bouquet of large yellow and white daisies she had made herself finished off the effect so well. Although I say so myself, we made a lovely couple that day and I was so proud of my beautiful Swedish wife. It was for me a dream come true. The ceremony itself was sweet and simple, taking place as it did in a light and airy office made special by some flowers and the kindness, professionalism and smiles of the registrar who appeared to relish the occasion as much as us, clever man that he was. The funny thing is that until I said 'I do', I had no idea how serious those two miniscule words are. It was a perfect morning and the lunch in the French establishment was wonderful.

Enjoying our meal and after coffee we all headed home to our flat where we ate our wedding cake made by those lovely ladies in the Cafe Yvonne and I frequented on Wimbledon Common. My Grandmothers were getting tired so my folks said they would take them home to Hertfordshire. I asked my mother if they would join us in the evening at which she laughed saying,

"I am sure you and your friends don't want a pair of fuddy-duddies like us to spoil your fun. No my son, you enjoy your evening, we have had such a lovely time already and you can't begin to know how pleased we are to see you and Yvonne married. We took small bets you know me and your dad, your dad won. He said you would be a fool to let Yvonne slip between your fingers and he also said, if there was one thing you were not, it was a fool. I on the other hand just wasn't sure you could settle down to a normal wedded life, what with your freedom loving ways and your wild goings on. But there you go, you turned out to be the exception that proves the rule and we are so pleased I was wrong. Your dad and I really wish you all the best of everything David. You have chosen a wonderful delightful girl who is intelligent enough to know who you are and what you need. "

At this point in our private conversation my dear sweet mother burst into tears. I hugged her to me and kissed her on her forehead. David and Gilly soon passed through the large living room window, this being David's favourite way of coming and going, saying they were looking forward to join us later that evening. Dono and Enid settled down for a kip on the two couches in the big room and Yvonne and I went to bed for a few hours rest before the madness of the coming evening.

We arrived at my Arab friends restaurant to find out what an extraordinary man Abbas was. 'Leave it all to me Gypsy I will make sure all is correct', sounded simple enough on the phone but what work he had put into those few words. Abbas met us on the stairs, this the entrance to his private world. Here with great ceremony he placed Arab head gear on my unruly locks. Then he handed over a gift to Yvonne of a very enchanting necklace made in the finest and most fabulous workmanship in silver and matching turquoise gems. Abbas then put it

around Yvonne's neck and she looked like a Princess. He then handed me a beautiful box, it held a pair of the most exquisite gold cufflinks with a miniature Swiss watch imbedded in the gold of one cufflink. As if this were not enough he also handed me a solid gold Key Ring and chain with Arab script embossed in blue and white Enamel. Etched with skill on the gold plaque hanging from the chain was the Arabic words, Allah be Praised. We both hugged and embraced Abbas, thanking him for his generosity but I could tell he had more marvels up his sleeve. Down the stairs behind him I saw coloured lanterns of glass leading to an Aladdin's Cave of wonders. Abbas had transformed his basement restaurant into a thing of outright beauty. Tables were laden with food on wooden planks that had tablecloths of embroidered workmanship wonderful to behold. The embroidery needles having made designs in coloured silks enough to make a rainbow bow its body in the deepest of respect. There was a roasted whole lamb on one table. Suckling pig on another. Ducks roasted and chickens boiled with sauces of every kind. There was Couscous, scented rice and vegetables of every description cooked in every way man had discovered. On the tables set for our guests were bottles of Abbas's best Moroccan wines, white, red and rose. Believe me, these wines chosen by Abbas could hold their heads high amongst the finest of French wines at any wine tasting. What with the warmth made by the lighting, the flowers pinned everywhere to the walls, the Arabic music, the wine the food and our dear friends, it was a night to remember our whole lives.

The night wore on in perfect harmony, the Hooker doing its giddy rounds too. Dono stood up determined to do the best man's speech. It was almost the last speech he was to make in his life. There, only for the fortune of where I happened to be standing for his unfortunate half drunken but well meant speech, goes Donovan today .

Don started on the lines of....

"Well here we are to see my dear Gypsy off into the realms of domestic bliss. Of all people I have ever known Gypsy is the last person I would have believed would marry. Of all the people I know I would have bet my bottom dollar dear Gypsy would stay single. I would have said that of all the people I know Gypsy should not marry for who would have believed such a thing possible or even desirable for a free minded man like Gyp to get hitched"

Before Donovan could finish off his speech there was a sharp strangled cry from behind me. Out of the corner of my eye I saw Abbas plunging toward where Donovan was standing a few short feet away. Abbass held in his eyes murder and held high above his head a cruel knife that was about to be plunged downward into the very centre of Don's terrified beating heart. Using my instinct, never letting another thought enter my mind but the thought to stop that knife blade from its destiny of being imbedded up to the hilt in the heart of my more than brother Donovan. As quick as thought itself I grabbed hold of Abbas's hand and forced the knife downward towards my own heart. Looking deeply into

Abbas's eyes there I saw what he had seen. Donovan had cursed our wedding on the very day of the pact. A thing of shocking importance and devastating consequences to an Arab way of seeing life. A curse that could only be lifted by the death of the one bringing down such evil intent on innocent newlyweds. Still fighting the downward stroke of that deadly sharp blade, I forced it nearer to my own heart until it cut my shirt.

"Abbas , Abbas," I called out. "Dono did not mean what you think he meant. How could he? He loves me even more than you love me."

My speech entered the very soul of my Arab friend and he heard the truth in my words. Coming back, back from a distance that was his arabesque inheritance Abbass controlled his utter anger at what he believed in the heart of his understanding Donovan had unleashed at our wedding feast. He smiled into my eyes dropping his knife into my hand.

"You are a good man Gypsy. Time will tell my dear brother. Let us pray for your sons and daughters yet to come. "

The atmosphere that had frozen became more like it had been and I asked Don and Abbass to give one and the other a brotherly hug. Granting my wish they complied with my request, upon which the party continued into the wee hours of the morning. The crazy thing about this episode, thirteen years later when Yvonne and I became divorced we received our Decree Narzi, this is the final date a marriage is considered legal... knock me down with a feather if the official last day of our marriage was dated May 10th. This was no other date than my mate Donovan's birthday. Coincidence?

Funny. Did Abbas's old knowledge detect something we in the west knew not? Had the unintended curse taken hold whether Dono meant it too or not?

Donovan's father Donald rather sweetly paid for the wedding party and handed me a thick envelope from Dono. In the envelope, two first class plane tickets to the West Indies. Dono had gifted us a honeymoon of three weeks duration in a cottage in the golf-course grounds of a very up-market hotel, in Nassau, Bahamas. Enough spending money was also there that we had no worries about doing whatever we wanted for those glorious three weeks in Paradise. Looking at the date on the tickets I realized they were booked two days in the future. That didn't give us long to pack our cases. Soon we were off and had the most amazing honeymoon thanks to the forethought and generosity of my dear mate Donovan.

A few months later back from our European gigs and me working on my sculpture in the little studio in the flat, Dono phoned from Scotland. Unbeknown to me he and his father had been searching for a small holding, as parcels of farming land were known in the Highlands of Scotland. This came as a surprise as I had no idea he was looking for land. To hear that the proposed purchase was on The Isle of Skye, a tiny island in the Highlands was also a revaluation. Donovan was excited by the prospect of using the three islands and mainland properties he had discovered as a Commune, and he wanted me to phone up our friends to propose the idea. Where Don had got this thought in his head of a commune I had no idea, although I took to it immediately. Without giving me any time to think he asked me to come up and join them to see the land he was so excited by.

On my arrival sixteen hours later on the beautiful Island of Skye, he met me in the company of a local fisherman who took us by boat to the three islands. This trip was organized for us by the Laird who owned the three islands for sale. The old buildings on the larger of the islands were extremely unusual. These were said to have been built from the natural rocks by just one man. He was totally alone for this mammoth task using methods which he kept secret from any of the highland fishermen. The second island was jam packed with many species of seagull also hundreds of rabbits put there in the distant past by a sea captain ran wild amongst the crying gulls. These birds were bigger and more aggressive than I had thought them. They were not afraid of men, swooping down on us viscously when we came near their scraggy nests and painted eggs of green and sand colour. The third island was smaller, full of seals spread eagled on the sandy coves or with their heads bobbing back and forth like broken puppets to the restless rhythm of the waves. Don believed it would be extremely easy to persuade our friends to join us and live in such wonderful idyllic surroundings. The big house on the mainland was a derelict but had the potential to be repaired. We would take it back to the Manor House it once was. The land attached to this manor house was well worked fields of corn sloping gently to the sea. There was also a four room cottage used at one time by the inhabitants as their local Post Office. This building was in good condition but in need of a new roof. I was as charmed by this little parcel of land as Donovan was.

"What do you think Gypo? Shall we buy it?" asked Don.

"Absolutely mate, it's a magic place," I said, getting me camera out and taking pictures to show our friends in England. "Dave Tilling would be very useful to organise the building projects if he and Roey would want to be part of this Commune " I suggested.

"Funny you should say that Gyp, Dave's the one I have been talking to about this idea of a Commune. He's for it lock, stock and barrel. He also has to move out of his studio in Bushy, meaning he can move down in a minute."

"Fantastic, could not be better," I said "We will buy some caravans and get your lovely old traveler's van down too," I said excitedly, beginning to get into the swing of it all.

The upshot was we purchased the land and buildings from the Laird. About eight couples agreed to join us in the highlands of Scotland, thrilled to be living a simple life on land and sea.

In a walled garden which we repaired, we started a vegetable garden. The locals said it would never work but somehow it flourished along with the chickens, ducks, geese and other birds. The Manor House was the first building to be tackled, Dave Tilling being in charge of the architectural plans and organising of our friends who each in their own way had a skill to bring to the job at hand. He with their help produced miracles. Sammy (who had once saved my life} was a keen gardener and was also an artist of finest talent. He took charge of the communal gardens with his Lady Lynn by his side. Donovan and I would leave this paradise every now and then to keep up with tours in Europe and the wider world.

I had decided to keep my flat on Wimbledon Common. It made it easier to get to and from the main airport for our never ending tours. The alternative would have been to take a plane from Glasgow to Heathrow then onward. Dono had his cottage in Hertfordshire still, where he could rest awhile before and after the hard work of the gigs. These different performances were slowly taking us around the world several times over.

CHAPTER TWENTY THREE
SKYE TO SKYE

We learnt a lot on the Isle of Skye. Once again I came perilously near to losing my life (in such a short span of years), this time on the dangerous single file road system that snaked its merry drunken way across the rugged and varied landscape of the Island. On this single track roadway there were passing places set at the sides of the road every quarter mile or so for traffic to pass each other in opposite directions. The story is quite funny in part. Me and Mick, a very good driver and a trusted friend left our caravans bright and early before the sun was up. I was driving the brand spanking new long wheelbase Land Rover which had been delivered by the dealer to our commune two days prior to this fatal departure. Our task, to buy a second hand caravan located on the mainland of Scotland. We knew of the Caravan Site through the local newspaper. Looking up the place on an old map we found it one hundred and thirty miles away, not bad we thought and at the price the owner wanted for the caravan, quite a steal. The upshot was that very morning, we were on the road.

Twenty miles from Waternish, our starting point, we turned a sharp corner only to find a bunch of sheep in the middle of the single track road. Luckily for them they scattered just in time to see another day, while we on that same corner on an upward slanting ridge, sailed off into the nothingness that awaited us. We zoomed off like a skater on ice caused by the small stones that were littering the sides of the road. Our Land Rover behaved exactly as if on oiled rollers and we catapulted into the air like a badly flown plane. Totally out of control and with all four wheels in the air we careened down a five meter drop of peat and rock infested bog land. It is a very strange thing to be sitting in a car seeing the landscape around you turn upside down for you are convinced it is the scenery turning, not the vehicle .

After the roof hit the ground with a deafening sound we continued our downward roll. On reaching the upright position I believed we had landed safely, me being a bit of a novice at driving off a Scottish mountainside. Like a fool I loosened my hold somewhat on the steering wheel only to find the Land Rover was still in motion. The rolling movement took me and smashed my nose into the dashboard. Shit, I thought, there goes me nose. With a peculiar intense clarity of thought I was preparing to see what other parts of my body would end up attached and belonging to me or scattered over the brand new interior of our spinning Land Rover. We flipped the whole four sided full Monty once again before we landed by a miracle in an upright position on the soggy terrain. I looked for Mick whom I had last seen sitting beside me. He wasn't there. Damn it, had he fallen out the open doors? Had the Land Rover crushed him to death as it rolled over him? Turning my head I found Mick in the back space behind the rear seats covered in murderous scythes, pitch forks, spades, huge hammers and picks that could take your head off in a second. Believe it or not when he shook himself free from this unwanted baggage he was totally unharmed. A few bruises were all he had to show for his adventure. As for me, apart from my nose that was bleeding slightly and swollen, I was unhurt too. Unfortunately the brand spanking new Land Rover looked as if it had been through the Second World War twice losing every battle along the way. Bedraggled and on its last legs, the dent in the roof from our first coming to earth huge and the front windscreen in an array of small octagonal cracks. The dented back doors stood wide open and no longer able to close. We were a sad mess, dents in the sides of the poor Land Rover were of many a shape and size. These drew my gaze to the front wheel; it was buckled at a sharp downward angle. This appeared to me to be an impossible angle and I believed the axle had snapped. On closer inspection however we found that it was only the rim of the wheel that was buckled. Looking in the peat bog where we had unceremoniously rested, we found the where with-all to take off the shattered front wheel and put on the spare. It wasn't much of an improvement, but with the two front tires now standing even along the same line we saw the whole Land Rover was at an obtuse angle tilted to the right. Mick and I jumped back into the Rover, choosing the four wheel drive. Mick slowly drove us uphill. Back onto the roads merciful flat tarmac I found rope behind the back seat and tied our back doors almost closed. We limped to the nearest garage where the owner nearly fainted when we explained the accident had only happened a few minutes earlier.

"Sit doown yee two before yee fall doown, yourn both be in shock from yon accident," he said kindly. Funny enough we felt O.K. I suppose it was relief that we had gotten out of this wreck alive.

"We still have about a hundred miles to go and then the return journey, do you think the Land Rover will make it?" I asked our canny mechanic.

"Goood God Mun, that's just aboot the finest engine that intelligent mun can make. Apart from what yon two have doon to the ootside, under yon bonnet she is like a wee piece o art, a dream is what she is. The mechanics of yon wee beasty will keep yee going fer another fifty years withoot a hitch," he said with confidence. Mick and I looked at each other.

"O.K. lets go for it," we both said. The journey was on. We believed it would go smoothly from that moment on. What innocent fools we were.

Following the map we found our destination easily enough and discovered the caravan was old, about twenty five years but well kept and sturdy. It would do us a treat for our newly extending family of friends.

Parting with the money and taking charge of the new purchase we set out on the return journey to Skye. All went well for the first fifty miles or so. We stopped by the wayside for a pee. It was here that Mick noticed a large bubble in the left hand tire of the caravan. It did not look good and upon close examination we realized the problem. The tire apparently was about as old as the caravan. This had been no problem whatsoever while the van was parked up but as soon as it was in motion the old rubber heated up and became very soft and pliable. The inside air pressure, although trying to be contained by the old inner-tube, was forcing a bubble to appear in the melting rubber of the wheel. Mick suggested we deflate the tire pressure as much as possible to lower the risk of it exploding. This we did. Getting on the road, hoping against hope the towing would go well and the old tire would last out the journey, we lowered the speed believing this would help the outcome. Now there is a destination on this roadway we were traveling known by the ominous title of. The Devil's Elbow. Believe me I am not making this up, this is all true. Look for a moment if you would at your left arm at shoulder height; now place your left fist on your lower chest. This was how the roadway looked. Behind the elbows apex on the left hand side was a drop of forty meters or so. After the elbow, the road dropped sharply downward to the right. To add insult to injury there was generally a thick swirling mist at the worst point of the elbow. Needless to say our tire burst with a loud bang about three miles before The Devil's Elbow.

What were we to do? We were hours from civilization. Not a garage for miles and sitting dangerously slurred across the roadway, the caravan's rear out. Nothing for it but to drive on the deflated tire hoping the rubber would hold up until we could find a safe place to park. My God what a to-do, the scenery was becoming more mountainous and the road narrowing in an upward twist then it fell downwards in long sweeps of road having thick metal buffers not allowing us to park or even slow down.

"Hell and High-water," called out Mick, "the bloody tire is alight," he informed me with panic in his voice. I looked in the cracked mirror just in time to see the flaming tire spin off of the rim. Luckily it landed in the middle of the roadway and not in dry highland pasture. We pulled over to re-assess our situation. Just then a lorry passed us by going hell for leather, blasting his horn like a Banshee on heat.

Damn and blast it, we could not stay where we were or some mad driver would pile into the back of us .We had to press on regardless using the metal rim of the caravans wheel, it was our only hope of getting safely from our present predicament. The only trouble being, the road was leading us relentlessly to The Devil's Elbow. The weight of the caravan was changing the shape of the metal rim flattening it out and turning it into the shape of a train wheel. This was OK but for the fact that the caravan was leaning lower on the left hand side and the Land Rover was angled {through the crash}, to the right side exaggerating the distance between the two making it hard to drag the van without the fear of it popping off the ball joint towing bar. We were climbing now to the climax of

The Devil's Elbow mountain.

"By Christ Mick go slow mate, I don't think we can make this sharp corner. Take the Land Rover as near to the middle of the road as you can or the caravan is going to topple over."

I turned my head to see the very thing I feared about to happen as Mick took the angle sharply. It was no good we were about to lose the van or worse still, be pulled over the huge drop with the weight of the caravan. There was just one hope and I saw it like a beacon in the night.

"Put yer foot down hard Mick for Christ's sake. The shock will stop the angle of fall and with luck, brace the van the other way." Mick being the good driver he was understood exactly what I meant and gunned the engine just at the correct moment to right the van's fall. It tilted on the reverse angle and slammed over to the roadway as we veered into the final curve like a racing car doing a circuit at La Mons.

"Fantastic you old Bugger," I exclaimed at his good driving. Mick just grinned sheepishly knowing how near we had come to being pulled over The Devil's Elbow or losing the newly purchased caravan to the drop. We traveled onward slowly in this fashion until even the rim gave way and turned into a square shape that threw the caravan up and down like a damn demented rabbit and dug a grove in the tarmac.

"Pull us in here Mick, let's try to get the bloody van's wheel hub off and drive to the nearest garage," I said, relieved we had found a pull in. With great effort we got the distorted hub off its three rusted bolts. With this trophy we drove the buckled Land Rover onward finding a garage not four miles from where we had parked the caravan. It was perfect, for there were old wheels surrounding the place like money in a smashed and broken piggy bank. The owner, it so happened was a Londoner looked at us as though we were the biggest roughs on earth. Asking where we were off to and what the hell the other car in the fight looked like, we explained to him as best we could our sequence of misfortunes. He softened to us a little when he heard my obvious London accent and took the distorted rim and hub from my hands.

"Not a chance in hell, never seen anything like this before," he said. "It's old, very old. Must have been made special for the caravan company. Has it got a spare mate? That's yer only chance. See here, it's very small for a rim and tire and only has three bolts to grip with, would never allow anything like this these days."

The garage owner was talking to Mick while I was looking at the old wheels outside where I spotted a tire and wheel hub of about the right size; it looked for all the world like it had come from a Mini.

"How about this one? It looks about right?" I asked.

"Yes you are right about the size but look at the holes they wont match up."

"I see that, but what's wrong with you drilling new holes in the rim to match the ones we have?" The garage owner looked at me.

"How far you say you are going? If not too far that canny idea of yours might just work at that." I brought the tire and rim over to him and he could see that the holes could be drilled with enough metal around them to be safe. He started measuring and drawing the marks for the new holes then took the hub to his big drill bench press that was tucked away at the back of his untidy workshop.

Soon the holes were drilled and with a file he put the finishing touches to his work.

"Now take me to your van lads so I can make a few adjustments if need be. Then I can tell you if it's safe to drive to Skye on the new wheel. Wouldn't be worth me life if I let you both go off when it was dangerous, me missus would have me guts for garters for the callousness of it. We don't want to read about your demise in the papers now do we? " .

As quick as you like we arrived at the broken caravan and our garage owner had the wheel hub screwed down in a moment. It looked the business alright.

"You know I believe it will work," was his remark.

"That's incredible," we intoned in our happiness.

"How much do we owe you for the wheel tire and your work?" I asked.

"Wheel and tire are free as some bloke left it for me. Just give me a couple of quid for the work and time."

"Not at all," I said and handed him a Fiver. "We really appreciate what you have done you have helped us out of a bind and no mistake. Thanks a million, now we can get on our way." I remarked. Dropping our friend off at his garage we headed for Fort William and the Ferry over to Skye. Thank God that was the end of our adventures that day and when we arrived at the site and the workings on the Manor House, Yvonne and our friends were overjoyed to see us in one piece. The rumours going the rounds of the Island had us both killed or so badly injured in the crash that we had been rushed to a hospital no one knew the address of on the mainland. Within two days of this happening I received a Telegram from Dono saying not to worry about the new Land Rover smashed up, he was just grateful that we were unharmed. Because of our drug bust it was such an effort to get back into America that if Dono was just going for a couple of gigs it was better for me not to go.

This was the case in this adventure on Skye, but while Dono was over there he heard for the first time of a character who would influence him for the entirety of his life. A Guru called The Maharishi Mahesh Yogi. Donovan heard of him through George and Patti and could not wait to meet the Guru and taking the first opportunity that came his way met the Master in America.

Weeks later we were due for a hug American Tour. Twenty six gigs, fifteen television appearances, ten wireless interviews and countless paper interviews. This was a long tour so I was asked to go to the trouble of getting a working visa at the U.S. embassy. The buggers had me take a medical. Hours later when they called me into the office I found they had a folder on me four inches thick. Music paper photos, pictures and articles from the bust, written reports on God knows what, all kinds of rubbish.

"Hey " I said to the Guy behind the desk. "I'm a British Citizen, how come you have all that information on me? Are you allowed to have all that?"

"That's very normal lad," he said honestly enough.

"We look out for those we think could be a threat to our America way of life and averse to our current policies, no matter the country they are from. :

"Are pop stars such a threat to your great big country then?" I said in mock horror.

"It's not only you pop stars we keep our eyes on, it's university students overly interested in politics. We keep our eyes on them in particular. You would be surprised how useful that can be if we need to use it against 'em later on in their life, especially if they do well on the political front and we can prove they have been naughty boys and girls." He laughed contritely. "You and Donovan for instance got some very nasty ideas Uncle Sam don't like. You been broadcasting your opposition a bit too loudly with our great and glorious fight with the bloody Vietcong."

"Not me mate," I said tongue in cheek. "I think it's great. Think it's absolutely fantastic you lot killing off your young kids and all to take over a country you have no idea what to do with, even if you win which in most peoples opinion you won't. Bet you anything your bloody kids ain't over there are they?" I asked him looking him in the eyes.

"Do you want this Visa or not young man? Unfortunately you seem to have passed the medical for drugs, nothing at all in your blood stream."

These were the sort of hassles one had to go through to get into the Land of the Free in the mid sixties. I bet they're even tighter now in these days of troubles.

The tour I am about to write about was superbly organised by a company know as Chartwell Artists. We had been recommended to these excellent tour specialists by the very smart singer and actor Davey Jones who was with the Monkees band. He joined us on the tour for about a week, not to sing but just for the company. Davey was a keen photographer and took loads of pictures at that time. He was also an island of Englishness in that sea of Americanism, being a great companion we enjoyed his high spirits no end. Chartwell Artists had luxurious houses they hired in the hills of LA which they sub rented out if need be to their clients. At their suggestion we hired a Lea- Jet to take us to the gigs that were five hundred miles or so away from Los Angeles. In this way we did dates in a few hours without having to spend lots of time in hotels. We would hire a room for a few hours near to the gigs for the pilots or if we were playing in a University that had its own landing strip as many did in the U.S. It would be possible to change after the gig and be in the plane within minutes and home in the hills above L.A. that same evening. We had a limousine waiting at the airport to meet us to take us home.

It was a great luxury and cost not much more than airfares and hotels would have cost in our normal way, bearing in mind that by now we were staying in the best suites in the best hotels money could buy. This new way of doing business made touring so much easier. Anything that did that was a God-send believe me. On a big tour like that I usually lost about three to four Kilos. It was weight I could not do without in my youth. On this tour Dono did The Hollywood Bowl twice in one week and filled it to overflowing both times. Donovan's reputation as a modern Shaman was made by a curious incident at that concert. During the first or second song it started to rain. It was an open air gig meaning for the audience it could have been a disaster. It must be said at that time of year it was an unusual weather occurrence. There were stirrings of unease in the audience and I was extremely worried about the electricity on stage and Don's connections to it as the high arch of the concert hall let the rain onto the stage below. In certain situations in those young days of electrifying music just touching a mike could electrocute a musician in rainy wet conditions. I was preparing myself to hustle on to the stage and take Dono off before such a fate could befall him knowing as I did he would go on to the very end to give the fans what they wanted. Blow me down with a feather if he didn't take the whole thing into his hands in the most peculiar of ways. He stopped singing. Gently he spoke to the thousands there.

"Hi my friends listen to me," he said in perfect confidence. "Put your hands together in a slow rhythmic clap, the rain will stop and pass on in peace respectfully to other places."

There was total silence then as Dono started to clap slowly, some of the audience felt the power and clapped along with him but most of the assembled personages there clapped along with little hope or belief in the reality of what Don had suggested. To the absolute amazement of all there, the rain fell lighter and lighter in a second and then lifted as if by magic. You can imagine how that effected those thousands of souls as their clapping turned into cheering and even more clapping for our hero and his seeming control over the very elements. It rained no more that concert and the fans loved every minute of his performance. That was the Sixties Magic; we youngsters would talk and discuss such ideas. It was as important for us as life itself to know that all things are ONE when it comes right down to it. The power in nature is the power of our nature. We can be as creative or destructive as those powers. It is up to each person and their intelligence to choose to destroy or to create. Not up to the whims of governments to indoctrinate us into these decisions by coercing the minds of the masses to follow the dictates of the industrial complex and the armaments industry. Yes we can destroy all before us, every past civilization has come to the same place in its history. Up until that time society had failed miserably to make the change to a better way of life at a certain unknown equilibrium in society.

Maybe it is that the future is so uncertain for our terrified and confused minds with the endless possibilities inherent in life. The certainty of disruption and destruction is more comforting to our intellect instead of the hideous deterrent it should be. Can it be that simple, can we be such cowards? Can we let the destructive powers of our nature come to the surface like a bubble of air through water? A stink of corruption rotting from the poison of our deficient nature hidden in the teary waters of our reptilian ancestral beginnings. And yet, in the beginning we had the courage to leave the comfort of the known Sea for the mysteries of the unknown Earth. At which point we discovered at our feet a miracle of understanding, another reality not inhabited by the destructive impulses but by the gloriously creative power. A myriad of life made in that living miracle that never ending time of creative thought that made all the creatures of our planet infinitesimal and mammoth. In the early movement of the Sixties we found these powers in our own creative thoughts, in our discussions, in our thinking in our need to understand and learn. This was the essence of the young and the way for many artists, musicians and creative thinkers of the time. The positivity of life's beauties and wonders were our God and our Direction. Their creative possibilities felt at the very core of our being.

Our knowledge was the awareness of hope and a need to understand our destructive natures to rain in our appalling negative responses. After the wonton destruction of the Second World War we felt compelled to change the world by our choice to a better freer place for Mankind. After all, had it not been paid for in the coin of death and cruel chaos through the loss of life in the previous generation brought about by unbidden War. It was a natural Yin -Yang affect that could have gone anywhere in its awareness. It is my belief that like many before us, our generation failed in our task. We bulked at its infinite ideas and found an easier less dangerous path in the hope that every human being could become a Buddha, Jesus or an Allah. A new realization was found and set out for us in the simple comfort of a new religion unheard of by most young minds of the sixties. It placated our uncertainties that were becoming too hot to handle. The fascination was a religion we were not familiar with, one I believe should never have been used by the new movement of youth as its Totem. Oh yes it had its treasures. It promised to take us on the enlightened path of Hinduism, Buddhism, a path to Sufism to The Way to `Zoism to one Ism and another Ism. It sweetly suggested we walk the well trod ways of the East leading us by shackled feet to self knowledge. We became interested in the Self above all other things. For me the sixties movement had at its very instinctual source encouragement for all concepts. Look within to find yourself by all means, but don't leave it there. Use your knowledge of what you have learned to advance thought and deed.

I have discovered a simple oxymoron. We are not alone because we are one. Birds amongst other unique creations discovered the idea of flight, fish discovered swimming, animals and insects discovered walking, but we humans my friends discovered the art of - Talking,   Writing, Sculpting,   Painting, Arithmetic,   The Arts of Physics and Science and Religion refined the Art of making things creatively by the use of our hands and minds combined, this among other wonders of our Nature too numerous to mention.

The few really Hip of our Generation stopped believing the Christian tenants of Man as the incarnate form of Evil. We knew and we believed in our uniqueness in a positive down to Earth way. There was ultimately no good or evil, there was only Choice. You knew who you were by your Choice. Where you should go, how you should get there, what you should do when you arrived there, these were your simple rights not the business of States. Our youthful destiny was not to critique or condemn any ones true choice but to know who they were by there choice and to know the courage it took sometimes to be the only one to make that choice.

The truth is always in the choice we arrive at; say what you will with your voice. We listened not to the direction other peoples words would sometimes take you. We understood this choice in our movement, we tried to control our thoughts to keep them in line with our deeds and actions. This in my opinion was a big part of the sixties creative process. It produced so much varied and diverse art and music in the young of Earth. But we were to lose so much of the sixties movement unintentionally by an exaggerated believe in The Self,   as an awareness, and by not concentrating on The Many as One ,concept that had in it the strength and the power to stop a bloody War in Vietnam.

Here for the first time my thoughts parted from the thoughts of my mate Dono. This made no difference to our everyday living after all freedom of thought was what we craved as much as freedom of motion. God bless your endeavors my dear friend, your creativity was still ballooning like a wayward moon in a star imbedded sky as you tapped into the Self. Through all your gossamer clouds of disappointment and hurt and need for the love of your life Linda that tried to bring you down, your ideas and your creativity led you skyward, up into an endless space of blue on turquoise wings through your beautiful songs and melodies. Strong and beautiful soul you were and still are my brother.

Here we will end this book for the minute but know there are many more stories where this lot came from, and we hope you are finding a sense of the Sixties through experiencing my time, for I had the luck to be at the centre of its magic.

THE END

Lightning Source UK Ltd.
Milton Keynes UK
UKHW021822220222
399082UK00006B/591

9 781291 527278